the
allotment
source
book

the
allotment
source
book

Caroline Foley

photography by Francesca Foley

NEW HOLLAND

Published in 2010 by New Holland
Publishers (UK) Ltd

London • Cape Town • Sydney • Auckland

www.newhollandpublishers.com

Garfield House, 86–88 Edgware Road, London
W2 2EA, United Kingdom

80 McKenzie Street, Cape Town 8001,
South Africa

Unit 1, 66 Gibbes Street, Chatswood, NSW
2067, Australia

218 Lake Road, Northcote, Auckland,
New Zealand

A catalogue record for this book is available
from the British Library

ISBN 978 1 84773 664 2

Editor: Emma Pattison

Designer: Geoff Borin

Photographer: Francesca Foley

Production Controller: Laurence Poos

Illustrations: Coral Mula

Editorial Direction: Rosemary Wilkinson

10 9 8 7 6 5 4 3 2 1

Reproduction by PDQ Digital Media Solutions
Ltd, United Kingdom

Printed and bound in Singapore by Craft Print
International Ltd

contents

introduction

England is not a free people until the poor that have no land, have a free allowance to dig and labour the commons.

Gerrard Winstanley (1649)

Allotments have had roller-coaster history. They sprang from the needs of starving farm labourers in the form of charity from landowners and the church; they gradually gained recognition, became almost a citizen's right, achieved great glory in the two world wars, and then fell into sharp decline.

Now, we have the great allotment revival. Waiting lists for plots have soared to unparalleled heights, running into tens of thousands of people and decades of waiting time. British Waterways, National Trust, Crown Estates, the Church, private landowners and railway companies are amongst the many who are offering land. Unused, brown-field sites and prestigious, inner-city building sites waiting for finance are under pressure to turn themselves over for temporary plots for 'meanwhile gardening'. Land Share puts gardens and gardeners together on the net.

Vacant concrete spaces on inner-city housing estates are being made into vibrant vegetable gardens in collections of builders' bags or palettes. In London, the Mayor has provided small pots of grant money for new 'food growing spaces'. At the opposite end of the scale and, by way of setting an example for green living, kitchen gardens have been installed with considerable fanfare at the White House and 10 Downing Street.

Knowing what to plant where and when to get the best result is quite a skill. So I was delighted when Garden Organic in Ryton, Coventry – the charity that promotes organic gardening – agreed to let me follow their planting plan for their show allotment through a growing season. Janet Reilly, the gardener in charge of the plot, makes a logical and easy-to-follow planting plan for the produce on rotation with clever companion planting, which we can all follow or adapt to our needs.

The legal chapter has been written by Dr. Richard Wiltshire, an allotment gardener, advocate, critic and policy analyst. He is author of the official guidance on good practice in managing allotments, *Growing in the Community* (2008), and *A Place to Grow* (2010), as well as a driving force behind the Allotments Regeneration Initiative. Richard clarifies the responsibilities of local authorities to provide plots and the need for clear arguments on the social and environmental benefits of allotments if they are to be prioritized in the allocation of funds. He explains what you can and cannot do with your plot to stay within the law and local rules, and what happens if your tenancy, or the site itself, comes under threat.

My own aim in this book has been to gather as much useful information as possible and to write a totally practical guide on how to avoid the pitfalls, make wise decisions and get the greatest satisfaction out of an allotment plot.

It has been an enormous pleasure to get swept up in this new wave of allotment energy. Things have certainly changed. Back in 1969 a select committee report on allotments* described the allotment holder as 'an individualist who considers his allotment to be as private as his home garden, who is seldom interested in anything beyond its boundaries, and is blind to his further responsibilities.' Now the opposite is true.

Many allotments have become self-governing and pro-active in raising grants for disabled plots, sensory areas for the blind, reading circles for schools and for equipment and facilities such as polytunnels, buildings for teaching and outdoor classrooms. They also play a vital role for our diminishing wildlife. Allotment holders welcome in the local community – asylum seekers, refugees, the homeless, people with learning difficulties or depression, isolated groups of women and the elderly.

Across England and Wales, allotments provide 18,000 hectares (45,000 acres) of green space, mostly in and around towns. They are little oases of peace in a busy world. It is cheering to see more and more nature reserves cropping up on sites. It is heart-warming to note how many allotments now have bee hives, to help save the threatened honey bee.

Not only do allotment people enjoy the best things in life – open air, unpolluted fresh food, exercise and companionship – but they also provide a great service to the community and to wildlife in the process.

Thorpe Committee of Inquiry into Allotments, 1969.

history of allotments in brief

1607 Midland Revolt. 'Captain Pouch' and his 5,000 followers protested against the enclosures. Ended in a pitched battle with 50 dead.

1649 Gerard Winstanley and the Diggers, or the 'True Levellers', anticipated the green movements. Saw the earth as a 'precious common storehouse for all'. Squatted on vacant and common land to grow produce. Finally evicted by the military from St George's Hill, Surrey.

1730s Agricultural Revolution resulted in mass unemployment among farm hands. Machinery replaced manpower. Particularly resented were the threshing machines, which took away the winter work. The old, open-field system began to be replaced.

1750-1845 Vast majority of Enclosure Acts in which 2.8 million hectares (7 million acres) of land was enclosed under 5,000 individual acts. One-third was common land. Less than 5 per cent was set aside for the poor. At the same time, the population of England and Wales increased from 5.7 million to 11 million.

1790s Concerned landlords and the Church started to set aside land as allotments for their workers and the 'deserving poor' – field allotments, cow runs, fuel allotments and potato grounds.

1815-1831 Napoleonic wars ended; 300,000 demobilized, adding to unemployment. 1816 Bread and Blood Riots, East Anglia. Anti-enclosure, anti-machinery riots. Town and country combined in protest against the industrial looms and the threshing machines that were taking their work. 1816 Commissioners to appropriate allotment land 'as they saw necessary'. 1830–1831 Captain Swing Riots. Groups of rioters moved from farm to farm, smashing threshing machines and setting fire to haystacks. Riots were quickly stamped out. Some 500 rioters were transported and 19 hanged. No immediate benefit to the workers.

1832 Labourers' Friend Society founded; this was an influential group including bishops, gentry and MPs. Its aim was to persuade landlords to encourage self-respect, independence and self-help in labourers, by giving them allotments.

1850s Rural population was dropping by 30,000 per year. As a result, allotments sprung up in the industrial towns and cities.

1884 Franchise Act gave labourers the right to vote.

1901 National Society started as a members' co-operative.

1908 Smallholdings and Allotments Act passed. Any six registered voters now had the right to demand an allotment where there was no provision. Land could be acquired by compulsory purchase.

1914–1918 Digging for DORA (Defence of the Realm Act). By the end of the war, there were 1.5 million plots.

1918 Scottish Allotments and Gardens Society (SAGS) was founded.

1919 Demand for allotments escalated to 7,000 applications a week. Words 'labouring population' (the last stigma) were finally removed and allotments were officially open to all.

1922 An allotment described as 'not exceeding forty rods which is wholly or mainly cultivated for the production of vegetables or fruit crops for consumption by himself or his family'.

1939–1945 Dig for Victory. Some 50 per cent of population grew food crops. There were 6,900 pig clubs. The people produced 70 per cent of vegetables, 25 per cent of eggs – one-fifth of the nation's food.

1947 500,000 wartime allotments had disappeared.

1950s Building boom. Developers sought to take over allotment sites.

1969 Thorpe Report commissioned by Ministry of Natural Resources to review decline. Among the report's findings were that only 3.2 per cent of allotment holders were women. It also noted the poor provision of amenities: only 50 per cent of allotments had piped water; only 2 per cent had WCs. It concluded that allotments should be made into leisure gardens in the continental style, with good facilities for the family.

1970 There were 22,250 hectares (55,000 acres) of allotments, but by 1996 only 13,350 hectares (33,000 acres) – a decline of 43 per cent.

1998 Parliamentary Select Committee Inquiry into The Future for Allotments. The Government agrees to some changes in planning guidance and to support preparation of a good practice guide.

2001 Growing in the Community, the good practice guide for allotment management advocated by the 1998 Inquiry, is published. Revised in 2008, and extended in 2010 with publication of A Place to Grow.

2002 Allotments Regeneration Initiative created to support the implementation of good practice by allotment associations and local authorities.

finding the plot

where to start

Getting hold of a plot these days is not quite as easy at it was a few years ago. Keep in mind, though, that generally people are entitled to go on more than one list, so they could be doubling up. More and smaller plots are being made available every week, and turnover can be rapid. In cities, particularly in the south-east, the unsatisfied demand is highest. It drops considerably as you head north or out into the countryside.

what's available?

Call the local authority and speak to the allotment officer officer (see www.name-of-the-place.gov.uk). Some large councils have several staff and informative websites. Smaller places will have someone with responsibility for the allotments, even if it is not their full-time post. Either way, they should be able to provide you with the full list including the private allotments. The local library should also have the information. Once you have established what the options are, check out the local ones to see if you like the look of them. Some sites have open days and will display a contact number and the number of vacancies, if any, on a board outside.

what type of site?

Statutory allotments

These are protected by Section 8 of the Allotments Act 1925. They are owned by local authorities and comprise 87 per cent of the total. They cannot be closed down without permission from the Secretary of State for the Department of Communities and Local Government. They are therefore comparatively safe from developers, especially if they are in full use. To close them down, the council must prove that they are surplus to requirements. They must show they have promoted and publicized the site and taken into account the people on the waiting list. If a site is closed down, adequate alternative provision must be provided. The best guarantee against closure, therefore, is to keep the site fully occupied.

Temporary sites

These are on land that is intended for other purposes and is being used for allotments meanwhile. These represent 5 per cent. Along with the privately owned allotments (8 per cent including those belonging to the railway companies) they are not protected from closure by law.

Community allotments

This is a new, unofficial term for plots that are gardened communally – school plots and those for disabled or minority groups. It has also come into popular use as a term for allotment sites that open up their gates to draw in the community at large.

management – how is an allotment run?

Fully run by the council

The local authority manages the site, collects the rents and is fully responsible for repairs and maintenance.

A well run site will be fully occupied and have no (or very few) neglected plots.

Participation

Plot holders take responsibility on an informal basis for minor repairs. They may have an allotment forum for the views of plot holders to be aired to the council.

Delegation

An allotment association takes responsibility for the day-to-day running. This might entail collecting rents, dealing with complaints and disputes and maintenance. The authority is responsible for major repairs and overheads.

Semi-autonomy

The allotment association leases the site from the council and takes full responsibility for running it.

Weighing up the situation

There are pros and cons to all the different categories. A good self-run site is likely to be the best bet. However, its success depends entirely on the quality of the people who manage it. The rents on their own with luck may just cover the administration. To get toilets installed or a trading hut will take a pro-active effort of fund raising. Taking the delegation route relieves the plot holders from the responsibility of meeting any heavy costs and the danger of not being able to replace a first-class team should they move on. The downside of relying on the council is that they are inclined to be stretched to the limit.

For advice on management and best practice, get hold of a copy of Growing in the Community published by the Local Government Association.

considerations

Distance from your home
If you take the bus or cycle, and are carrying tools, will you get there after a hard day at work?

Facilities
In an ideal world, you want good access and well-maintained paths. You do not want a site with too many neglected plots as these may affect yours as weed seed blows in.

• Easy access to water is essential, though not required by law. It usually comes in the form of standpipes along the length of the paths backed up by water butts. Good security is vital. Allotments often suffer from vandalism.

• A shed is of great benefit. If there isn't one supplied, it is worth asking about any rules e.g. maximum size if you decide to erect one yourself.

• A first-class site might have a clubhouse and a trading shed. Lavatories are becoming more common every year, particularly where there are disabled plots. Where plumbing is a problem a 'tree bog', 'compost toilet' or a 'leaching bed' can be installed.

• Enterprising management may raise money to hire or buy machinery to share – rotavators, shredders and mowers. They

Ideally your plot should be easy to reach from home. The luckiest plot holders have their plots right on the doorstep.

may put on events, lectures and open days to include the local community.

The organic site

The truly organic allotment site is catching on slowly. Generally, committees resign themselves to discouraging chemicals rather than banning them, as this is difficult rule to enforce.

Some allotment sites are fortunate in having woodland and water nearby, which makes them an oasis for wildlife. Others will make a wildlife area, which will help to keep a healthy balance between pests and predators.

Affiliations

Is the allotment site you favour a member of the National Society of Allotment and Leisure Gardeners? Roughly one-third of all allotment sites are members of NSALG. Member sites can call on them for advice and use their insurance scheme as well as buy a wide range of seed at around half the normal price. Their magazine, *The Allotment and Leisure Gardener*, covers local, national and international allotment news. Affiliated to NSALG is the Scottish Allotments and Gardens Society (SAGS). Members of SAGS can also join NSALG. There is no similar allotment society in Northern Ireland.

What are the rules?

Following the First World War, a hungry, largely unemployed populace began to sell the produce and flowers off their allotments to make a little money. In 1922, selling off the plot was made illegal. However, small-scale sale of produce at the level of farmers' markets for excess produce with the money going back into the site is now quite commonly allowed and accepted. Allotments vary in strictness. Some are run on near-military lines while others are more liberal and boil the rules down to a simple, single phrase – 'Use it or lose it.'

Typically rules are:

- no subletting your plot or using it for trade or business;
- if you vacate your plot, rent must be paid up to date and your belongings be removed within two weeks;
- you may not transfer your tenancy without permission, give your key to other people or allow them to visit your plot unsupervised;
- you must display a number board on your plot, lock gates behind you, inform the management of a change of address and allow them entry to sheds or other structures when requested;
- if you have a shed it must be well maintained;
- dogs must be kept on leads;
- at least 75 per cent of the plot must be cultivated by the end of the first year and be free of weeds;
- it is forbidden to bring rubbish onto the site, block or dig up communal pathways, wash crops or tools in water troughs or use a hosepipe or a sprinkler;
- you may not go onto other people's plots without permission;
- you must not be abusive, violent or a nuisance to other people;
- children must be kept under control; no livestock e.g. rabbits, homing pigeons or chickens are permitted without permission.

Other rules may concern a ban on barbed or razor wire, no trees, only trained fruit trees or only trees that don't overhang into other people's plots. There are sometimes restrictions on bonfires.

Water is usually supplied from stand pipes which may be some distance from the plot. Collect as much rain water as possible in water butts.

There are often restrictions on the size of sheds, greenhouses, polytunnels and other structures.

If you want to keep hens, ducks or rabbits you will need to get permission from the Site Manager. Under the Welfare Act of 2006 it is an offence to fail to provide a suitable environment, appropriate diet and fresh water. You must allow them to exhibit normal behaviour, house those that are social creatures together and protect them from pain, injury, suffering and disease.

choosing the plot

Before taking on a plot, do a little research. Most allotments have open days – a good opportunity to meet people and learn about the site.

size – whole plot, half or quarter?

As allotments sprung from the needs of the 18th century peasant, it could be said to be entirely fitting that the arcane measurements – the pole, the perch and the rod – are still customarily used in allotment circles. All three are the identical measurement, the distance between the back of the plough to the nose of the ox, or 27.5 m (30¼ yd). The full-sized allotment of 10 poles therefore is 275 sq. m (329 sq. yd). This was considered the right size to supply a family with vegetables all year round.

This is a large area to keep up to scratch unless you are able to give it almost daily attention through the growing season. A wartime cropping plan recommended that half the plot be taken up with potatoes. This was calculated to bring in a massive 450 kg (10 cwt) a year, which is more than a family is likely to need these days. So be realistic as to how much time you will actually be able to spend on the plot and how much produce you and

your family will actually consume. You can grow plenty of crops in half a plot, or even just a quarter one. These are becoming more commonly available now as the demand for plots continues to soar. The most common mistake for newcomers is to be overambitious, only to find that they have taken on a little more than they can handle. The best way to get the low-down is to chat to other plot holders.

If there is a choice of plots check out:
- **The neighbours** Your plot will be a place to relax and unwind, so it is important that you will get on well with your neighbours. It is also a good idea to avoid a neighbouring plot with a lot of weeds, which will seed themselves all over yours.
- **The soil** This can differ on different parts of the same site. Look at neighbouring plots to see if the plants are growing well.
- **Aspect** The ideal aspect is south facing. You should be able to move your beds to face in that direction unless the plot is on a slope, in which case the beds would need

to go across it, or if it is shaded by trees on one side.

- **Weeds** If the plot is full of perennial weeds, it is going to be a big job to clear it.
- **Access** Good access means less barrowing of manure etc.
- **Water** It is a great advantage to be near a tap as water is heavy to carry.
- **Shelter** Wind is very damaging to plants.
- **Privacy** If you like a bit a peace and quiet when you garden, a corner plot might suit you best.
- **Frost pockets** You can't grow food in them.
- **Overhanging trees** These will make the plot too shady for growing produce, and the tree roots will soak up nutrients and moisture from the soil.

The lease

Rents vary but are always the best bargain in Britain, bar none. Legally, rents are set at what a tenant can 'reasonably be expected to pay'. The average rent is between £25 and £50 a year, possibly with additional concessions for retired allotment holders. Some of the parish church allotments are as little as £1 per annum.

The lease will include provision for a tenancy to be ended by either party. If the authority wishes to end a tenancy it will need to give a year's notice, expiring on or before Lady Day (25 March) or after Michaelmas (29 September) each year. However, if the tenant fails to pay the rent or breaks the rules, one month's notice is all that is required.

A hard path is a bonus for easy access and deliveries.

preparing the ground

weeds, earth and wind

Once you've procured your plot, do a mini survey to establish a few facts about the soil, the weeds and the wind. You may need to tackle all three before you can really get going.

Making a rough sketch will concentrate the mind. Mark the plot out roughly to scale. Put in any existing features – the shed, water butt, paths or trees. Observe the orientation of the plot and mark it on the plan. You want vegetables to grow north to south, if possible, so that the plants won't shade each other. If there is a damp patch, it might be a good place for a pond. If you find any frost pockets mark them in as useless for growing vegetables. Ground frost can appear even when the air temperature is above 2°C (36°F).

Check on the wind. You may need to put in wind-breaks. Mark the direction of the prevailing winds (usually south-westerly) on the plan.

weeds

Unless you are one of the few lucky exceptions, you will need to clear the weeds before you even start on a new plot. Though some weeds have their uses, none is desirable in the vegetable beds as they will compete for nutrients, water, light and space.

Identify which weeds you have. Annual types are easily kept under control. Perennial weeds need a firmer hand.

Annual weeds

Annual weeds are those that grow, flower, seed and die in the course of one growing season. They propagate themselves by seed, sometimes many thousands per plant. To get on top of them, therefore, it is vital to prevent them from flowering and setting seed. If you don't have time to tackle the problem straightaway, be sure to deadhead them before they have any chance to set seed. Watch also for little seedlings that spring up from seeds blowing in from other plots. There are various ways to deal with annual weeds.

Hoeing As annuals generally live in the top layer of the soil, they can be kept down by hoeing and hand pulling. Through the growing season, keep your hoe to hand so you can catch them young, before they make much root. Only till a few centimetres deep to avoid damaging nearby plants or bringing up more dormant weed seed to the surface and the light where it can germinate.

Shading

Mulches Once you've cleared the ground shade new seed out with a mulch. A 5 cm (2 in) layer of mulch between plants will dispose of most annual weeds. As the mulch is loose, any rogue seedlings that do appear can be pulled out easily. Suitable mulches, which will also benefit the soils as the worms take them down, include horse and other animal manures as well as leaf-mould. Spent hops are sometimes on offer from breweries, while spent mushroom compost, composed of horse manure, peat and chalk, from commercial growers, is alkaline and suitable for neutral to acid soils. All need to be rotted down well before using, to get rid of any pathogens and chemicals. Grass mowings are rich in nitrogen and make a moisture-retaining mulch. Use sparingly as they can get slimy. They can also be spread over newspaper to keep down weeds for short periods as they rot down.

Close planting Plant closely and thin late so there isn't much room for weeds. Broad-leaved plants – potatoes, courgettes and cabbage – are effective in shading out annual weeds. If you feel you are losing the battle, give your plants a head start against the competition by transplanting, using pregerminated or chitted seed, or by fluid sowing.

The stale seedbed Prepare the bed for sowing. If the weather is cold, warm it by covering with polythene or fleece for a couple of weeks. This will encourage the weed seeds to germinate. Hoe them off before sowing your seed. Your plants should get a head start and be up and going before any more weeds appear.

Perennial weeds

Perennial weeds go on from year to year and are a more serious proposition. If you have lots, you need to take sweeping measures. Most can spread from their roots as well as from seed. Dock and cow parsley grow massive taproots. Couch grass, ground elder and willow herb make a tangled underground network, while the roots of coltsfoot, horsetail, creeping thistle and bindweed have very deep storage roots. The roots of bindweed have been found at the bottom of wells. All are difficult to dig out cleanly and will sprout from the tiniest section of root left in the ground.

Rotavating perennial weeds is counter-productive. It transforms the look of things only for the briefest moment. Ultimately, it will only make things worse. As the roots get chopped up each section will turn into another plant and so multiply itself even more. Another disadvantage is that

A 5 cm (2 in) layer of mulch will keep annual weeds at bay and prevent evaporation.

Many perennial weeds have an extensive root system and will resprout from the smallest piece of root left in the ground.

Horse or mare's tail (Equisetum arvense) is a common garden weed flourishing in poor damp ground. It produces thousands of spores and the roots can go down as far as 1.5 m/5 ft.

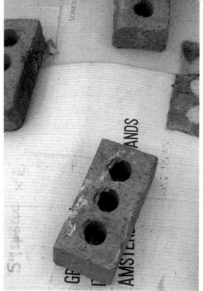

far left *If you make slits in weed suppressing black plastic you can grow plants through them.*

left *Plastic sacks firmly weighed down with bricks to deal with tough perennial weeds in time.*

opposite *To clear perennial weeds by digging them out, loosen the soil first and go back to tackle the weeds with hand tools making sure that you get every bit of root out.*

rotavating can, in certain circumstances, damage the soil structure by creating a 'hard pan' – an impermeable layer which will adversely affect the drainage.

Some of the best ways to deal with perennial weeds are as follows.

Excluding light No plant can live without light. If you have tall weeds, scythe or strim them down. Cover the area with heavy black plastic buried at the edges and weighed down with stones or bricks. For really bad weeds, like mare's tail, layer thick wodges of newspaper, or heavy cardboard, overlapping and pinned down under the heavy black plastic. This is turn can be heavily weighted down with stones or timbers.

The length of time you need to keep the ground covered depends on the particular weed. Some will be gone within the year, while the most persistent can take three years. However, if you make cross slits in the plastic to allow in water or use porous horticultural plastic, the land needn't be wasted. You can plant small plants of vigorous growers – potatoes, marrows or pumpkins – through the slits.

Mowing If your allotment plot is covered in thick grass and weeds, scythe or strim it down and keep it short. Only lawn weeds – low-growing 'rosette' weeds, like daisies – will survive constant mowing. When you are ready to plant, take off the turf, bury it upside down about a spit down and cover with the topsoil. It will soon rot down into good loam. Another method is to make a turf stack. Stack the turfs upside-down and cover with black plastic or hessian-backed carpet, to cut out the light. The stack should become friable and crumbly after six months or so.

Flame gunning A flame gun is a portable gas torch in use in agriculture since the 19th century. It gives off the right heat to rupture the cell walls several hours after exposure to the flame; it doesn't kill the plants by burning them. You can tell if the treatment has been effective by pressing a leaf between finger and thumb after the treatment. If it leaves dark green finger-prints, then it has worked. Weeds are flame gunned at about 71°C (160°F) for a single second. In agriculture, flame gunning is generally used for clearing small weeds in the carefully calculated time between

sowing a crop and the seeds emerging. It has the advantage of not disturbing the soil with the consequence of bringing more weed seed up to the light to germinate. Tough perennials may need several treatments of flame gunning. It cannot be used when the soil is mulched. Obviously flame gunning should be treated with respect. It's wise to check with the management before going ahead.

Hand digging Water well. Start digging away from the plant to loosen the soil. Lift the weed from beneath, then go back and sift through the soil with a hand tool searching out broken-off fragments, which could turn into new plants.

This works but it is painstaking. Be realistic. You may not be able to deal with the whole plot immediately. By law, allotment holders are expected to cultivate the first quarter in three months, and three-quarters by the end of the first year and the whole plot after that. So, if you are going to have a big battle with the weeds, aim to get one-quarter well weeded and planted within three months. If necessary, put the rest of it under hefty light-excluding cover until you have time to attack it.

the soil

Getting the soil into top condition is the key to successful organic growing. To grow plants on poor soil is like building a house on sand. Good soil is teaming with life and nutrients – fungi, algae, bacteria, worms, vegetable and animal remains, air and water. The organic gardener's maxim is to look after the soil and let the soil look after the plants. Plants in top health give better yields, have resistance to pests, will shrug off diseases and spring back from adverse weather conditions.

If the plot is lush with stinging nettles, chickweed and dock, you can be fairly sure that the soil is fertile.

Dig up a little soil and analyse it. Healthy soil has an agreeable, earthy smell. A thriving worm population will tell you that it is friable and will be easy to work. Ideally, there should be two or three worms on every spadeful of soil you dig.

Check the type

Pick up a small handful half an hour after rain and roll it between thumb and fingers. Clay soil is sticky, sandy is gritty and silt is silky. Loam – the best soil of all – contains roughly equal amounts of all three. If it moulds into a ball, it will be silt or clay. Clay goes shiny when rubbed. Chalk will slip through your fingers, while peat is dark and crumbly.

Clay soil is rich in minerals and nutrients. It can become waterlogged, is slow to warm up in spring, tough to dig and will cake in the heat. Brassicas, which like firm planting, do well on clay. Avoid treading on it as it will become hard and

A good wheelbarrow is essential on any allotment and is particularly useful for moving large quantities of soil.

compacted. Winter weather will break it down if you dig it over and leave it in rough clumps in autumn. Incorporate sharp sand, grit and plenty of organic matter to lighten it so that air can circulate and water drain through it. With a little work, clay can become workable, good soil.

Sandy soil is free draining and easy to work. It warms up quickly in spring. It is a light soil, particularly good for salad crops, roots and legumes. It can be too free draining so that nutrients are washed through it, or 'leached', by rain. It is often low in potash. Adding well-rotted compost or manure will help to bind the particles together and retain nutrients and moisture. Leave any digging until spring and keep it covered through winter, to minimize leaching.

Silt is an alluvial soil from river banks. It lies somewhere between clay and sand. It is easily compacted but holds on quite well to nutrients. Treat as for clay soil.

Chalk is free-draining, poor soil. It is full of lime, which makes it alkaline and inhospitable to many plants. It is often low in potash. Organic matter will help to bulk it up and counteract the alkalinity.

Peat comes from wetland, is light and easy to work, and is fertile but acidic. It retains water when wet but dries fast, when it has a tendency to blow away. Adding lime will make it more alkaline, while organic matter will give it substance and weight.

While each type of soil is very different in character, there is one simple cure for all types. A few years of the addition of generous quantities of organic matter applied regularly will transform each type. It will lighten clay and silt and make them more free draining and quicker to warm up in spring. It will enrich poor chalky soils and counteract the alkalinity. It will give peaty soils more body and weight.

Soil pH

The pH (potential of Hydrogen) is a scale of acidity/alkalinity. It goes from zero to 14. The ideal for plants and micro-organisms is smack in the middle at seven – neutral. Above seven is alkaline, and below seven is acid. Some plants have a preference for a little more acidity or alkalinity. The majority of food crops prefer soil on the alkaline side – pH7.5 – but potatoes are best planted in acid soil – pH5–6. Neither plants nor the micro-organisms that feed them can survive extremes at either end of the scale. However, real extremes are unusual.

How to test your soil's pH Collect three or four small samples of soil from different parts of the plot. You can send them off for a full analysis, as advertised in gardening magazines or though the Royal Horticultural Society (RHS), but a cheap kit from a gardening centre is probably all you need.

If the soil is too acidic, add lime to counteract it. Ground limestone (calcium carbonate) and dolomitic limestone (calcium magnesium carbonate) are the organic choices. Do not add them at the same time as manure as they react against each other. General practice is to lime in autumn and manure in spring.

If the soil is too alkaline, garden manure and compost will send it in the right direction. Test every year to monitor progress. While you can tip the balance and improve the soil, you cannot completely change its character.

Soil profile

If you are being thorough, or have worries about drainage as water is sitting in pools, dig a small hole around 90 cm (3 ft) deep. This will reveal some horizontal bands – the topsoil, the subsoil, broken rock and the bedrock below.

If the soil is too acidic for the crop, add lime. Avoid putting it on at the same time as manure.

Topsoil The first layer, the topsoil, is noticeably darker than the rest. This is the layer that feeds the plants. Check the depth. About 45 cm (18 in) of topsoil is right for soft fruit. Fruit trees need about 60 cm (24 in). Most vegetables will be happy with 38 cm (15 in).

The soil structure is the way particles clump together. If you can see plenty of holes and cracks on the exposed face you can be sure that there is plenty of air going through. If not, then you need to open it up by adding organic matter or raising the beds.

Subsoil This is lighter in colour. It contains few plant nutrients but its structure affects drainage. It is important that water can flow away and air can get to the roots. Test it by pouring water down the hole to see if it runs away. If it doesn't, it could be due to compacted airless topsoil or an impermeable barrier in the subsoil known as a 'hard pan'. This can usually be broken up with a pickaxe, or loosened with a fork, and kept aerated with regular additions of organic matter.

garden compost and manure

Compost

To get your soil into top condition you are going to need a plentiful supply of compost. Aim for a big heap as you need a good quantity to get the full effect – around 5 kg per square metre (12 lb per square yard), applied annually. The sooner you start building a compost heap, the better. Whereas a commercial-sized heap will heat up in a matter of days, a small heap can take all winter, or two or three months in summer, to rot down.

Making compost is the speeding up of a natural process that will bring life to the soil. As animal and vegetable remains rot down, the heap heats up and the population of helpful micro-organisms will burgeon. As the heap cools down, worms and insects join in.

The final result is humus – gardener's gold. It dramatically improves soil texture, structure, water-holding capacity and drainage. When the compost is ready, it will have reduced by half its volume, it will be sweet smelling, dark and crumbly. The original contents will be unrecognizable.

Compost bins The best plan is to have three compost bins – one ready to use, one rotting down and one being filled. You need a container without a bottom so that the worms to get in. Small gaps are important for air circulation but you don't want gaping holes as they will let the heat out and dry the compost. A lid or cover will keep the rain off and you will need access from the side or top to turn the compost

The ideal is a row of compost bins – one ready, one rotting down and one in the making. The sacking blanket gives extra warmth.

and get it out. For fast composting, make the bins at least 1 cu. m (35 cu. ft).

There are many types on the market including recycled plastic bins. Occasionally these are given out free by the council. However, on a plot an excellent, no-cost compost bin can be made from three pallets nailed together at the corners with a fourth tied on to make a door. Push straw, old sacks or newspaper into the gaps and make a lid from a piece of board. Wood is the best material for compost bins as it has insulation and it 'breathes'.

Compost activators To speed up the action, use a compost activator every 15 cm (6 in) or so through the heap. A little rotted compost from an old heap will get the process started. Farm manure, human urine, nettles, seaweed meal, poultry or pigeon droppings, comfrey leaves and blood, fish and bone are all good activators. Lime helps if the heap smells sour or if you are on acid soil.

What to compost You can compost anything organic – kitchen scraps, tea bags and coffee, eggshells, wood ash, hair, newspaper and cardboard, natural fabrics, garden prunings and weeds.

However, if you are not sure that you will achieve maximum heat, it is prudent to leave out perennial weed roots, weed seeds (which might survive the experience), fish and meat (which might attract rodents) and diseased material. The topgrowth of potatoes often contains potato blight and potatoes may sprout again, so don't take the risk. Brassica roots may have club-root. Cat and dog faeces should never be used for compost where you are growing vegetables. Evergreen plants are slow to decompose. Keep them separate. Pine needles are acidic and can

make a good mulch for acid-loving plants such as blueberries or be used for paths.

How to make compost Start off the heap with something coarse and twiggy (sticks or straw) to let in air from the bottom. Build it slowly as and when you have suitable materials or go for a fast, big heap. To do this, collect and save a good assortment of materials, aiming for about one-third green (wet) materials to two-thirds of dry ones. Fill a few dustbins full of different things before you start. You might pick up extra material from outdoor markets and greengrocers. Chop up woody materials into short lengths and crush the tough stalks or be prepared to pull them whole out at the end. Cut fabrics up into small pieces. Tear newspaper into strips.

Water any dry materials, such as straw, paper and cloth. Squeeze them out. If you have too much green material, particularly grass mowings, you will end up with a slimy mess. You want moisture, but not sogginess, which will make the heap putrefy. Aim for squeezed sponge dampness. Mix your ingredients together. Let the heap settle by itself.

A couple of turnings at intervals of a few weeks will speed up rotting and give you the opportunity to check on progress and make adjustments. Dig out the whole heap onto a plastic sheet and add whatever it lacks – more water or green material if it's too dry, more shredded dampened paper, rags or straw if it's too wet. Mix it up again, add some more activator and fork it back. To get full value from your compost when it is ready, use it in early spring.

If you don't have enough material to make much difference to the heap, bury kitchen and garden waste about 30 cm (12 in) deep in a trench. Cover with soil and

An effective leaf mould container can be made out of a length of chicken wire. The sticks at the bottom are to raise it for air circulation.

allow it to rot down. Make holes, fill them with potting compost and plant greedy feeders, such as courgettes, through it. Bean trenches are often prepared in this way in autumn for the following year. Many people put a layer of mowings or a few comfrey leaves in potato trenches before planting.

Sheet composting looks unsightly but is another way to make use of small amounts of kitchen and garden waste. Lay thin layers of compost between vegetable rows and let it rot down where it lies on the soil.

Leaf-mould Compost is broken down quickly by bacteria, while leaf-mould is broken down gently by fungus. After a year it can be dug in, to improve soil structure, opening it up for air and water, as a peat substitute and for home-made seed and potting compost. As it can hold up to 500 times its weight in water it makes a great water-retaining mulch. If you leave it for a second year it will turn into humus. If you want to speed up the process, shred the leaves by running a mower over them first.

Collect the leaves in a cage of chicken wire or in black plastic sacks with holes punched into them. Add a little water. No further action is needed except to push the pile down as you add more leaves, and to water it in dry summer months. If you and other plot holders need more leaves, the Parks Departments will often deliver them free of charge.

Animal manure

Well-rotted horse manure is another great traditional soil improver. The urine in it provides nitrogen and potassium, and the manure and straw bedding will bulk up the soil. Do a little research, however, before obtaining any from an unknown source.

Animal manure must not be used fresh as it will scorch the plants, rob them of nitrogen and may be full of pathogens – possibly horrors like wormers, antibiotics, weed-killers or hormones. Once rotted down, however, it will be transformed into a great soil conditioner. On straw it should only take 3–6 months to rot. On wood shavings it will take a year.

As with compost, the bigger the heap, the better and the more quickly it will rot down. A good-sized heap would be 1.5 m (5 ft) high and wide. Speed it up by turning the sides into the middle from time to time. If the top and sides are covered with polythene or a tarpaulin, more heat will be created. If hot enough this will kill off lurking weed seeds and prevent the nutrients from being leached by rain. When ready, the manure will be dark, crumbly and pleasant smelling as well as teaming with small, bright red branding (fishing) worms.

Using animal manure For vegetables, spread the well-rotted manure thickly on the soil in winter, for the frosts to break it down even further. The worms will till it for you, dragging it down into the soil. However, if you need to lime the soil in autumn, spread the manure in spring. If applied at the same time they will react against each other and the nitrogen will be wasted.

Green manures

Green manures, until recently regarded as agricultural rather horticultural crops, are now widely used by plot holders. They are even introduced in tiny spaces such as the greenhouse. They are fast-growing crops that can be slotted in for a few weeks or up to a year or more when there are gaps or when you want to leave a part of the ground fallow. Green manures are cut down when young and dug in, adding fertility and improving soil structure. The tops will provide you with masses of good material for the compost heap.

If you have empty beds that you are not ready to plant, or a gap between two different crops, a green manure crop will make a quick-growing, temporary cover, blocking out the light to keep the weeds down. If you wanted to take some time off in winter, a covering of winter green manures, such as grazing rye or winter tare, will protect the soil and keep your plot looking cared for while you are away.

As the roots bind the soil together they are beneficial for light soils and they prevent erosion and leaching by rain. Heavy clay soils benefit from the types of green manures that have roots that will break it up, such as buckwheat and Italian ryegrass, helping drainage and drawing nutrients and minerals from the depths.

The leguminous types, such as clovers, winter beans, trefoil and lupins, store nitrogen in the roots, which is released into the soil as they rot down when dug in. Nitrogen is good for leaf growth. So these green manures are

far left *The bigger the manure heap, the quicker it will rot down.*

left *Manure is ready to use when it is sweet smelling and full of branding worms.*

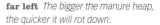

Phacelia tanecetifolia has ferny leaves and lavender flowers which are so attractive to hoverflies that it is used in agriculture for biological control against crop pests.

Trefoil is useful for resting overused soil and improving fertility. The plants can be left in the ground for a year or so but should be clipped occasionally to stop them going woody.

particularly useful when followed by a leafy brassica crop.

Most have flowers that attract beneficial insects. Though the crops are usually dug into the soil before they flower, it is worth leaving a few in the ground for this reason. Alternatively, keep a patch especially for beautiful crimson clover and the forget-me-not blue of Phacelia flowers. You could include a few in your wildflower area. Another idea is to sow crimson clover underneath established fruit trees. It will look a picture and work like a magnet for bees and butterflies. Green manures make good cover for the pest controllers such as beetles, frogs and toads.

Sowing green manure Before sowing green manure rake the ground to a fine tilth. Usually the seed is broadcast by throwing it as you walk up one side of the bed and across the top. If the area to be sown is small, large seed (from, for example, field bean or lupin) can be sown individually by hand.

Cutting down Cut down green manures before they flower or when you need the ground. Dig them up, chopping up the foliage with a spade as you go to speed up decomposition. Light annuals, such as mustard or buckwheat, can be hoed off. Cut down tougher specimens, such as Italian rye grass or grazing rye, and leave for a few days before digging them in roughly. A second digging usually will get the last roots out. If the plants have become woody, put the tops on the compost heap and dig in the roots only. Some of the perennials, such as clover, trefoil and rye grasses, may regrow and will need to be hoed off or covered with mulch. Break up any tough lumps with a sharp spade. If you are on the no-dig system (see page 46), leave the residue on the surface to act as a mulch, or compost it.

When to sow and plant after green manuring Green manure that has been in for only a few weeks will rot down quickly and a new crop can go in within a few days. A more mature crop will take as long

as a month – longer for the grazing ryes. The rye grasses inhibit seed germination while they rot down. Either wait for a few weeks before sowing the next crop, or use transplants, rather than seed, as they will not be affected.

Types of green manure Fenugreek, mustard, *Phacelia* and buckwheat are fast-growing, leafy plants that can be slotted in six- to eight-week gaps when the ground is cleared between crops.

Winter tare, grazing rye, winter beans and Italian ryegrass are sown in early autumn when many vegetables are lifted and can stay over winter, to be dug into the soil the following spring – a productive way to leave the land fallow.

Alfalfa, red clover and trefoil can be left in the ground for a year or so but should be clipped occasionally to stop them going woody. These are useful for resting overused soil, improving fertility or giving you a break.

Keep in mind crop rotation. Winter beans, clover and lupins are legumes. Mustard and fodder radish are brassicas.

Green manure plants
Alfalfa, lucerne

(*Medicago sativa*) LEGUMINOSAE
Nitrogen fixer. A few months or up to three years. Growing to 1 m (3 ft). If left long term, cut the tops off before they go woody and put them on the compost heap, to encourage fresh growth. Agricultural fodder crop with massively deep roots, up to 4.5 m (15 ft) long, which draw up nutrients to the topsoil. Dislikes wet, acid soils.

Beans, field

(*Vicia faba*) LEGUMINOSAE
Nitrogen fixer. Agricultural broad beans, originally grown as animal fodder – hence

the expression 'full of beans'. They have deep tap roots which help to excavate the soil and add organic matter to the subsoil. Sow September to November to overwinter Very hardy. Best in moist loam. Foliage will sprout again when cut down. Moderately easy to dig in. Dry seed for following year.

Buckwheat

(*Fagopyrum esculentum*) POLYGONACEAE – knotweed family. Anywhere in the crop rotation. Tender annual. 90 cm (3 ft). Sow in April or when the soil warms up. Fast grower, producing plentiful organic matter. Can be cut down in June. Good, short-term green manure for resting the soil in spring before the tender vegetables – tomatoes, aubergines, peppers – are planted in June. Has deep roots, which break up heavy soils and draw up nutrients. Smothers weeds. Copes with poor soil. Flowers attract helpful hoverflies.

Crimson clover

(*Trifolium incarnatum*),

Essex red clover

(*T. pratense*),

and white clover

(*T. repens*) LEGUMINOSAE
Nitrogen fixers. Hardy perennials, growing up to 30 cm (12 in). Crimson clover prefers light soil and has gorgeous, red flowers, which are loved by bees. Sow March–August or leave over winter. Red Essex clover prefers good loam. Sow April–August for 3–18 months. Crimson and red clovers are fairly easy to dig in. White clover is a long-lived perennial with a deep taproot. It is good for long-term green manuring. It has dense foliage to suppress weeds and is very attractive to friendly predators. However, repeated use of any clover can bring on 'clover sickness'.

Fenugreek

(*Trigonella foenum-graecum*) LEGUMINOSAE
Rarely fixes nitrogen in the UK. Semi-hardy annual. 60 cm (24 in). Possibly best fast grower. Bushy plants have weed-suppressing foliage. Plant late spring–summer. Grow for up to three months in well-drained, moisture-retentive soil.

Lupin

(*Lupinus angustifolius*) LEGUMINOSAE
Agricultural lupin. Sow spring for a slow-maturing summer crop. 50 cm (20 in). Takes 2–3 months to get to the digging stage. Seeds are sown rather than broadcast. Deep-rooting lupins improve soil texture, fix

White clover is good for long-term green manuring. It has dense foliage to suppress weeds and is very attractive to friendly predators.

nitrogen and are effective in suppressing weeds. If left to flower, they are attractive to beneficial predators. They are poisonous, possibly ruling them out for the allotment.

Mustard

(*Sinapsis alba*) BRASSICACEAE
Tender annual for couple of months in summer or early autumn. Rapid growing and weed smothering. Needs moisture and fertile soil. Reduces soil-borne pests and diseases. Once mustard starts to flower, it goes over quickly, so dig it in. This is easily done. Good green manure for summer.

Trefoil is usually dug in before flowering when used as a green manure. If you leave a few plants to flower however, it will draw in bees like a magnet.

Phacelia

(*Phacelia tanacetifolia*) HYDROPHYLLACEAE – waterleaf family. Anywhere in the rotation. Semi-hardy annual. Growing to 90 cm (3 ft). Ferny leaves. Bright blue flowers attractive to beneficial insects. Grow for a couple of months in summer or for 5–6 months in winter. Easygoing regarding soils and easy to dig in.

Ryegrasses – Hungarian grazing rye

(*Secale cereale*)

Italian ryegrass

(*Lolium multiflorum*) GRAMINEAE Grass family. Anywhere in the rotation. Tough, hardy annuals used for overwintering on almost any soil. Sow August–November. Considered to be best green manures for soil improvement. Dig out a couple of months before you need the land and let them rot down. The disadvantages are that their tough fibrous roots are not easy to dig up.

Trefoil

(*Medicago lupulina*) LUGUMINOSAE Nitrogen fixer. Hardy biennial. Summer grower. 30 cm (12 in). Sow March–August. It takes three months to grow and is a good crop for overwintering. Not fussy about soil except will not survive in acid. Makes dense foliage.

Winter tare

(*Vicia sativa*) LEGUMINOSAE Nitrogen fixer. Hardy annual. 75 cm (30 in). Fast-growing, bushy vetch providing good leaf cover. Dislikes drought. Prefers alkaline soils. Sow in March–May or July–September for three months. Reasonably easy to dig in. Five-star green manure for fixing nitrogen quickly and suppressing weeds.

wind

Though plants need a good air flow round them they will not prosper in winds. Even mild winds dry out the topsoil, plant roots and leaves. As vegetables are juicy plants, they are particularly susceptible to dehydration. Wind stress has the effect of producing smaller plants, with smaller leaves and flowers. This makes them less attractive to pollinators and helpful predators. When the ground is frozen, overwintering crops are not able to take up water to replace moisture blown out of their leaves.

If you are on a windy site, put up windbreaks. It is reckoned that shelter will increase production by up to 30 per cent. To be effective windbreaks need to filter the wind and diffuse it. A solid barrier is counter-productive because wind is like a tidal wave: when it hits a solid barrier it will shoot over the top at full force.

If the wind is on the mild side of the allotment, plant a natural windbreak in the form of tall plants such as trained fruit trees or a summer screen of Jerusalem artichokes. If the wind is more severe, a hedge – not always allowed on allotments – is highly effective. A mixed native deciduous hedge would be of great advantage to wildlife as well as you. Lathe and wattle fencing or trellis will look attractive and be doubly useful as you can grow crops up them. You can buy plastic netting for the purpose, which you could also use to back up the hedge until it grows up.

A windbreak is effective up to six times its height. So a 2 m (6 ft) windbreak would protect the 12 m (40 ft) in front of it. Small plants can be protected by bigger ones running alongside them or a strip of green manure like grazing rye.

the division
of space

divide and rule

On the principle of divide and rule, start by splitting the plot up into manageable chunks. You needn't use traditional squares and rectangles – triangles, circles, ovals and diamond shapes are equally good.

components

Important components for consideration of a place on your plot are:
- shed, greenhouse, polytunnel, cold frames, seating area, water butts and nursery bed;
- compost bins, manure heaps and leaf-mould;
- windbreaks;
- beds for annual vegetables on rotation, for perennial vegetables, soft fruit, trained top fruit, herbs and flowers;
- raised beds;
- climbers on supports and screens for privacy;
- paths;
- a pond;
- children's beds.

Structures
The shed, greenhouse, polytunnel, cold frames, seating area, water butts and nursery beds would normally be grouped together for ease of working. The roof of the shed or greenhouse can be used for catching rainwater to be siphoned off into water butts below. If you choose a shed where the pitch of the roof isn't too steep (30 degree maximum) you could green roof it (see Meadow on a roof, page 335). The south-facing side of a shed might make a handy sheltered position for seedbeds and cold frames. Near the shed (and the kettle) would be a natural place to sit.

Composting areas
Compost bins usually go at the far end of the plot to avoid flies and the smell of decaying vegetables being anywhere near where you might work or relax. If you get a delivery of manure you will probably want it at the nearest delivery point and as far from you as possible. Arrange compost and manure heaps near the main path so that you can load and unload a wheelbarrow easily. If you are on a slope, have the heap at the high end so you go downhill when it is loaded.

Windbreaks
If you are on a windy site, decide what kind of windbreak you would like and which

would be most effective – a plant screen, trellis or fencing, a hedge or netting.

Beds for different crop types

A grid pattern for your plot is probably the simplest and most practical solution. For annual vegetables you will need at least four defined beds so you can move each group around every year on the rotation system (see page 72). There is no need for the beds to be the traditional oblong strips. However, whatever shape, ideally they should be no more than 120 cm (4 ft) wide so that you can reach across without treading on them and compacting the soil. If you want them to be bigger than this, you can get round the problem by working off planks or putting in stepping stones at strategic points.

The beds for annual rotation vegetables should be sheltered and in full sun. To avoid them shading each other run them north–south.

Most permanent plantings will need separate beds. Asparagus, which lasts for 20 years or more, needs a bed to itself.

Cane and bush fruit are long-term fixtures (blackberries and hybrids keep going for up to 25 years) and may need supports, such as post and wire or trellis. Top fruit – apples, pears, plums, cherries and peaches etc. – are usually grown flat as trained trees on fans, cordons or stepovers. Many allotment committees don't allow any trees – not even fruit trees as they may cast shade on the plot for the next tenant or the neighbouring one. Strawberries will need to be moved to a different spot every third year and can be slotted in wherever there is a gap.

The perennials, such as artichoke, rhubarb and seakale, can go in borders around the edge of the plot. They don't need a position in full sun. In gaps grow some comfrey for a free supply of fertilizer and wild flowers for the bees and friendly predators that will help to cope with the pests.

You might like to have some scented flowers and herbs around your seating area. The Mediterranean herbs, such as lavender, rosemary and thyme, enjoy

above left Having a bench so that you can enjoy the evening sun is one of the great pleasures of having a plot.

above Polytunnels can extend the season at both ends and are a cheaper alternative to a greenhouse.

How to make a raised bed

You will need: four boards of the same height, sawn to the appropriate length; four stakes – 5 x 5 cm (2 x 2 in) to the width of the board plus 15–20 cm/6–8 in and sharpened to a point; drill; screws long enough to go through the timber and into the stake; screwdriver.

1 *Gather your materials and tool together, ensuring that the boards and stakes are the correct size.*

2 *Bang the stake into the ground to the right height. Drill through the upright into the board and secure with a screw. Repeat for the other board.*

3 *Fill with compost or soil.*

baking in the sun and their aromatic scents are known to have a soothing effect. Place the seating area to face south for day-long sun, east for morning sun, or west to catch the last rays of the evening.

You might like to give the children a little plot to themselves.

Raised beds

If your soil is poor, raising the beds gives you the opportunity of starting afresh. It also opens the possibility of taking on the no-dig system (see page 46) and provides easy access for gardeners in wheelchairs (see Gardening for the disabled, page 67). Other advantages are that beds with sides will contain the soil and prevent heavy rains from washing away, or leaching, the nutrients. They will stop soil spilling over onto the paths as the beds get higher once you start adding organic matter on a regular basis. An edging of old planks is the usual method. Logs sawn in half lengthways are a good alternative. While untreated hardwood railway sleepers make excellent edgings, those treated with coal tar creosote contain harmful chemicals. Coal tar was never intended for use by the public and has never been available for sale. It was intended for use for telegraph poles and railway sleepers.

Supports and screens

Supports for beans or fruit can be triple purpose. They can be a climbing frame for the plants, provide a low-level windbreak and give you a screen behind which you can retire peacefully with your newspaper.

Paths

Paths need to follow the most direct route from A to B – otherwise, in practice, they won't be used. It is ingrained human nature to take the shortest route, even if it means

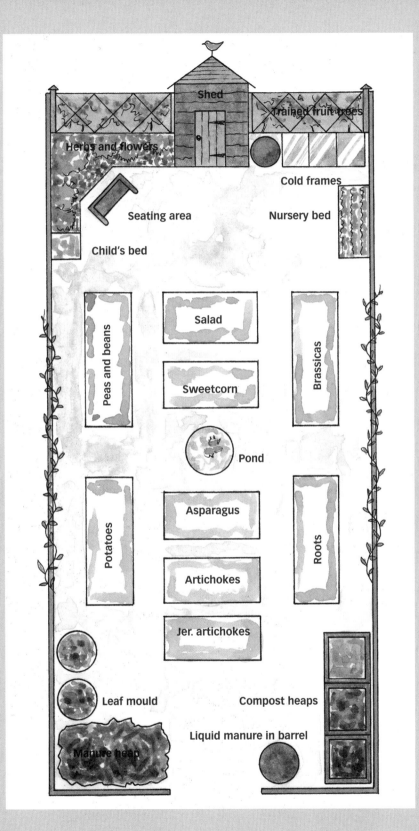

Shed

Trained fruit trees

Herbs and flowers

Cold frames

Seating area

Nursery bed

Child's bed

Peas and beans

Salad

Brassicas

Sweetcorn

Pond

Potatoes

Asparagus

Roots

Artichokes

Jer. artichokes

Leaf mould

Compost heaps

Liquid manure in barrel

Manure heap

Draw up a simple plan showing where everything on your plot will be situated.

opposite A simple and attractive path can be made with a layer of hefty plastic to keep the weeds at bay covered with wood chip.

right *If you are laying down paving, leave it loose until you are absolutely sure that you have the path in the right place.*

far right *A log makes an informal edge to separate the path from the bed.*

taking a running jump over a flowerbed. Work out how the paths will link the compost heap to the flowerbeds, and so on. The main paths should be wide enough to push a loaded wheelbarrow through with ease and without brushing the plants. Plan a network of paths. Some need be only wide enough to get behind the plants (such as soft fruit) to tend them.

When starting out, it is probably best to have temporary paths. These can be anything from trampled earth to mown grass. Wood chips make luxuriant paths. If you are on a weedy site, a covering of hefty plastic underneath will deal with them in time. If you have access to paving slabs, lay them down loose on a bed of sand until you are sure that the paths are where you want them.

Ponds

A substantial pond or source of water on the site is wonderful for wildlife. If there is none, even a tiny pond on your plot will be

Making a pond with a butyl liner

1 Dig a hole. Put the subsoil and topsoil in separate piles. A good shape for a small pond is like an inverted sun hut, with the deepest point in the middle and a gentle shoreline all round.

2 Lay a board over to check that the levels on the outside are equal.

3 Remove sharp stones. Line the hole with soft sand as an extra precaution.

4 Cut out the lining, allowing plenty of overlap all round.

5 Line the hole with the lining and hold it in place with stones or bricks.

6 Drop some subsoil into the bottom of the hole and layer it on the sides to hide the liner and provide a growing medium. Don't use topsoil as you want to keep fertility low.

7 Add water slowly. You may need to let the liner out to prevent it from going into folds or crumpling.

8 When the pond is full, cut off excess liner cautiously. Build up the banks with subsoil and pack it down hard. Fill any gaps with stones to hide the liner and to keep the edges in place. Put topsoil on the ground around the pond for planting and fill any cracks and crevices.

helpful for biodiversity. A south-facing spot out of wind and away from trees is ideal. You can provide a little shade for creatures that want it with the planting. An old sink, cattle trough or ready shaped pond liner will serve the purpose. Ideally it should be 60cm (2ft) deep at some point, to stop it freezing at the bottom where creatures gather to hibernate. Otherwise shallow waters are best. Most aquatic invertebrates live in the top few centimetres. You will need to make a gentle sloping shoreline so that creatures can drink and wash in safety.

The addition of water from an established pond will kick-start the wildlife. Within days beetles, dragonflies, water boatmen and pond skaters will appear under their own steam. Water snails often arrive by air on the legs of water birds. Add a little frogspawn for slug control. For biodiversity, don't put in fish as they are inclined to eat everything.

Beds for children

One way to get young children interested in gardening is to make them a little plot of their own. Site it in a sunny spot in the centre of activity – somewhere near the shed and seating area. A raised bed, knocked up from old planks or recycled from an outgrown sand pit, will bring scented flowers up to a child's nose level while keeping everything contained.

Young children like instant gratification, so ease the way for them and prepare the ground. As a finishing touch you could mark out the initials together in little plants or pebbles. Pumpkins and squashes grow at speed and come in wonderful pantomime shapes. Buy tools of the right size and weight for a child. Though, non-edible gourds are fun for children to grow as ornaments. Sunflowers sprout within a week and you will see a growth spurt on every visit. Mark off how much they have grown in each week or have sunflower races. Cut the deadheads off at the end of the season, remove the petals and hang them off trees for the birds.

Nasturtiums flower non-stop and come in sunset colours. Children enjoy finding 'faces' in pansies and snapping the jaws of snapdragons. The flowers of canary creeper look like small birds. Most children love to eat home-grown sweet cherry tomatoes and strawberries. Buy them little plants.

If children catch a few caterpillars, they can observe the metamorphic cycle. A pond will be endlessly fascinating especially if there are frogs in it. Some seed merchants have a special 'kids' mixes' to attract the creepy crawlies. To round off the entertainments when all else palls, you could put paving for hopscotch or a giant snakes-and-ladders board.

The dig / no-dig gardening debate

Traditionally in Europe, soil is dug or tilled to remove weeds, to loosen the soil, get air through it and to incorporate compost and manure down into the lower levels. Farming practice is to allow the land to stand fallow without being tilled to recover itself every so many years.

The arguments against digging are that it is detrimental to the food web in the fragile topsoil, that it brings weed seed up to the surface where it can germinate and that it damages the soil's structure. Also digging moves nutrients to lower levels of the soil, where there is less oxygen and where they are less available to micro-organisms.

The no-dig method

Before you adopt the no-dig method, always get rid of perennial weeds. You need to have considerable quantities of organic matter to hand. The principle is to keep adding thick layers (10–15 cm/4–6 in) of mulching materials such as manure, compost, leaf-mould, spent mushroom compost and old straw. This will be taken down by the worms and other soil life, aerating the soil. Their excretions will bind together the soil crumbs. When you want to plant, it is permissible to excavate a small hole in the topsoil. Potatoes, however, are grown entirely on the surface.

Alternatively, if the soil is really poor and thin and the perennial weeds are overwhelming, you can practise no-dig gardening by covering the soil completely with a sheet mulch such as impenetrable, thick layers of wet, biodegradable material (newspapers or cardboard) to black out the weeds over several years. Then you make new compost on top of them using the same mulching materials with the addition of good topsoil or proprietary compost and plant and sow into that.

how will you garden?

Do you want to go one step further than organic gardening? Though permaculture, biodynamic and forest gardening were originally devised for greener agricultural solutions, they can be effectively adapted to the allotment plot.

the bioneers

Modern organic agriculture

Sir Albert Howard (1873–1947) is known as the father of modern organic agriculture. He believed that the health of soil, plant, animal and man is one and indivisible. A British botanist and agricultural adviser in charge of a government research farm at Indore, India, his job was to teach Western agricultural techniques. However, he found that he could learn more from the Indians, particularly the connection between healthy soil and the health of the people, livestock and crops. He invented the Indore method of composting, and he documented and developed organic farming techniques. He spread his knowledge through the Soil Association (UK) and the Rodale Institute (US). His 1940 book, *An Agricultural Testament*, inspired many farmers and agricultural scientists who furthered the organic movement, including Lady Eve Balfour of the Soil Association and author of *The Living Soil*.

Biodynamic gardening

Rudolf Steiner (1861–1925), Austrian scientist and philosopher, developed the biodynamic concept from a series of lectures given in 1924 which were subsequently published as *Spiritual Foundations for the Renewal of Agriculture*. They were composed for a group of German farmers concerned with the decline in soil fertility on their farms. Steiner's philosophy of 'biological dynamism' – or 'biodynamics' – took a holistic, cosmic view that embraced the influence of the solar system on our planet. His aim was to heal the earth, thereby restoring soil fertility.

Central to biodynamic gardening is the belief that all the forces of nature need to be in harmony to create a healthy growing system. Each month the moon moves through 12 constellations of the zodiac and each is associated with one of the four elements – earth, water, fire and air. There are also favourable times for different forms of cultivation – digging, sowing and harvesting. Each biodynamic entity (e.g. the allotment plot) has a unique fingerprint in terms of microclimate and micro-organisms. The ideal practice is to produce everything from within it.

Organic gardening

Lawrence D. Hills (1911–1991), nurseryman and author, was introduced to organic gardening by Rudolf Steiner's Biodynamic Agricultural Movement. In 1949 Hills was asked to oversee and manage the growing of a million celery plants on 20 hectares (50 acres) of Fenland in Norfolk. He planted 100 Russian comfrey offsets – 'the plant that was to change his life'. The result was a successful trial on feeding fresh-cut comfrey to cattle, horses and pigs to provide fodder mineral-rich with calcium and phosphorus.

Research into Victorian farming literature threw up the letters of a 'constant reader', a certain Henry Doubleday, who developed the F1 'Doubleday's Solid Stem Comfrey' or 'Russian Comfrey'. He had spent 30 years researching comfrey, which he believed could hold the key to feeding a hungry world. On his death, his family burnt his papers believing they had little value. As a result, Lawrence Hills founded the Henry Doubleday Foundation.

The aims of the Henry Doubleday Research Association (HDRA) were to promote organic farming and gardening and to encourage research into comfrey. His book Russian Comfrey sprung from his work at his trial grounds in Bocking, Essex, where he developed the variety, Symphytum x uplandicum 'Bocking 14'. Unlike other forms of comfrey, it can only be propagated from cuttings and doesn't spread. The publication of Silent Spring by Rachel Carson (1907–1964), he said, defined his future. However, though the

book makes the case, it offers no solutions. Hills decided that his mission henceforth would be to find some. HDRA, now Garden Organic, continues to grow and promote organic gardening.

Permaculture

Bill Mollison (born 1928), University of Tasmania ecologist and winner of the Alternative Nobel Prize (1982), is known as the 'Father of Permaculture' – 'permanent agriculture' or 'permanent culture'. It encompasses many disciplines – architectural, agricultural, conservation issues and the needs of communities everywhere. It is about using human brainpower to design and devise ways to create a more sustainable world using the natural resources without waste or damage to the planet.

Typical design ideas for gardens would be solar and wind power and natural water purification with reed beds. 'Zoning' puts those plants that need most attention conveniently close by. As the edge of the pond, field or wood is generally the most popular habitat for wildlife, so the 'edge effect' – making wider and longer edges by using wavy contours – will provide more prime land for flora and fauna. Chickens will eat pests and decayed fruit and do a bit of hoeing for you as well as providing eggs and supplying manure. A movable hen house is a good idea for a rough area. The no-dig method (see page 46) is a classic piece of permaculture.

Forest gardening

Robert A. de J. Hart (1913–2000), a British farmer and writer, was the champion of 'forest gardening', or 'agroforestry'. He had studied agricultural forest gardens in tropical countries for 30 years before setting up a small model forest garden in

Shropshire in the 1960s. The principle was to mimic the layers found in natural woodland using edibles instead of woodland flora and fauna. The layers go in 'stacks' from edible herbs at ground level up to fruit trees as the top level. Once established, a forest garden should be self-maintaining apart from pruning and mulching.

He recommended starting with an orchard of standard fruit trees planted around 6 m (20 ft) apart all ways. In between these would go dwarf varieties of fruit trees. Under and between them would be planted fruit bushes such as currants (Ribes) and berry fruits (Rubus) as they can take a little shade. On ground level there would be herbs and perennial vegetables as well as roots, beneficial fungi and climbers. Clearings would have to made for common vegetables as they need sunshine.

allotment forestry

In 1991, Geoff Sinclair, a forester in Essex, decided he could no longer stand by and see people buying canes from China to support their peas and beans, when they could be using local hazel peasticks and bean poles. If they did, they would be supporting Britain's coppiced woodlands, which were already in near-terminal decline – 90 per cent down during the 20th century along with rustic crafts and traditions associated with them.

He took over four allotment plots in his local Ipswich and grew a hazel woodland from seed. Next he started an annual Bean Pole Festival with a grand sale of peasticks and bean poles. He held workshops and master classes in wattle-work for raised beds and turfed seats, rustic chairs and benches, bentwood archways, cloches, hooped border edgings and he even made a coracle or two. From his website www.allotmentforestry.com he spread the message. Geoff's point is that by using locally grown twigs you will be supporting British woodlands, the environment, wildlife, rural employment and be preserving valuable skills and traditions.

His efforts have brought great and just rewards. In 2008 National Bean Pole Week sprung up supported by the Forestry Commission with coppicing events and activities right across the UK. The Small Woods Association and the Green Wood Trust, which runs courses in woodland management and coppicing, have joined forces to make a linked network of sustainably managed coppiced woodlands across the UK with a national directory of growers and craftsmen.

clockwise from top *Young hazel being cut down for bean poles. On average, once established, and depending on the soil, the poles are ready for coppicing every four years. To get the best price, buy young plants from commercial forestry suppliers and plant 1–2 metres/yards apart to make a coppice; an obelisk bean support can be made out of hazel twigs stuck into the ground and woven together at the top into a top knot. Runner beans need more substantial bean poles up to 2.40 m/8 ft lashed at the top with wires; simple arch made from beanpoles and twigs.*

opposite, clockwise from top *The floor of the hazel coppice carpeted with wild anenomes; little is needed to craeate a simple arch other than a few nails and a hammer, or screws and a drill; rustic fence of upright hazel bean poles; woven fence of hazel twigs.*

the dig for victory plot

English teacher, Pru Coleman, became interested in wartime gardening when she came across Dig for Victory propaganda films put out by the Ministry of Information in the 1940s. As an experienced allotmenteer, with two derelict plots already brought up to scratch and a few prizes under her belt, she was looking round for a new challenge.

What impressed her in the wartime films was the high standards, the emphasis on skill and correct cultivation, the utterly serious approach to feeding the family. She started to read around the subject – Arthur J. Simmons' *Vegetable Growers Handbook* and *Wartime Allotments* and *Your Garden in Wartime* by Mr C.H. Middleton – the household name in radio broadcasting of the time. The didactic approach of these wartime gardening books appealed to her sense of perfectionism.

Not content with merely reading about it, Pru was inspired to recreate a wartime plot accurately. The result is an enchanting cottage-garden affair with vegetable plots almost entirely sown with seed that was used in 1939–1945. Complete authenticity is in the pipeline. Though many of the war varieties are still going strong, others have faded out: for example, trench celery and, because they take up space as well as time, tall peas and marrows. Her experiences to date have convinced her of the value of deep cultivation, old-fashioned digging and the correct spacing for maximum yields.

Pru Coleman's immaculate plot is inspired by Wartime allotment literature. To make it as authentic as possible, the emphasis is on the serious nature of growing food using traditional methods.

the showman

When Allan Kimber, a security engineer, took on an allotment 20 years ago, he decided that he would aim for no less than show standard in all that he grew. True to his word his winnings include first prize in Britain in the National Allotment Gardens Trust Competition; first for best allotment plot in the Birmingham and Black Country in the NSALG competition and first in the City of Wolverhampton, City Allotment Competition. He has not failed to be placed in local competitions over the last 15 years.

He avoids short cuts. He works on his plot four hours a day. He buys quality compost for each stage of growth and top-quality seed, often specialist showman's seed. Being an engineer, his plans are precise and his plot is run with military precision along with a certain panache.

Tricks of the trade include growing runner beans over an arch so that the beans are encouraged to grow down perfectly straight. Celery is blanched with wrap-around collars of roofing felt. Glass is placed underneath marrows so they can glide across without blemishing their skins.

Crops are staggered with sowings every two weeks to get the timing synchronized with the shows. Carrots and parsnips are grown in a bottomless barrel of sand with a core of compost ideally suited to them. A submerged pipe gets water and plant food down to the base encouraging them to grow ever deeper and longer.

Why not have a go?

Around August, many towns or villages put on a flower, produce and craft show. Among these are some 3,000 societies affiliated to the Royal Horticultural Society (RHS), where you can pick up a prestigious RHS medal. The RHS Horticultural Show Handbook sets out the rules that are followed across the country. It gives invaluable tips on growing, point-scoring and presentation.

clockwise from top *Alan Kimber checks his runner beans; beans trained over an arch to encourage them to grow straight; onions laid out in groups for selection for final selection.*

opposite, clockwise from right *Show onion 'Kelsae'; onions on display; mixed exhibit at the Village Show; peas lined up for the show.*

bee-keeping

Allotment people are rising to the occasion and stepping in right across the country to help the honey bee. This is vital work as the honey bee is under serious threat worldwide due to the parasitic varroa mite, which has left few honey bee colonies surviving in the wild.

Keeping bees is a fascinating hobby and an important, ancient craft skill to pass on to future generations. Along with it come the benefits of increased pollination on the allotment as well as the production of honey – an average of up to 18–27 kg (40–60 lb) a year per colony. Once trained and set up, it shouldn't take more than an hour or so a week to keep bees.

A few pointers on how to start. Get the agreement of the management and find a good location on the edge of the site, away from crowds. Apiaries make excellent use of a derelict corner. Ideally the entrance should face south-east towards the rising sun and not be under dripping trees. The hive is best sited behind a fence or hedge and where the bees have a clear path up to 3 m (10 ft), the height at which they usually fly. There should be water nearby and bee-friendly plants.

Keeping bees takes knowledge and skill. Information on all aspects on setting up and training is available through the British Beekeepers' Association (www.britishbee.org.uk) and their countrywide district associations. They recommend a taster day of beekeeping before signing up to an introductory course. Beginners usually start with a four-frame nucleus of quiet, easy-to-handle bees with a fertile, young queen, some workers and few droves. In the course of the first year this will burgeon into a full colony, by which time both beginner and they will be all set to get going in style.

opposite *Checking for honey.*

left *The 'smoker', essential equipment for calming bees.*

above *Hives need to be in a sheltered, peaceful, south-east facing site so that the bees can enjoy the rising sun.*

top *A hive raised on bricks consisting of bottom board, two 'supers' (boxes filled with frames of combs) and an outer cover or lid.*

forest farm peace garden

Up on the airy plateau of the Peace Garden, doves – a symbol of peace – flutter about a dovecote while the blades of a wind turbine rotate serenely and loftily in the breeze.

By the 1990s the allotments at Hainault, Redbridge, were derelict. By good fortune the site was rescued with American grant money aimed at setting up a therapeutic garden for refugees and asylum seekers. Though the original remit hasn't changed, the garden has expanded into a uniquely welcoming place for the local community at large.

The ethos follows the permaculture tenets of 'People care, Earth care and Fair share'. People are offered the opportunity to heal themselves with the support of the community. The Earth Care is the transformation of a once-derelict site into a fruitful place. For Fair Share, everything is provided free and the produce is shared.

The garden is so inspiring that the volunteers (25 a day on average) throw in their skills, whether they are people skills or those of practical application. Projects have included ponds and waterways, a show garden, a forest garden and a compost toilet. There are informal teaching sessions on everything from bee-keeping to making hawthorn syrup as well as health advice from a professional herbalist.

Next in the pipeline is the Redbridge Community Food Project. The plan is to convert yet more of the wasteland into vegetable and fruit growing. This would be a commercial exercise, aimed at bringing locally grown, organic food to the local community, providing long-term volunteering placements, training opportunities, communal food events as well as a further 25 allotment plots for asylum seekers and refugees.

this page, clockwise from top *The dovecote, symbol of peace; all produce is for sharing; live willow arch.*

opposite, clockwise from top left *Raised beds in the communal area; individual plots; the Peace Garden is a therapeutic place where people can find companionship in calm surrounding; an average of 25 people volunteer to help every day.*

keeping livestock

Section 12 of the 1950 Allotment Act allowed plot holders to keep hens or rabbits, so long as it was 'otherwise than by way of trade or business'. You will need the approval of the council or landlord who may well put a ban on cockerels. It is expected that the birds will be well kept and not be a nuisance. For those starting out, the Poultry Club (www.poultryclub.org) is a great source of free advice. They will help you to choose among the 300 UK breeds: broilers for meat, layers for eggs, dual-purpose, large fowls or bantam, exotic, historic or show birds. They provide tips on handling, health, feed, housing and how to protect them from dogs, foxes and badgers. The Henkeepers Association (www.henkeepersassociation.co.uk) is an information and campaigning network for people with a small garden flock.

During the Second World War, chickens were commonly kept on allotments and people even grew the wheat to feed them. Now they are regaining popularity on allotments. Cockerels are generally not allowed.

gardening for the disabled

There are plenty of practical steps that can be taken to smooth away difficulties for the disabled gardener, and there are charities to advise and help finance them. For wheelchair users, you can introduce raised beds (see page 42) that can be reached across with ease, lightweight tools that are hand operated, an easily accessible source of water and smooth, non-slippery paths wide enough to turn the chair around. For people with mobility problems, trolleys, caddies, carts and carrying belts are available.

Thrive, based in Battersea Park, London and near Reading in Berkshire, run training courses, workshops and weekend courses for professionals including one with Coventry University that leads to a Diploma in Social and Therapeutic Horticulture. They are involved in advising and assisting 900 gardens nationally. Their website (www.carryongardening.org.uk) gives practical advice and tips for wheelchair users, partially sighted people and people recovering from strokes and heart attacks. For their National Blind Gardeners' Club they also produce a quarterly magazine, Come Gardening, which is available in large print, braille or on CD.

Gardening for the Disabled (www.gardeningfordisabledtrust.org.uk) is a voluntary organization based in Kent, providing grants to individuals for them to adapt their gardens or plots to their needs. When applying for a grant, applicants need to join the society and provide a note from their GP, social worker or occupational therapist describing their disability.

The wheel chair user needs to twist around to work on staight-sided raised beds. Providing foot holes or knee space can be make gardening from a sitting position more comfortable. Paths leading to the bed need to be wide enough for a wheelchair to pass, possibly with extra room to turn.

What's happening on the allotment?

* Harvesting fruit, courgettes lettuce, beans.
* Sowing japanese greens.
* Looking out for pests and diseases.
* Trying to keep cabbage white caterpillars at bay!

making a
planting plan

planning your plot

The line-up of plants for an allotment plot consists of perennial and annual vegetables, fruit trees, soft fruit, flowers and herbs. Work out a plan tailored to your particular desires and needs.

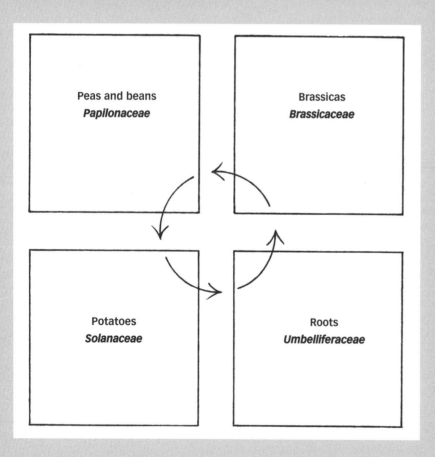

Peas and beans
Papilonaceae

Brassicas
Brassicaceae

Potatoes
Solanaceae

Roots
Umbelliferaceae

If it is likely that you will be there only at weekends, you would wise to plan for an easy-care plot. If your main interest is cooking and you are short of time, you might decide to restrict yourself to the most desirable vegetables – those that taste remarkably better when freshly picked or are expensive to buy. If you are a good-weather gardener, concentrating on summer produce and putting the plot to bed through winter with some green manures might be the approach for you. On the other hand, you may want to take on a full plot to feed family and friends all year round.

Whatever you decide the heart of your allotment plot is likely to be four or five beds of various vegetables on the rotation scheme.

A simple plan of four or plots on the rotation system is a must for any successful allotment.

crop rotation

Crop rotation was been practised since the ancient Greeks with good reason. The principle is to avoid a build-up of pests and disease in the soil that is particular to one family of vegetables. Just as you may have family weaknesses and strengths, so do vegetable families. Vegetables that are related have a tendency to catch the same diseases and to attract the same pests. Rotation is not by any means foolproof but it is a good limiting factor.

The most important family groups to rotate are *Brassicaceae* (cabbage family), *Papilionaceae* (peas and bean family), *Solanaceae* (potato family) and *Umbelliferae* (carrot family or 'roots'). If you have four areas, each year two beds are given manure (which is acid) and two are limed to make them more alkaline. As you move around, each bed will receive manure one year and lime the next, so the pH (acid/alkaline) should stay in balance.

Year 1 Manure the soil for the potato family (*Solanaceae*). It likes a rich soil on the acid side.

Year 2 Lime the same bed for the carrot family (*Umbelliferae*), which covers the root crops. It prefers a light alkaline soil.

Year 3 Manure the same bed again for the pea and bean family (*Leguminosae*). It takes nitrogen out of the air and stores it in the roots. When the plants are harvested, the roots will be left in the soil to fertilize the brassicas (cabbage family) the following year. Let the ground settle over winter as brassicas like to be planted firmly.

Year 4 If necessary lime the soil before planting the brassicas, as their worst enemy – club-root – doesn't prosper in alkaline soil.

The principle is to keep the groups moving together, one bed forward each year always in the same direction.

the main family groups

Brassicaceae
Plants with four petals in the shape of a cross.
Cabbage family Brussels sprouts, broccoli, cabbage, calabrese, cauliflower, Chinese cabbage, kale, kohlrabi, mibuna and mizuna greens, mustard greens, pak choi, radish, rocket, seakale, sprouting broccoli, swede, texcel greens, turnip.

Papilionaceae
Plants with pea-shaped flowers; legumes.
Pea and bean family Asparagus pea, broad bean, French bean, peas, mangetout, snowpea, runner bean.

Umbelliferae
Plants with flowers that form umbels (like umbrellas).
Carrot family or 'roots' Carrot, celeriac, celery, Florence fennel, Hamburg parsley, parsley, parsnip.

Solonaceae
Plants with funnel-shaped flowers with five petals like their relative deadly nightshade.
Potato family Aubergine, chilli, pepper, potato, tomato.

top *The carrot family or 'roots' (Umbelliferae), have umbrella-like flowers adored by bees.*

above *The cabbage family (Brassicaceae or Cruciferae), have cross-shaped flowers and are known as 'crucifers'.*

good partners with these main family groups

Most plot holders find that they need more room for their potatoes than they do for their root vegetables, so then you can join in more families. When you get gaps – say between harvesting the first early potatoes and while you are waiting for the weather to improve before you can plant out your young tomato and pepper plants – you can improve the ground and keep it covered with speedy green manures. Buckwheat is ideal for a tight six week gap in summer.

Beetroot and onions with the carrot family

As they like the same soil, good companions for the carrot family (*Umbelliferae*) are the beetroot and onion families.

The beetroot family (*Chenopodiaceae*) includes: beetroot, chard, good King Henry, perpetual spinach, red orache and spinach. The onion family (*Alliaceae*) includes: garlic; Japanese bunching onion; leek; globe, pickling and Japanese onions; shallots; spring onion; and Welsh onion.

Curcurbits with the potato family

The cucumber family (*Cucurbitaceae*), or curcurbits, which includes courgette, cucumber, gherkin, marrow, pumpkin and squash, enjoy rich circumstances and easy living, so they fit in well with the potato family (*Solanaceae*).

The flowers of potatoes, tomatoes, aubergines, peppers (Solanaceae) have flowers that resemble those of the deadly nightshade.

perennial and other useful vegetables

Perennial vegetables

The cardoons and globe artichokes, good King Henry, rhubarb, scorzonera, seakale and sorrel are perennials so they need a semi-permanent position. Asparagus lasts for at least 20 years and needs a bed to itself.

Jerusalem artichokes, which take up a lot of space, also need their own bed so that they can be dug out completely at the end of the season before they become a nuisance. They make a tall summer screen.

Saladini

Salad crops, lettuce, chicory, endive, corn salad, summer purslane, Chinese leaves etc can be slotted in odd gaps.

Other vegetables

New Zealand spinach, salsify, scorzonera and sweetcorn don't belong to the main family groups and can be fitted in where there is space. However, it is good practice to take note of where they are and move them to somewhere different the following year.

fruit

Soft fruit

Strawberries are replaced every three years. They can be slotted into gaps, taking little space, or else they can be grown in containers.

Although red- and whitecurrants can be grown as cordons, they are usually grown like gooseberries as goblet-shaped bushes, each on a short 'leg'. They grow to about 2m (6ft) high and wide. Blackcurrants are grown as free-standing bushes and need to be planted 1.2–1.8 m (5–6 ft) apart,

depending on variety. If you want to grow a lot of soft fruit, think about putting up a fruit cage.

The blackberry – the wild, thorny bramble of our hedgerows – has been tamed by crossing it with raspberries and dewberries (a wild European relation of the blackberry). This has resulted in myriad hybrids and thornless types with less vigour. Even so, these need to be grown up strong supports.

Top fruit

Apples and pears, peaches and plums are generally trained to grow flat against a trellis, fence or wall on allotment plots. There are also dwarf varieties.

flowers

Flowers will bring in the predators and the birds who will eat the pests, as well as the bees to pollinate. They will disguise and camouflage your crops from pests that go by sight and smell. There are many flowers that you can eat or use for edible decoration.

planning ahead

A well-organized gardener is a step ahead with a planned succession to make the most of the land and the growing season. If you sow seeds under cover or in the seedbed in late winter and early spring, there will always be young plants in the wings ready to be transplanted to centre stage as crops go over. Alternatively, in the growing season, a row of lettuce or a quick crop of young carrots can be slotted in gaps, with the seed sown in situ. This kind of planning sounds impressive, but once you get the hang of it it's dead easy and good fun.

garden organic

This is the plan of the exemplary allotment plot followed from April to October at Garden Organic, in Ryton near Coventry. As it is a show allotment, an educational place visited by many schools and groups of people interested in organic growing, it has to be a model of horticultural excellence, highly productive and look good for visitors all year round.

It is run by Janet Reilly, one of the team of professional gardeners there. She has designed it along the lines of an overflowing cottage garden. The four large beds on rotation are in the centre and around the edges are fruit trees, herb beds, drifts of wild flowers, a fruit cage, a little shed and the compost bins.

Janet makes a clear planting plan at the beginning of the year, which she follows, but nothing is set in stone. When an uncatchable rabbit was discovered living under the shed, wading through vegetables at night, she put in extra rows of flowers between the rows of vegetables for tight planting because rabbits like open ground. This year she is testing the theory that slugs don't like red vegetables, so she has sown red cultivars of cabbage, lettuce and kale.

As the carrot fly travels low and in straight lines and can be defeated by erecting a low barrier, Janet sows a row of tall coriander on one side and scarlet flax

(*Linum grandiflorum* 'Rubrum') on the other. Apart from being useful, the flax flowers untiringly for months and sets off the green-leaved vegetables a treat.

All the beds are edged with lettuce and flowers, mostly marigolds. The favoured nasturtium is 'Alaska', a form that doesn't run. Tagetes 'Golden Gem' is the single marigold that is best for attracting useful predators. Viper's bugloss (*Echium vulgare*) is grown in the rotation beds next to the peas and beans as slugs like to congregate underneath it where they can be rounded up.

Around the four rotation beds are more flowers for beneficial insects. Wallflowers are grown along with the brassicas in the seedbed as they don't mind being uprooted. Marigolds and basil are grown with the tomatoes. The dwarf morning glory (*Convolvulus tricolor*) works well with the beans. The four beds are large so all work on them is done off boards.

From the comfrey (the non-seeding *Symphytum x uplandicum* 'Bocking 14' variety) three cuts are taken every year for the compost heap. It is so full of moisture that the thick stems rot down without needing to be chopped up. As you will see from the following plans, the ground is always covered, if not with crops then with green manures or flowers. Apart from those plants that don't take to being transplanted, such as root vegetables, the produce is started off site ready to be slotted in at the appropriate moment.

clockwise from top left Jan Reilly weeding the brassicas; large quantities of wild flowers are grown to encourage predators as pest controllers; brassicas are kept netted against flying pests. French marigolds to encourage predators protect them also.

APRIL

All beds will have been topdressed with garden compost at the rate of two barrows to 5 sq. m/sq. yd. In bed 2, the young peas will be protected by bottle cloches. Dwarf morning glory (*Convolvulus tricolor*) will be sown around the beans. Buckwheat is grown in bed 3 for two months, until the weather is right for the tomatoes, aubergines, cucumbers and peppers to go in. French marigolds (*Tagetes*) and basil will be grown with the tomatoes. Chards and beetroots will go in with onions in bed 4 as companions in due course.

BED 2
Bean family
Legumes (*Leguminoseae*)

Pea 'Ambassador'
Mangetout 'Carouby de Mausanne'
Broad bean 'Express' (three rows)

BED 1
Cabbage family
Brassicas (*Brassicaceae*)

Turnip 'Purple Top Milan'
Kale 'Redbor'
Calabrese 'Fiesta'
Brussels sprout 'Nautic'
Summer cabbage 'Golden Acre'
Cabbage 'Marner Freurot'
Lettuce 'Rubens Red'

BED 3
Potato & cucumber families
(*Solanaceae* and *Cucurbitaceae*)

Buckwheat
Potato 'Colleen'
Potato 'Orla'
Potato 'Amorosa'

BED 4
Roots, beet & onion families
(*Umbelliferae, Chenopodiaceae*
and *Alliaceae*)

Onion 'Senshyu Yellow'
Linum grandiflorum 'Rubrum'
Parsnip 'Tender and True'
Onion 'Red Baron'
Linum grandiflorum 'Rubrum'
Carrot 'Resistafly'
Carrot 'Yellowstone'
Coriander
Lettuce 'Bedford'

JUNE

In bed 1, as the summer cabbages and calabrese are harvested, the gaps are filled with oriental vegetables. Brussels sprouts are moved into their permanent positions. In bed 2 , the broad beans and mangetout are being harvested now and it is now warm enough to plant out runner and French beans, which are trained onto wigwams. In bed 3, the early potatoes will be replaced by squashes. Now the danger of frost has past, the tomatoes, outdoor cucumbers, aubergines, peppers and chillies will be planted out. In bed 4, the Japanese onions have been harvested, making room for Swiss chard and beetroot.

BED 2
Bean family
Legumes (*Leguminoseae*)

Runner bean 'Hestia'
Dwarf French beans 'Purple Queen'
Pea 'Ambassador'
Runner bean 'White Emergo'
Broad bean 'Express'

BED 1
Cabbage family
Brassicas (*Brassicaceae*)

Turnip 'Purple Top Milan'
Kale 'Redbor'
Mustard greens 'Giant Red'
Kohlrabi 'Azure Star'
Mibuna greens
Brussels sprouts 'Nautic'
Cabbage 'Marnier Fruerot'
Lettuce 'Rubens Red'

BED 3
Potato & cucumber families
(*Solanaceae* and *Cucurbitaceae*)
Buckwheat
Potato 'Colleen'
Potato 'Orla'
Potato 'Amorosa'

BED 4
Roots, beet & onion families
(*Umbelliferae, Chenopodiaceae* and *Alliaceae*)
Linum grandiflorum 'Rubrum'
Beetroot 'Red Ace'
Swiss chard 'Lucullus'
Red and green lettuce
Parsnip 'Tender and True'
Onion 'Red Baron'
Linum grandiflorum 'Rubrum'
Carrot 'Resistafly'
Carrot 'Yellowstone'
Coriander
Lettuce 'Bedford'

AUGUST

In bed 1, the turnips and summer cabbages have been harvested. In bed 2, the broad beans are over and two new sets of runner beans have replaced the old ones. A block of sweetcorn was planted out in July. In bed 3, there is a fine harvest of cucumbers, tomatoes, aubergines, peppers, courgettes and chillies. In bed 4, the carrots, onions and beetroots are being harvested and young leeks are being dropped into the gaps.

BED 2
Bean family
Legumes (*Leguminoseae*)

Sweetcorn 'Golden Bantam'
New runner bean 'Hestia'
New runner bean 'White Emergo'
Echium vulgare

BED 1
Cabbage family
Brassicas (*Brassicaceae*)

Kale 'Redbor'
Mustard greens 'Giant Red'
Kohlrabi 'Azure Star'
Mibuna greens
Brussels sprouts 'Nautic'
Lettuce 'Rubens Red'

BED 3
Potato & cucumber families
(*Solanaceae* and *Cucurbitaceae*)

Cucumber 'Crystal Lemon'
Tomato 'Yellow Perfection'
Capsicum 'Ring of Fire'
Capsicum 'Golden California
Wonder'
Aubergine 'Black Beauty'
Aubergine 'Hative de Barbentane'
Courgette 'Rondo di Nizza'
Beetroot 'Red Ace'
Red lettuce 'Roxy'
Red-edged lettuce 'Lattughino'

BED 4
Roots, beet & onion families
(*Umbelliferae*, *Chenopodiaceae*
and *Alliaceae*)

Linum grandiflorum 'Rubrum'
Leek 'St Victor'
Beetroot 'Red Ace'
Swiss chard 'Lucullus'
Parsnip 'Tender and True'
Linum grandiflorum 'Rubrum'
Carrot 'Resistafly'
Carrot 'Yellowstone'
Coriander
Lettuce 'Bedford'

WINTER

In bed 1, there is still produce for winter – sprouts, cabbage, kale and calabrese. When these go over in the new year, the bed will be emptied and sown with clover and grazing rye. In bed 2, the ground is cleared. Winter tare and grazing rye green manures are sown in strips. In bed 3, a bean trench is dug and will left open over winter in anticipation for next year's crop, when it will be the legume bed. *Phacelia* is sown here and will be dug in two weeks before the beans go in next year. In bed 4, grazing rye and field beans will keep the soil covered over winter. Next spring, on the rotation system all the beds will make one move anti-clockwise.

BED 2
Bean family
Legumes (Leguminoseae)

Winter tare and grazing rye

BED 1
Cabbage family
Brassicas (Brassicaceae)

Kale 'Redbor'
Mustard greens 'Giant Red'
Brussels sprouts 'Nautic'

BED 3
Potato & cucumber families
(*Solanaceae* and *Cucurbitaceae*)

Bean trench

BED 4
Roots, beet & onion families
(*Umbelliferae, Chenopodiaceae* and *Alliaceae*)

Grazing rye and field beans

plant list

vegetables

Aubergine 'Black Beauty' Prolific purple fruits

Aubergine 'Hative de Barbentane' Prolific, bred to withstand cooler temperatures

Beetroot 'Red Ace' Strong grower. Bolt resistant, dark red

Broad bean 'Express' The fastest to mature from early spring sowings. Particularly good for freezing

Brussels sprouts 'Nautic' Resistant to white blister, ring spot and powdery mildew

Cabbage 'Golden Acre' (summer) Medium heads. Good cooked and raw

Cabbage 'Marnier Fruerot' (summer) Red ballhead, good fresh or suitable for long-term winter storage.

Calabrese 'Fiesta' Good for late summer and autumn

Capsicum 'Golden California Wonder' Sweet, mild, yellow pepper

Capsicum 'Ring of Fire' Fiery chillis that get hotter as they turn from green to red

Carrot 'Resistafly' Early; good carrot fly tolerance

Carrot 'Yellowstone' Late; easy to grow yellow carrot

Courgette 'Rondo di Nizza' Round Italian variety

Cucumber 'Crystal Lemon' Lemon-like fruits

French bean 'Purple Queen' decorative, purple pods and bright pink flowers

Kale 'Redbor' Red-tinged leaves that turn magenta in cooler weather

Kohlrabi 'Azur Star' Decorative plant with bluish leaves and lilac bulbs. Said to be the earliest and the best tasting. Resistant to bolting

Leek 'St Victor' attractive, blue-purple leaves. Very hardy

Lettuce 'Bedford' Resistant to aphids and mildew

Lettuce 'Lattughino' loose-leaf type with frilly, red-edged leaves

Lettuce 'Roxy' big, slow-to-bolt lettuce with blistered, red leaves

Lettuce 'Rubens Red' A large cos lettuce with dark green leaves overlaid with deep red

Mangetout 'Carouby de Mausanne' Tall mangetout with lovely, pink flowers

Mibuna greens Generally trouble free. Can be eaten as seedlings or be left to mature

Mustard greens 'Giant Red' ornamental, easy to grow

Onion 'Red Baron' Red-skinned variety

Onion 'Senshyu Yellow' Popular, reliable Japanese overwintering variety

Parsnip 'Tender and True' Old favourite with good flavour. Resistant to canker

Pea 'Ambassador' High-yielding, reliable. For continuous summer crops sow every three weeks

Potato 'Amarosa' A rare, first red early

Potato 'Colleen' An Irish first early with good resistance to blight and scab

Potato 'Orla' Highest blight resistance in a first early, plus resistance to scab and blackleg

Runner bean 'Hestia' Dwarf variety with red and white flowers

Runner bean 'White Emergo' high-yielding, white-flowered variety

Sweetcorn 'Golden Bantam' Classic, open-pollinated variety

Swiss chard 'Lucullus' Green and white form. Abundant, big tasty leaves and succulent, white midribs

Tomato 'Yellow Perfection' Golden tomatoes. Early and prolific. Excellent for slicing

Turnip 'Purple Top Milan' Early cropper, bunching turnip. Excellent harvested when golf-ball size

flowers

California poppies (*Eschscholzia californica*).

Comfrey (*Symphytum x uplandicum* 'Bocking 14').

Dwarf morning glory (*Convolvulus tricolor*)

Evening primrose (*Oenothera caespitosa*)

French marigold (*Tagetes*) 'Golden Gem'

Lungwort (*Pulmonaria officinalis*)

Lupin (*Lupinus polyphyllus*)

Marigold (*Calendula*)

Mullein (*Verbascum*)

Nasturtium (*Tropaeolum*) Alaska Series

Red orache (*Atriplex hortensis*)

Scarlet flax (*Linum grandiflorum* 'Rubrum')

Scorpion weed (*Phacelia tanacetifolia*)

Tansy (*Tanacetum vulgare*)

Valerian (*Valeriana officinalis*)

Verbena (*Verbena bonariensis*)

Viper's bugloss (*Echium vulgare*)

Wallflowers (*Erysimum cheiri*)

herbs

Chives

Coriander

Garlic chives

Lemon balm

Lemon verbena

Rocket

Sorrel

fruit

Autumn raspberries

Blackcurrants two bushes

Blueberries

Gooseberry

Greengage 'Reine Claude de Bavay'

Compact upright tree

Japanese wineberry

Redcurrants two bushes

Strawberries renewed every three years.

gathering the stock

what to look out for

Buying seed and small plants to fill a whole plot can amount to a substantial outlay when starting from scratch. Take account of your actual needs and tastes and the quantities you really will enjoy growing and using. You can cut down the cost by sharing and taking a few shortcuts.

'collections' of seed

These give you the chance to try out different varieties for the price of a single packet. Many types of vegetables have summer and winter varieties – the winter ones being suitable for storage or hardy enough to stand out in the cold in winter. Others, often the newer cultivars, can be sown any time throughout the growing season, sometimes through winter as well.

plug plants

If you miss out on sowing at the right time, you can buy plug plants, which should arrive by post at the optimum moment for planting out. Although plugs or young plants are more expensive than a packet of seeds, there will be no waste and time and effort can be saved.

small plants

Some types of vegetables – courgettes, tomatoes, aubergines and peppers – are so prolific that most people only need two or three plants to provide the whole family. It saves bother and time to buy a small plant in a pot, though admittedly you don't get the same choice of varieties.

free sources of plants

Your own seed

Saving your own seed (see pages 151–152) is generally very worthwhile, though it is not necessarily easily done on an allotment where seed can be blowing in from all around and cross-pollinating.

Cuttings

You may be offered free offcuts or bits of root of a perennial by friends – Jerusalem

artichokes, soft fruit, garlic, seakale or rhubarb. Be wary of importing disease but otherwise accept them gratefully. Take cuttings yourself of shrubby herbs such as rosemary and thyme.

Where not to economize

Seed potatoes and the first garlic bulb must be bought from a reputable nursery. Seed potatoes should be certified free of pests and disease. Soft fruit also (with the exception of red- and whitecurrants as they have no certification) should come with a guarantee of good health. After that, you can keep up your own supply of soft fruit and garlic (though not potatoes) for many years to come.

seed

Apart from particular plants that don't respond well to being moved (e.g. root vegetables, many of the oriental vegetables and sweetcorn) it is generally more effective to start seed at home and transplant rather than growing it in situ.

Young plants are less likely to be eaten or squashed than tiny seedlings. It is also easier to keep an eye on them if they are on your windowsill. Another advantage is that plants spend less time in the allotment beds, so you can make optimum use of the space. Growing seeds in biodegradable modules gives young plants the least possible 'transplantation shock', especially if you harden them off slowly to prepare them for a drop in temperature.

buying seed

Send off for the free catalogues provided by seed merchants or browse through them on the web. Seed merchants offer a vastly wider choice of varieties than the garden centres, where there is usually space to display only bestsellers.

When buying seed look for:
● disease resistance;
● new introductions – often they have great merits as a result of research;

● old and heritage cultivars – if they are still in the catalogues they must have something valuable to offer;
● organic seed, which is grown without man-made chemicals and on clean land. Most seed companies have an organic range and there are several specialist organic seed merchants;
● RHS Award of Garden Merit (AGM) displayed on seed packets. The award is given only after extensive trials for outstanding excellence, for plants that do not need specialist growing conditions or care, have a good constitution and are widely available.

different types of seed

F1 hybrids
These are the result of the scientific crossing of two parent lines, resulting in reliable, uniform results. F1 stands for 'first filial generation'. With vegetables, the breeders usually concentrate on vigour,

flavour and – important for the organic grower – disease resistance. They often manage to breed out undesirable characteristics.

It is an expensive and lengthy business to get a new cultivar registered since the Plant Varieties and Seed Act was passed in 1973. The Act was designed to protect the consumer from fraudulence in the seed business. As a result, new cultivars are very carefully researched and tested before breeders are willing to bear the expense. Therefore, new cultivars should have merits that are worth checking out.

The downside of F1 seed is that it is more expensive and that often the entire crop will mature at the same time. This is not desirable for the home grower unless the aim is to freeze in bulk. Of course, you can sow a few at a time to space out the crops. Don't save seed from F1 hybrids as there is no guarantee as to how it will turn out.

Pelleted seed

Pelletted seed makes fine or irregular-shaped seed easier to sow accurately. Individual seed is enclosed in an inert, clay-like substance, which breaks down on contact with water.

Seed tapes

These are designed for trouble-free, perfect spacing, to avoid thinning. The tapes are biodegradable.

Primed or sprinter seed

This has been germinated and then dried. It must be sown within two months. It is usually more successful than untreated seed if you are sowing early in the season or in adverse conditions.

Too many seeds?

It is a good idea to have a seed-sharing scheme with your neighbours as there may be too many seeds in one packet for a single family. With beans and peas there are likely to be 40–50 seeds. For carrot and cabbage it is often 500. For kale 2,500 – enough to feed an army! Work out how many plants you want, and add a failure margin for bad weather, bad luck or any duds. There is a UK statutory minimum germination rate for seeds. This varies from plant to plant. While most have a near 100 per cent rate of viability, others are more unpredictable. Carrots need to have only a 65 per cent success rate. Some seeds store much longer than others if kept in the correct conditions of dryness and dark. Others, such as parsnip, which can have 350 seeds in a packet, should be bought fresh each year.

The pre-germination test

You will need: a waterproof container; kitchen towel; clingfilm; water; newspaper or something similar to cover the container and keep out the light.

1 Line the container with a thick layer of kitchen towel. Water it until it is sodden.

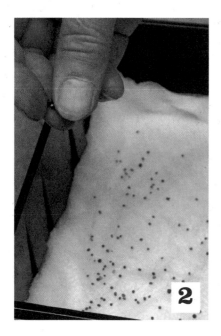

2 Sprinkle on a few seeds.

3 Cover with clingfilm, cover it to block out the light and put in a warm place such as an airing cupboard

Pregerminated seed

Pregerminated seed is useful for tricky customers such as cucumbers and other tender plants, when conditions are too cold for them. It is easy to pregerminate them yourself – a handy technique if you are not sure whether seeds are still viable. To pregerminate seed, put them on wet kitchen towel in a seed tray (or on a plate) covered with a plastic bag, and keep them at about 20°C (68°F). If all is well, they will start to sprout roots and leaves within three weeks. With large seed such as peas and beans it helps to soak them overnight first.

Seed from grocers

In allotment circles, there is a good success rate in growing from seed that has been dried for cooking, particularly the pulses. It is certainly worth a try if you are willing to take the risk of it not working out. Check that the seeds are viable, before planting.

Heritage seed

The Heritage Seed Library is run by Garden Organic. This is a library for seeds that haven't been registered under the Plant Varieties and Seed Act (1973). Each year members of the library can choose some six varieties of unregistered vegetable seeds. These are varieties that may have been overlooked in the first place, been dropped from popular seed catalogues for one reason or another or were family heirlooms that have never been in the catalogues. Due to the expense of getting cultivars registered, these varieties are easily lost. By joining, members may get something wonderful and unique to grow in their own gardens. Garden Organic tests the seeds to make sure that they are a true variety, and their notes and observations will arrive with the seeds. The Heritage Seed Library is open to everyone, with the serious purpose of maintaining the genetic diversity of vegetable stock for the future.

4 *Leave for two or three days, then check daily for signs of life. If less than 50 per cent germinate, you may decide not to continue.*

4

equipment

Equipment can be as basic as using yoghurt or ice cream pots, old tins or even rolled up newspaper or kitchen roll tubes as containers for your seedlings. Anything will do, providing that the containers are not toxic to plants. It is important to make adequate drainage holes as plants need air around the roots.

heated propagators

If you have a propagator providing controlled heat from below and space to start plants off at home, you will be well ahead of the game. Propagators provide the ideal conditions of warmth at root level and a cooler ambient temperature above. However, you can also propagate seed very well in an airing cupboard and on a light windowsill out of direct sun.

containers

Modular planters

If you are sowing seed big enough to handle and are buying new containers, select the module, 'plug' or cell style of planters, in which each individual seed has its own compartment. They more or less eliminate possible damage to the roots when transplanting.

Biodegradable containers

Other good inventions are biodegradable products made from paper and peat alternatives. When you are ready to transplant, you can plant them as they are in the biodegradable containers, completely avoiding the possibility of root damage.

Long biodegradable tubes, or root trainers, are ideal for plants with long roots such as sweet peas and runner beans. The shape of the pot directs the roots downwards, which will help the plant seek out water in the depths of the soil later.

Polystyrene cell blocks

These give insulation and are a good idea for seedlings raised in a cold greenhouse. They usually come with a presser board to pop out individual plugs. Some have capillary matting, a tray for water underneath, and a cover so you are all set to raise your seeds on the windowsill, only needing to top up the water from time to time.

Clay pots

Clay pots are porous and so your seed is less likely to suffer from overwatering or drying out, but clay pots are less hygienic than plastic ones. New developments are biodegradable pots made from coconut shells and grain husks. They look like plastic and will last five years unless damaged. When broken they can be thrown on the compost heap and will rot down within 18 months. Clay pots are porous so your seed is less likely to suffer from overwatering or drying out. They are warm in winter and cool in summer, and are more stable than plastic pots and considerably heavier. They are excellent for long term plantings.

opposite *If you are stuck for a pot, rolls of newspaper are adequate for seedlings. They can be planted complete later to rot down without disturbing the roots.*

Old tins are decorative and come free. Even more so than plastic, they can get too hot for the roots if left in the sun and can be blown over easily, especially if they get top heavy. Don't use tins that have contained toxic substances.

Guttering

A short length of plastic guttering is ideal for starting off peas and beans. When they are ready to go out you can slide the seedlings off effortlessly into a prepared furrow outside, without the roots noticing.

cold frames

A cold frame is ideal for hardening off young seedlings. It is the halfway house between a greenhouse (or windowsill) and the outside world. Basically a box with a glass or plastic lid, it offers a degree of protection against the weather. On sunny days the 'light', or see-through glass or plastic lid, can be lifted off or opened. The standard types are made of aluminium or wood. Some new versions are made entirely of see-through plastic. If you are buying a wooden cold frame, look for the letters 'FSC' (Forest Stewardship Council) to make sure it comes from a sustainable source. Alternatively you could make one yourself.

hotbeds

If you have access to fresh stable manure, you could try a hotbed. It is an adaptation of the cold frame, with the advantage of providing bottom heat like an outdoor propagator. Victorian gardeners made great use of them on large estates for out-of-season crops and early delicacies for the house. It is a great idea for the allotment, especially for those who don't have the luxury of a greenhouse or propagator. It makes an interesting

challenge, is free (unless you pay for the manure), low-tech and energy saving.

You need a cold frame lid with glass or plastic windows and a good heap of stable or farmyard manure with straw in it – so fresh that it steams in the cold. If you find you haven't got enough, mix the manure with up to an equal quantity of newly collected leaves. The bigger the heap, the higher the temperature you will achieve. To get a hothouse temperature of 27°C (80°F) the heap needs to be 1.2–1.5 m (4–5 ft) square once it has settled down. However, useful warmth can be generated from a hotbed half that size.

Making a hotbed

Turn the manure and straw once or twice each day, shaking the fork to break it up and to get it well mixed for about a week. Decide whether you want to dig a pit or build the hotbed on the ground. A pit will keep things tidier and give some insulation. If you have cold, wet soil though, it's better to make the hotbed on the surface.

For the pit method, dig a hole about 30 cm (12 in) deep, reserving the topsoil. For a surface bed, remove the topsoil and make a flat base. The dimensions of the heap will depend on how much manure you have and the size of the frame. Allow for a 30cm (12in) border around the frame for stability.

Pile the manure into the pit, beating it down so that it will stay firm and flat. Aim for a compact, squared-off pile. Leave for a few more days for the steam to escape and for the heap to settle. Add a 10 cm (4 in) layer of topsoil. Check the soil temperature – if it is more than 27°C (80°F) wait a few days until it cools down.

Cover the heap with the cold frame, leaving a little chink for gases to escape. Make holes and fill them with seed and potting compost. Sow your seed in them. An adaptation of this idea is to use your existing compost heap. Square it off, add a layer of potting compost and cover with a cold frame.

polytunnels

A small polytunnel does much to extend the season, even bringing plants right through winter with a little luck and good management. Polytunnels vary in size from walk-in types, now quite commonly seen on allotment plots, to plant-sized ones. Either will keep the soil warm, protect plants from late frosts, from animals and some pests. You can make your own small polytunnel with lengths of hose reel bent over (or children's hoops sawn in half) for the framework with clear plastic sheet on top. For maximum sun, run it east–west. Erect it on a calm day in a sheltered spot.

Walk-in polytunnels usually come in kit form. Erecting them is well within the ability of the capable DIY person. The types with a sheet treated with anti-fogging agent are worth the extra cost. They will last longer and neither you nor the plants will suffer from condensation and unwanted drips.

In a polytunnel, the ventilation, the shading and the temperature are controlled manually by you. Ventilation is a question of opening and shutting the vents or doors, making sure to shut them in the cooler months at night and to have them open all day in summer. The change in temperature between day and night can be quite dramatic. When the temperature is hot in summer, the plants will need extra watering.

Cold greenhouses

A small greenhouse is a step up from the polytunnel as you can regulate the airflow

Polytunnels come in packs these days and can be assembled by a capable DIYer in a single day.

and temperature changes more easily. On an allotment, polycarbonate glazing is recommended, being 200 times stronger than glass and more or less vandal proof. Most small greenhouse are virtually square – 1.8 x 1.8 m (6 x 6 ft) or 1.8 x 2.4 m (6 x 8 ft) – with a glass roof, so they are absorbing sun on all sides and from the top.

Site the greenhouse on a flat base in any direction that suits you but not under shady trees. One advantage to placing it east–west is that you can put your sun-lovers on the south side and those that like cooler conditions on the northern one.

Cleaning the greenhouse

To get rid of pests and disease, a greenhouse needs a thorough cleaning annually – usually in autumn but it can be done early spring. The warm, humid atmosphere, which makes good growing conditions, is also ideal for pests, unfortunately. Some elbow grease put into hygiene and keeping an eye out for the first signs of trouble go a long way to avoiding trouble.

Take out and inspect all plants, and cover any tender specimens with fleece if the weather is cold. Wash down the glass or polycarbonate with soap, water and disinfectant. The latest organic disinfectants made from citrus products are effective and harmless to plants. Having clean glass will help the light levels through winter. Be thorough and remove any grime that has collected in the joints between the panes. As hosepipes are generally not allowed on allotments, resort to a plastic plant label to get into the cracks and crannies. Put all old compost on the beds outside. It is best to do this on a fine and breezy day

so that the greenhouse will be clean and dry for the plants to go back inside. Old flowerpots also need a good scrub while you are at it.

Insulating the greenhouse

After the autumn clean, you may want to add insulation. Bubble wrap is good.

Pest control in the greenhouse

If pests get out of control, the greenhouse, being enclosed, is the ideal situation for biological control. Use sterilized compost and separate tools for the greenhouse.

nursery or seedbeds

Having a nursery bed in top condition will save the effort of bringing the whole allotment up to scratch. The seedling vegetables can stay there in comfort to be transplanted to their permanent positions when they are ready and there is a space. It's the ideal place for slow-growing plants, such as brassicas, that don't mind being moved, or for any young plant that you want to keep an eye on.

Preparing a seedbed

If you have heavy, wet clay, make a raised bed (see page 42) for good drainage for growing on young plants. Ideally, the bed should be partially prepared the autumn before, by digging, mixing in plenty of organic matter and leaving it to settle through winter.

A couple of weeks before you are ready to sow in spring, warm the soil with clear polythene. This will encourage any dormant weeds to germinate so you can dispose of them before you start.

Befeore sowing, break up lumps of soil by bashing them with the back of a

spade. Rake patiently until you have a fine tilth – crumbly soil in small particles that seeds can push through effortlessly. Keep the rake as near parallel to the soil as possible. Drag stones and debris out on the pull and smooth on the push. Sprinkle on some general-purpose fertilizer if necessary. Finally, you may need to flatten the surface by walking up and down on it. Do this when the soil is reasonably dry. Don't stamp. You are aiming for a flat, lightly firmed surface, not a compacted one.

how to grow from seed

Important points to bear in mind when growing from seed:
- pay attention to the directions on the packet and follow the instructions about sun or shade considerations and cultivation tips;
- avoid planting your seeds too deeply. The seed carries within it all it needs to germinate but only has the power to grow a limited distance. It needs to reach the light before it runs out of steam. A general guide to planting depth is two-and-a-half times the size of the seed;
- seeds need warmth, moisture and air to germinate. Cold, waterlogged conditions are likely to be fatal;
- sow fine seed sparsely, to save time thinning the seedlings later;
- use common sense on the sowing times – you know your local weather best. Manufacturers often recommend the most optimistic sowing times. Plants sown at the optimum moment for them often catch up with those sown earlier;
- decide whether to sow directly outside or to start seed off under cover or in a nursery bed and transplant later.

sowing

A good sowing technique is at the very essence of successful allotment growing. Get this right and you'll be well on your way to producing a bountiful crop.

composts for sowing

Don't take shortcuts with compost for seedlings. Use new seed and potting compost or multipurpose compost. These contain everything that seedlings need – the right texture for moisture retention, aeration and nutrients. They are also sterile – free from weeds, pests and diseases.

sowing under cover

Fill a container with compost, leaving space at the top for watering. Shake it from side to side to get a flat surface and firm it down gently. A firming board, or piece of timber cut to the size of the seed tray with a handle on the top, is useful for this. Otherwise press down with the bottom of another flat-bottomed seed tray of the same size.

Water the compost thoroughly before sowing, or else sit the tray in water afterwards and let the compost soak it up by capillary action. You shouldn't need to water again until the seeds have germinated. Though rainwater is generally best for plants, for seeds it is safer to use sterile tap water.

If the seeds are big enough to pick up by hand, make holes with a dibber (a pencil or chopstick will do the trick) to the right depth and drop them in. Fine seed should be scattered through finger and thumb – carefully, to achieve an even distribution – on the top of the compost. Cover the seed by sieving a thin layer of compost over it.

Cover the tray or container with polythene or a sheet of glass and put it in a warm place. Unless it contains one of the few plants whose seed germinates better in the light, put the container in the dark or, if you are using a propagator, cover it to block out the light. Check every day for signs of life. As soon as the first seedling makes its appearance, take off the cover and put the seedlings in a light place but out of direct sunlight and draughts.

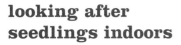
A thriving allotment is a wonderful reward for your hard work.

looking after seedlings indoors

Watering

The most common problem with seedlings is 'damping off', a fungal problem caused by excess moisture or poor hygiene. Keep the seedlings just moist. Always use tap water. Water slowly at the base to avoid disturbing the seedlings or, safer still, let them soak up water from below.

Light

If you are growing seedlings on a windowsill, their container needs to be turned every day to get even light all round. An alternative is to put the container in a box with the back lined with kitchen foil to reflect light.

Thinning

If they become overcrowded, seedlings need to be thinned out. Growing them too close together leads to competition for water and nutrients, and it can cause weak growth or even disease. Water the compost well before you start, then pull or ease out the surplus seedlings, leaving the strongest ones in place (an ice-lolly stick is an effective tool). If they are entangled, pinch them out at the base without disturbing the others.

Pricking out and potting on

When seedlings grow too big for their container, or if they are ready but the weather is too cold for them to go outdoors, you will need to prick out and pot on the seedlings. This is best done when the plants have two 'true' leaves. The first leaf-like apparitions are not leaves at all but part of the seed.

Before pricking out, water the seedlings well and allow to drain. Using a dibber, gently ease out the seedlings, taking as much compost with them as you can, to avoid disturbing the roots. Replant in pots or trays with more space for the plants to develop. If you need to support the plant, hold it by the leaves, not the stem, which is easily broken. If you have grown seedlings singly in modules, tip them out and plant in bigger pots to the same depth.

Hardening off

Acclimatize young plants to the outside world in stages. Start by keeping them under cloches or in a cold frame, lifting off the cover by day and putting it back at night. Protect them from fluctuations in temperature until they can cope.

Transplanting into the allotment

The danger with transplanting is that young plants can get 'checked', or they suffer from transplanting shock, due to root damage or drying out. To avoid this:

- where possible, grow seedlings in biodegradable plugs or modules;
- work at a steady pace. Have the land raked to a fine tilth, watered and lined up for planting before you start. Roots dry out fast as soon as they are out of the soil;
- move the young plants in the cool of evening or on a dull day;
- water them well the day before and keep them watered after transplanting, until they are completely restored.

sowing seed outside

Once the soil is warm enough, most seed can be sown outside. Some – notably root vegetables, cucumbers and sweetcorn – don't transplant well and are generally sown where they are to remain growing. Onions usually go straight out as they don't take up much space.

Optimum sowing temperatures

The seeds of the hardiest plants – cabbages, cauliflowers, radishes, sprouts and turnips – will germinate when the temperature has reached a consistent minimum of 5°C (41°F). Carrots and parsnips need a slightly warmer 6°C (43°F). By warming the soil and using a protective cover, it is reckoned that you can keep the temperature above 6°C (43°F) for an extra three to four weeks at each end of the growing season.

Tender vegetables, such as French and runner beans, sweetcorn and tomatoes, need a minimum of 12°C (54°F), which is unlikely until June in most places. Err on the cautious side. It is better and safer to grow fast when conditions are at their optimum.

Seed trays with cells are ideal for sowing the seed of plants without tap roots.

How to sow seed

1 Fill a container with good drainage or a seed tray with seed or multipurpose compost leaving a small gap at the top. Water well.

2 Sprinkle or place seeds sparsely and evenly on the surface.

3 Cover thinly with perlite or sieve over a thin layer of compost.

4 Cover with a plastic bag or clingfilm. Keep warm, in the dark and covered (e.g in the airing cupboard) until there are signs of germination. Take off the covers and put in the light but out of direct sunlight.

Sowing patterns

The traditional way to sow is in parallel rows or drills. These work particularly well for beans, peas and other climbers that need supports. If the row goes north–south the plants won't shade each other. The advantage of a straight row is that you know exactly where the seeds are as long as the ends of the row are marked. However, any geometric pattern will do. Blocks or squares are easy to net and good for low broad-leaved plants. As they grow, their leaves will shade out weeds and keep in moisture.

How to sow seed in the allotment

Fine seed is held in the palm of one hand and fed or pinched through finger and thumb of the other. Mixing fine seed with a little silver sand as a spreading agent can help to distribute the seed more evenly. Make a furrow with the side of a hoe. If you want to sow a wide area (e.g. with a wildflower mix or green manure), the technique is to walk down one side and across the bottom or top, broadcasting it with a wide arm movement.

Large seed can be picked up individually (e.g. melon, broad bean or peas) and 'station' sown individually either in a furrow or by making a series of holes with a dibber and dropping them in. Usually three or four seeds are planted together. After germination, choose the strongest seedling and thin out the remainder.

Station sowing

2 *To get a straight row use a peg (or scewer) and line (or string). Guided by the string use the side of the hoe to make a furrow.*

1 *Rake forwards and backwoods to achieve a fine tilth.*

3 *Place the seeds one by one in the furrow. Finish by drawing some soil over the seeds. Alternatively, you can make holes with a dibber and drop the seeds individually.*

propagating

The vast majority of vegetables that we grow are either annuals or are treated as such for maximum performance. Annuals – or plants that germinate, flower, fruit and die within a single year – can only propagate themselves from seed. However the perennial vegetables, herbs and fruits can be propagated vegetatively from cuttings for fast growing, free plants.

propagation from cuttings

Herbaceous plants, shrubs and trees can often be propagated by cutting off bit of root or stem. The resulting offshoots will be identical to the parent plant. Golden rules for success with cuttings are to use:

• healthy stock – watch cuttings and promptly remove any part that is beginning to wilt;

• clean, disinfected tools and scrubbed pots;

• sharp cutting tools so that wounds heal fast;

• fresh proprietary compost. For hardwood cuttings going into garden soil, make sure that it is weed free and has sharp drainage;

• the correct method for each type of cutting.

Types of cuttings

Semi-ripe cuttings These are taken in late summer when the growth has slowed down. Choose a healthy new shoot that hasn't flowered. It should be a little stiff at the base and floppy at the tip and 7.5–10 cm (3–4 in) long. Either pull it off the stem to make a little 'heel' or cut it off just below a node with a sharp, clean blade. If you are not going to plant the cuttings straight away, store them in a plastic bag and keep them cool.

The ideal conditions for semi-ripe and softwood cuttings are a humid environment, indirect light and warm soil temperatures. These conditions may be created by keeping cuttings under glass or in plastic bags in dappled shade. Semi-ripe and softwood cuttings are ideal for lavender, rosemary and thyme.

1 Mix equal parts of perlite or silver sand with potting compost. Fill a container allowing for space at the top for watering. Water well. If it is a heel cutting, tidy it up by removing ragged edges with a sharp knife. Strip off all the leaves apart from about four at the top. Pinch out the topmost bud.

2 Plant in a flowerpot, using a dibber, spacing cuttings 7.5 cm (3 in) apart. Plant almost to the level of the leaves, but not touching.

3 Cover with a clear plastic bag. Blow in it to increase the carbon dioxide and seal it at the top.

4 After about two weeks, cut small holes into the bag to let in air.

5 Two weeks later. Hopefully there will be roots appearing out of the bottom of the pot, the sign that the cuttings are ready to pot on. If no roots show, wait a little longer.

How to take a semi ripe cutting

You will need: a craft knife, containers, potting compost, perlite or sand and a cloche to keep in moisture.

2 Alterntively cut it off carefully just below a node.

4 Mix well. Fill the pot leaving a gap at the top for watering. Water thoroughly.

1 Choose a healthy new shoot in late summer. Don't let it dry out. Take a heel by pulling it off the stem at a join.

3 The ideal cuttings medium – equal parts of perlite or sand with potting compost.

5 Pinch out the top most leaves. Strip off the lower leaves of the cuttings, leaving three or four on top. Trim off any ragged edges.

6 *Make a hole with a dibber and plunge the cuttings in up to (but not touching) the first leaves.*

7 *Cover with a cloche to keep in moisture and place in the shade.*

Softwood cuttings These are taken in spring from soft new growth in much the same way as semi-ripe ones. The cuts are made just below nodes as these are the fastest-growing parts of the plant. Being earlier in the season, softwood cuttings need to be kept warm – at 18–24°C (64–75°F) – in order to root. They can either be kept in a propagator or, failing that, set in a warm place like the airing cupboard covered with a clear plastic bag. They need to be kept moist. Remove the bag for half an hour two or three times a week to stop the cuttings rotting off. Softwood cuttings should root in 6–10 weeks.

Hardwood cuttings Hardwood cuttings are taken between autumn and spring and are generally used for propagating deciduous trees and shrubs such as black-, red- or whitecurrants and gooseberries. In October, choose a healthy, straight shoot from the current season's growth and about the thickness of a pencil. Cut a length about 20 cm (8 in) long.

Trim the cutting just above a bud at the top end using a slanted cut and then make a straight cut below a bud at the bottom of the cutting. This is to remind you which way up to plant the cuttings. Remove any large leaves, sideshoots or all but the topmost four buds. Wound the bottom cut slightly to help rooting. Cuttings will generally root happily without rooting powder, although you can use organic versions based on seaweed.

Make a V-shaped slit in the ground where you will keep them and put some sand or sharp grit at the bottom for drainage. Push the cuttings down so that only the four top buds show. It is generally best to cover hardwood cuttings with cloches or keep them in a cold frame over winter. They should have rooted by spring.

propagation by root division

Dividing up the roots of perennials has the merits of being simple to do, of providing you with new plants instantly and of rejuvenating the parent plant at the same time. Wait until the plants are three or four years old and well established. Divide them when dormant. Discard the old centre.

Rhubarb and seakale There are two methods: you can dig up the entire plant, cut it into sections with a knife, and then replant the sections making sure that there is some root and some shoot on each division; or you can leave the plant in the ground and sink two spades back to back right through the roots and prise the plant apart. The latter method is the tougher option.

Asparagus Lift the whole plant with care and, using pressure from your thumbs, pull it apart into two pieces without breaking the roots. You may need a knife to finish off dividing it.

Artichokes and cardoons These produce little offsets next to the roots. Choose a healthy offshoot. Without moving the parent plant, use a sharp spade or a knife (ideally one with a curved blade) to cut down into its root to separate the offshoot. Cut the leaves back by a third and replant the offset.

Jerusalem artichokes and garlic Keep back some tubers of Jerusalem artichokes and replant them in spring. You can cut them through at the joints for more tubers. The first garlic needs to be bought from a garden centre. After that, keep a few bulbs back. Pull these apart in autumn and plant the cloves individually.

1 Once the rhubarb is well established and about five years old, it benefits from being divided up. Work around the plant, some distance away from it, using a hefty garden fork.

2 Ease the rhubarb out of the ground – it doesn't matter if some of the roots snap.

Dividing rhubarb
Your will need: one or two strong garden forks, a spade and a sharp knife.

3 Cut it into several pieces, with a spade or sharp knife, making sure that each piece has some root and shoot. Replant about 2.5 cm (1 in) below the surface

propagating soft fruit

Runners

Strawberries put out runners, which need to be clipped off while you are harvesting the fruit so as not to exhaust the plant. After fruiting has stopped, around July, allow four or five runners per plant to grow. When long enough to reach the ground, bury small pots of compost in a circle around the plant and pin down the strawberry runners with a hairpin of wire. Runners usually root within six weeks. Sever them from the parent plant and grow on.

Suckers

Raspberries To propagate, dig out any suckers along with plenty of root. Inspect the sucker carefully for any signs of disease and then plant it separately. Only propagate from young stock in the peak of good health.

Blackberries and hybrids In July or August, make a small hole about 15cm (6in) deep in the ground and bury the tip of a healthy shoot. Once it has made roots in the following spring, sever it from the parent plant with about 30 cm (1 ft) of stem. Dig it up and replant.

Propagating strawberries from runners

You will need: a flower pot, compost and a hairpin of wire.

1 *Choose healthy runners when long enough to reach the ground.*

2 *Fill a flower pot with compost and bury it next to the parent plant. Secure the runner down with a hair pin of wire to keep it in contact with the soil.*

3 *When you see signs of growth it can be severed from the parent plant and allowed to grow on.*

looking after
your plants

water, protection, food and supports

Good gardening is about understanding the individual needs of plants. It is providing them with their ideal conditions, food and water at the right time, supporting climbers, staking plants against winter windrock, protecting plants from being eaten by pests and sheltering them from cold weather and wind. For the best results, grow plants in their optimum season, fast and skilfully so that pests and disease don't get a look in. Unless you are seeking an extra challenge, go with nature, never against it.

watering

All plants need water, a precious commodity on the allotment, but it can be given with discrimination and a little know-how. Ways to conserve water include:
● collect as much rainwater as you can in water butts. Rainwater is the best water for plants and will be at the right temperature for vegetables sensitive to cold, such as tomatoes and aubergines. The one exception to using rainwater is for seeds, when it is safer to use sterile tap water;
● sink short lengths of pipe, an inverted water bottle with the bottom sawn off, or a flowerpot next to plants that need plenty of water. This way, you can target the roots with precision, without wasting a drop;
● make a moat around plants;
● put on thick mulches in spring after a good rainstorm, to keep the moisture in the soil and prevent it evaporating;

● improve the water-holding capacity of the soil by incorporating plenty of organic material every year;
● when planting in containers, add water-retaining granules;
● water in the cool of the evening or first thing in the morning, to avoid evaporation. Morning is better as wet soil at night is ideal for foraging slugs and snails;
● protect plants from drying winds by using windbreaks.

Watering techniques

Watering seeds in situ Dribble water into the seed drill before planting outside. Watering from overhead can make the soil 'cap', or form a crust, making it difficult for the seeds to push through. If you need to water after the seedlings emerge, use the finest rose on the watering can.

Watering seeds under cover Soak the compost in the seed tray – this should provide enough moisture until the seeds have germinated. Keep them moist by sitting the tray in water or by watering carefully at the base.

Watering transplants Transplants are particularly vulnerable and need nursing until they establish. Soak before and water well after transplanting and continue to keep plants moist. Water every day (or even twice a day in dry weather) carefully at the base of the plants.

Watering barerooted fruit trees and shrubs As soon as the plants arrive, soak them for a couple of hours and plant them straightaway, or, if this is not possible, heel them in to prevent them drying out. In their first season, until they get their roots down and can bring up moisture from a good depth, keep plants thoroughly watered on a regular basis.

Green vegetables These need constant moisture but don't overwater as this can produce too much soft growth attractive to pests.

Plants that need to be kept constantly moist

Those with little root Seedlings, cuttings and transplants, barerooted trees and shrubs. Also, plants that have a tendency to bolt should anything upset the smooth passage of their growth. Lettuce, true spinach, rocket and some orientals fall into this group.

Fine horticultural mesh can be used through-out the growth of plants as it lets in air and rain water.

Greedy feeders Tender plants that grow at speed – tomatoes, courgettes, marrows, peppers and chillis – will not perform well if deprived of water. Also, green vegetables as the effect of watering is leaf growth.

Plants that profit from a good watering at specific times

For plants that are grown for their pods and seeds – peas and beans – you don't want too much leaf growth. Keep them on the dry side until they flower. At this point they could do with some help and generous watering will boost production. For plants grown for their roots and tubers, such as potatoes, a soaking when marble sized is proven to help the crop.

How to water established plants and when

A sprinkling of water is counter-productive. This is because the plant will start to look for water near the surface – the first place to dry out. The aim of watering is to get the plants to grow their roots downwards, to seek out the more constant moisture that can be found in the lower depths of the soil. For established plants a rough guide is 11 litres per square metre (2 gallons per square yard) once a week in the growing season, or twice a week when it is hot or when you see any signs of wilting. Water slowly at the base of the plants, to avoid damping off and waste.

Testing the moisture content of the soil Test the moisture in the ground by digging a hole about 23 cm (9 in) deep. If it is damp at that level, established plants should be able to tap into it. Alternatively, buy a cheap soil moisture meter.

When to reduce watering Slow down on watering as winter approaches for plants that will stand out in winter (sprouts and winter greens). You don't want a lot of lush growth that will be knocked back by cold weather. In winter itsself, cut the watering right back as plants just tick over then.

plant protection

Nowadays most edible plants are grown, at least for part of their lives, under some form of protection against pests and cold. The stronger plastics are the only real deterrent for birds as they are not hoodwinked for long by bird scarers in any form.

Horticultural fabrics

Modern horticultural meshes and fleece take care of a lot of problems in one fell swoop. They are designed to let in light, water and air so crops can be grown under them throughout. Brassicas, which are sitting targets from aerial and ground attack, are really best doubly protected throughout their growth with netting on top and cabbage collars below.

A complete covering, or 'floating mulch', speeds up growth. Allow a little slackness. Bury the edges of the fabric so that you can let it out as the plants grow or weigh it down with stones. If you have raised beds with wooden edging, the fleece can be stapled to the sides. If you are covering entire crops, check thoroughly for any pests that might be trapped inside first. Weed well because the weeds will enjoy any extra luxuries too.

You may need to lift the fabrics to weed or for plants to be pollinated.

An old drinks bottle sawn off at both ends offers some protection against pests, wind and weather.

opposite, clockwise from top *Fine horticultural mesh can be used throughout the growth of plants as it lets in air and rain water; wide netting deters pigeons; a flowerpot or an old tennis ball works well as a cane topper to protect from injury.*

Fleece Made of polypropylene, fleece is so light and airy that crops hardly feel it. It provides warmth while letting in light, air and water so crops can be grown to maturity under it while being protected against pests. The one disadvantage is that it will get dirty and tear after a year or two. New inventions include more durable fabrics that can be washed at the end of the year.

Mesh fabrics Mesh fabrics made of plastic last longer than fleece, especially if they are UV treated. They don't keep the plants as warm but are just as effective against pests. As they let in more air, diseases are less likely to develop. They can also be used for a floating mulch. Mesh comes in various gauges.

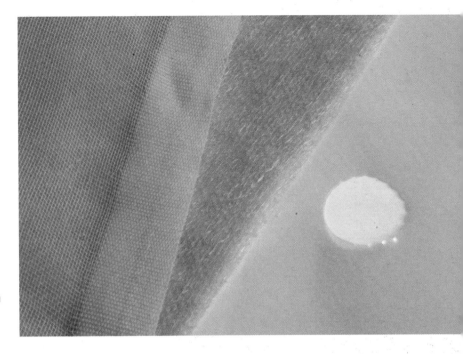

Enviromesh, gauge 1.35 mm, will protect against cabbage root fly, carrot fly, cabbage white butterfly, pea moth, cutworm, cabbage whitefly, leaf miners and many species of aphids. It is tough enough to deter birds, including pigeons, rabbits and cats.

Micromesh, gauge 0.6 mm, will protect all these plus every type of aphid and the tiniest pests like the flea beetle, onion fly and vine weevil.

Ordinary polythene Ordinary polythene sheet is useful for warming large areas of soil by a degree or two. The problem with polythene sheeting as a cover is that it is non-porous, so can create sweaty conditions to foster fungal diseases in summer and harbour slugs.

Aerated polythene This is a good warmer for outside seed sowing. It has holes punched through it large enough for

above left The cane tops here prevent the netting from slipping down the canes.

above right The belt and braces approach. Brassicas protected from ground attack with collars and from aerial attack by flying pests with netting.

pollinating insects to circulate, so you do not need to lift it to allow access for pollination.

It is worth having a role of aerated polythene to hand as it has myriad uses, such as an instant insect-proof curtain to the greenhouse or to cover a few hoops for a little polytunnel in a cold snap. Every year there are new inventions so it is worth checking the catalogues.

Cloches

A seedbed with a cloche cover works in much the same way as a cold frame. But whereas cold frames are fixtures, cloches can be lifted on and off and moved around the plot from one set of plants to another. Some are designed to cover multiple plants and others are for individual ones. Tunnel cloches work in much the same way as small polytunnels (see page 128-129). The bell-shaped ones look good on individual plants or you can use old plastic water bottles with the bottom sawn off and the top left open for ventilation. They will warm the soil for early spring sowing if put on two weeks before sowing or planting.

Winter warmth

Polystyrene Pots in the cold greenhouse will be kept a few degrees warmer if you stand them on a sheet of polystyrene during the winter months, and you can protect your winter salads from frostbite by growing them in polystyrene boxes. These boxes should be made from polystyrene sheets glued together with a see-through sheet of glass or clear plastic on top. A sheet of polystyrene under your seed trays is also a good insulator and will help to prevent cold creeping up from below.

Bubble wrap As temperatures drop below zero, bubble wrap comes in handy for lagging your pipes and for 'double glazing' the greenhouse or cold frames.

below left *An easy poytunnel construction. Sections of old hose serve as well as commercial hoops.*

below right *For extra warmth use fleece instead of netting.*

Making nettle string

You will need: tall nettles, thin rubber gloves and a key ring with keys attached or similar.

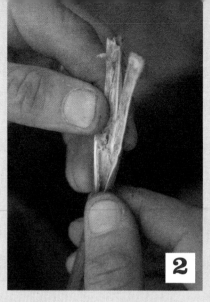

2 *With your thumb nail, split the outer skin.*

4 *Remove the inner strands.*

1 *Strip off the leaves – if you have let the nettles die back, most of the sting will have disappeared*

3 *Continue down the length of the nettle.*

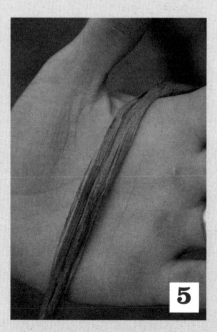

5 *Take the inner strands and thread them through the key ring and twist the strands until they begin to buckle.*

above *Nettle string in use.*

left *A tomato plant tied with a figure of eight knot.*

6 *Holding onto the ends firmly, release the key ring. It will twirl round at speed making the strands into rope. Tie the ends.*

Making a mini polytunnel

You will need: two children's hoops (or a length of hose pipe), polythene, horticultural fabric, netting or fleece sufficient to cover the desired width and length with enough flak to tie the ends, hairpins of wire, stones or bricks to hold the fabric in place on the sides.

2 *Insert the hoops, pushing them down firmly into the soil*

4 *Cover with the fabric.*

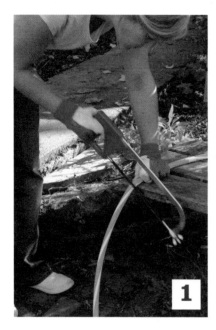

1 *Saw the hoops in half or saw off four equal lengths of hosepipe.*

3 *Repeat until you have a row of hoops to the same height and width.*

5 & 6 *Tie the ends into a knot and secure.*

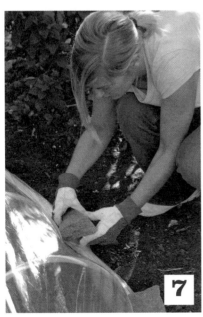

7 Weigh down the sides with stones or bricks or pin the down with wires.

8 For access or on warm days, the covers can be lifted.

Viper's bugloss (Echium vulgare).

food

Apart from the compost and manure that is applied annually, you can boost both soil and plants with organic fertilizers, which come from plant, animal and mineral origins and do not harm the soil or the populations of micro-organisms within it. For those who prefer not to use animal extracts there are all-vegetable alternatives.

The standard practice is to apply a topdressing of an all-round fertilizer such as blood, fish and bone or seaweed meal prior to planting. Most organic fertilizers work on slow-release principles. This is better for plants as they will be encouraged to grow strongly in a measured and controlled way.

There are also liquid feeds, proprietary brands and home-made ones. These work fast as a tonic for flagging plants. They are useful for tired specimens that have been overwintered, plants in pots with limited resources as well as fast-growing, greedy feeders such as tomatoes, cucumbers, squashes or calaloo (Amaranthus). Liquid feeds are short-term solutions, handy as backup.

The type of feed you use depends on the plants, whether you want to improve the fruit and flower or to put on leaf growth.

Nutritional needs of plants
Major elements for plant growth are NPK – nitrogen (N), phosphorus (P) and potassium (K) – plus trace elements and minerals.

Major elements
Nitrogen (N) boosts leaf and shoot production. As a component of chlorophyll, it gives plants their greenness. A shortage of nitrogen is revealed by stunted, pale leaves. Nitrogen is a good booster for leafy vegetables. However, overfeeding with nitrogen will produce fast, sappy growth, which will be attractive to pests and make plants vulnerable to disease and frost. Don't overfeed fruiting or root vegetables with nitrogen as it will encourage leaf growth rather than fruit and flowers.

Phosphorus (P), or phosphate, stimulates healthy growth throughout the plant. It is associated with roots. A sprinkling is commonly used in planting holes to help establish new shrubs and trees. Only small quantities are needed. A deficiency of phosphorus will be evident by stunted growth and discoloration on the older leaves first. A deficiency on very acid soils is not uncommon.

Potassium (K), or potash, is the nutrient for the size and quality of flowers and fruit. It gives plants resistance to pests and disease. Any lack of potassium will result in small fruit and flowers and yellowing leaves.

Magnesium (Mg) is also a constituent of chlorophyll, the greening agent. If there is a shortage of magnesium, it is usually caused by insufficient organic matter in the soil. The effect is a yellowing leaves starting from the veins.

Sulphur (S) also helps to form chlorophyll. As with magnesium, it is unusual to find any shortage in soil containing plenty of organic matter.

Calcium (Ca) helps in the manufacture of protein.

Trace elements
Where the content of organic matter is high, It is unusual to find any shortage of these micronutrients. It can be difficult, even for experts, to pinpoint deficiencies as symptoms can be similar. If concerned, send off for a professional soil analysis.

Manganese (Mn) helps to form chlorophyll and protein in the leaves. A lack is revealed by stunting and yellowing in the younger leaves.

Iron (Fe) contributes much the same as manganese. A shortage is not uncommon in highly alkaline soils.

Copper (Fe) and zinc (Zn) activate enzymes.

Boron (B) is an important element throughout the growing tissue. A shortage causes corkiness in fruit and root crops.

Molybdenum (Mb) helps to produce protein.

Fertilizers

Seaweed This is a wonder plant. Seaweed meal builds up the humus structure and water-holding capacity of the soil. It is known to increase root mass, which helps plants to take up moisture and nutrients from the soil. For roots it is best applied on planting and then four weeks later. The extract is an excellent all-round tonic for promoting strong growth and disease resistance. Though low in macronutrients, seaweed contains the full range of 60 trace elements – minerals, vitamins and the essential amino acids and alginates. Plants sprayed with seaweed extract are less attractive to aphids. You can buy seaweed in many different forms and combinations. It is against the law to collect seaweed unless it is lying loose on the beach. If you have some, wash it well and spread it out thinly to cure for up to a month (this is a smelly process). When ready, you can use it as an activator on the compost heap, or as fertilizer for beets and brassicas.

Comfrey Another miracle worker is comfrey, with its roots that penetrate deeply into the subsoil, some 1.2–3 m (4–10 ft), and are fast and greedy mineral gatherers. Whereas most varieties will spread and be virtually impossible to dig out, *Symphytum x uplandicum* 'Bocking 14', developed by Lawrence D. Hills, can be propagated only from cuttings and won't spread.

Growing comfrey Buy offsets of *Symphytum x uplandicum* 'Bocking 14'. Choose a weed-free site in full sun. Clay soil is ideal. If planting on thin soils, apply manure. Comfrey can be planted at any time apart from January and February. Keep it well watered during the first summer and remove any flowerheads for the plants to build up strength. The following spring, feed with a high-nitrogen fertilizer and put on a good mulch of manure. Comfrey grows fast and needs plenty of nourishment.

Harvesting comfrey Around April, comfrey usually has its first cut of the year, with shears or a sickle. Chop it back to 5 cm (2 in) from the ground when the new season's shoots are 30 cm (1 ft) high, and leave overnight to wilt.

This first cut is usually aimed at the potato patch. Dig the potato trenches deeper than usual to allow for it. Lay the comfrey along the trench at 0.5 kg (1 lb) per 30 cm (1 ft). Cover lightly with soil and plant the seed potatoes. As the comfrey heats up, it works like a small compost heap, giving the potatoes a racing start and providing them with a balanced plant food.

The second comfrey cut can be used in trenches for the beans and peas. The comfrey will hold moisture and release potassium – particularly associated with improving fruit and flowers through the summer. Later on, comfrey will benefit tomatoes, raspberries or gooseberries if piled between rows to keep down weeds and provide slow-release nourishment.

Comfrey in compost When applied as a 5–10 cm (2–4 in) layer on top of 10–15 cm (4–6 in) layer of woody herbaceous material, comfrey will create plenty of heat as it rots down to give the compost heap a flying start in autumn. It is also good added to compost throughout the growing season.

Grass cuttings These contain 2–5 per cent nitrogen. They rot down to almost nothing but can become slimy. The key is to spread thinly – no thicker than 2.5 cm (1 in) or they will start to heat up. They can be incorporated thinly into the topsoil, be spread around crops as a nutritious mulch or be used on the compost heap as an activator.

Red Campion (melandrium rubrum).

Liquid fertilizers Liquid feeds can be used a foliar spray or as a soil drench. Home-made feeds or compost 'teas' are excellent in every way and have the advantage of costing nothing; their only problem is the powerful stink that they give off. Many find this hugely off-putting. Keep them as far away from you as possible and tightly lidded.

Alternatives are to buy pellets or 'odour-free' products such as comfrey pellets and seaweed liquid feed. Comfrey pellets are soaked for three days before they can be sprayed on. There are also combinations of comfrey and seaweed with added alfalfa or lucerne (another deep rooter and mineral finder).

Home-made liquid feeds It is easy to make your own first-class liquid fertilizers or 'teas'. The luxury product for your own liquid feeds is a barrel with a tight-fitting lid (to keep the smell inside) and a tap. The alternative is to tie up the particular product in a 'tea bag' of hessian sack or similar and to suspend it in a barrel or old dustbin on a crossbar and leave to fester for a few weeks in the barrel. As a rule of thumb, the 'tea bag' should be about one-tenth to the volume of water. The resulting liquid is normally diluted at least 4:1 and should look like weak tea. This is an inexact science. Strain it before watering or spraying it onto the plants or the ground.

If using tap water, leave the water overnight before using it to get rid of the chlorine. Don't spray home-made liquid feeds on parts of the plant that you are planning to eat.

- Comfrey: fill the barrel with the comfrey and let it rot down. The resulting black liquid can be siphoned off through the summer as wanted. At the end of the season, the dregs can be thrown on the compost heap. Stir from time to time. Comfrey is a very juicy plant so it doesn't need water to rot down into liquid. Dilute it at the end.
- Nettles: make a good general tonic and are high in potassium and calcium. Those gathered in spring are richest in nutrients. They are not suitable for alkaline soils.
- Manures: Chickens, duck, pigeon or rabbit, horse or sheep manure can be treated in a similar way. Let the manures rot down for six months before steeping them in water. Dilute these 20:1, as they are potent.
- Real tea: cold, stewed tea makes a high-potash liquid manure and is a quick way to give plants invaluable compost.
- Fish tea: this can be made in the same way as real tea, but using old bones or rotting fish. It is very effective, but the smell is truly indescribable!

Dried fertilizers Some fertilizers have an all-round action while others can be targeted to a specific problem.
- Blood, fish and bone-meal is a balanced, NPK all-round fertilizer.
- Hoof and horn is rich in nitrogen and works on a slow-release basis. It needs to break down, so apply it to the soil a week or more before planting.
- Seaweed meal is a slow-release, all-round tonic with all the trace elements. It contains hormones that promote photosynthesis and protein production, and also helps to create humus in the soil.

- Most dried manures have all the trace elements but are low on NPK.
- Chicken manure is high in nitrogen. Potent. Use sparingly. Good activator for compost.
- Bone-meal is rich in phosphate for root growth. Usually applied as a base dressing when planting shrubs and trees.
- Rock phosphate is a good alternative to bone-meal for dog owners who don't want their plots dug up or dislike using animal products. It promotes rooting, particularly for shrubs and trees.
- Fish meal contains nitrogen and phosphate.
- Rock potash is a useful source of potash alone.
- Epsom salts are a soluble form of magnesium alone.
- Wood ash from your own bonfire is high in potassium and has some phosphate. Exact quantities of each depends on the type of timber.
- Ground limestone increases alkalinity. Adds calcium.
- Dolomitic limestone increases alkalinity. Supplies calcium and magnesium.
- Gypsum Calcium. Does not affect the pH.
- Volcanic rock dust. A by-product of the quarrying industry. Contains a wide range minerals and trace elements.
- Green-bracken products High levels of potassium and nitrogen.
- Blood meal provides high nitrogen. It is so potent and fast acting that it is generally not recommended. If overapplied it can burn plants with excessive ammonia.

Making comfrey tea

1 Chop up comfrey and leave it to rot down in a barrel with a tightly fitting lid and a tap.

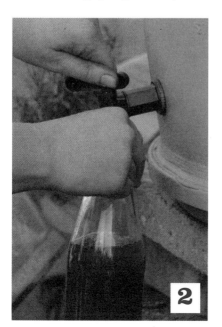

2 After around a month, it can be siphoned off into bottles, diluted and used as required.

Cleverly hand woven string mesh for runner beans to climb.

supports

Climbers need support to prevent them sprawling, being flattened by rain or covered in mud. Also, once on supports, it is easier to weed around them without causing damage. Pruning, watering, keeping a pest and disease watch and harvesting crops also becomes simpler.

Put the supports or stakes in before sowing or planting. Normal practice is to make special supports, but many plants can also be grown up a trellis or any other form of support you happen to have. Beans and gourds look very decorative growing over an arch with their pods or fruits hanging down.

Some climbers, including French and runner beans, cling by twining themselves as they grow up the support and so won't need tying in once they've taken hold. Runner beans are vigorous, growing to 2.4 m (8 ft) so will need hefty supports. The usual method is either a big wigwam or a row of tall poles lined up and crossed at the top. The less vigorous French beans grow well up a light wigwam. You can even grow them up a sunflower. The secret of doing this is to get the host plant established before introducing the bean.

Some of the cucurbits, melons, squashes and certain types of cucumbers have a climbing habit and bear heavy fruits. Outdoor crops can be trained up supports in the same way as beans. Heavy fruits are sometimes put into nets attached to the support to take the weight off the plant.

Peppers, tomatoes and aubergines may start to flop when the fruits get heavy. Put in short stakes and tie in the stems, or tie string around all the stems to enclose them in a bunch and keep them upright.

Dwarf and 'semi-leafless' peas don't need support, but the other pea types are quite bushy, cling by their tendrils but don't grow very tall. You can box them in with stakes each side of a double row, using horizontal wires or netting across the framework, or you can stick in twiggy, branching peasticks along the rows, or else string up a net.

Apart from the free-standing bush types, soft fruits are generally trained on a post-and-wire system or they are trained against a wall or fence using vine eyes or nails and wire.

Free-standing trees are planted with a short stake. A little buffeting by the wind strengthens the young tree.

Ties

It is important that tree ties don't cut into the plant. The best ties stretch or can be loosened. For tree stakes you can buy little, plastic belts with buckles that can be let out or soft plastic tubing, which stretches. Old nylon tights make excellent ties for larger plants. For smaller plants, soft string is fine. Always tie in a figure of eight, as this makes a buffer between the plant and the stake and it protects the plant from rubbing.

Hazel pea sticks just stuck into the ground are good supports for peas or broad beans. Heftier hazel bean poles are ideal for runner beans. Lash them at top with strong string or rope.

end of the growing season

the harvest

One of the loveliest things of growing your own is being in touch with the seasons. At the end of the summer, when the evenings get shorter and there is a nip in the air, it is time to gather in the summer harvest, collect seed for the year to come, to make provision for wildlife and prepare for the winter ahead with a fully stocked larder.

In the allotment, harvesting goes on all year round. Even in the depth of winter there will be out-of-season crops salads and oriental saladini growing under some form of protection, as well as hardy winter greens and roots braving the elements outside. By May, the first asparagus is ready to cut, and early peas and broad beans are in season. A few weeks later, in June, there will be the new season's potatoes and strawberries. From July to October everything ripens all at once and the race is really on. It is a good idea to have a storage plan.

Some useful harvesting rules are:

● avoid damage. Store only perfect specimens. Eat the rest up quickly. Broken tissue invites fungus and bacteria. Rough handling can lead to bruising;

● use a clean, sharp knife for trimming. A clean cut will repair fast;

● cool down the crops straight after lifting. The ideal time to harvest is early in the morning on a cool day. Move the crops from the ground to the shade of a tree, to the shed or refrigerator with due speed;

● store crops so that they don't touch each other. Wrap apples individually. Store root vegetables in compost or sand. Check regularly. Remove any that show the first signs of rot;

● unless you are going to eat straight away, aim to pick when the produce is on the very verge of perfection as it continues to grow after it has been harvested. Tasting is the best test. If in doubt, sample one.

vegetables

Brassicas

Broccoli and cauliflowers are made up of flower buds, which will spoil if allowed to open into flowers. Pick the broccoli buds regularly to prevent this. Cauliflowers are ready when the whole head is white and smooth.

Brussels sprouts are picked from the bottom up and taste better after a frost. Clear away yellowing leaves as you go.

Cabbages are ready when they feel solid to the touch. If left too long, they will keep growing and split. If you want to store tight-headed cabbage, dig it up with the roots before the frosts.

Kale and Swiss chard Pick the outside leaves as you need them. Leave the centres to grow.

Kohlrabi Harvest when young as it coarsens quickly.

Storing brassicas Most brassicas store for only a few days wrapped and refrigerated. However, tight-headed winter cabbage can be kept for a couple of months in a cool place if it has its roots still attached.

Potatoes

First early potatoes are ready when the flowers appear.

Maincrops are ready when the tops go brown and dry. Dig from the outside, taking care not to spike the tubers. A potato fork with blunt tines is the best tool.

Storing potatoes Earlies should be eaten within a few weeks. Maincrops can be stored right through winter. After lifting, keep them in the dark in a moderately warm place (10°–15°C/50°–59°F) for a couple weeks. This will encourage a corky layer of tissue to form on the skin, which will protect the potatoes and will heal any small cuts or abrasions. Afterwards, store them at 5°C/41°F in potato sacks. Continue to keep them in the dark at all times, to prevent poisonous green patches.

Legumes

Runner and French beans should snap crisply when bent over.

Broad beans can be eaten in their skins like mangetout when very young or else be left to mature.

Mangetouts are harvested when the seeds are barely visible.

Peas If you hold pea pods to the light you can judge if they are ready.

Storing legumes Freezing or drying. To dry beans, hang the whole plant upside down or pick off the pods and spread them out to dry off naturally in a frost-free, airy place. Store in airtight jars.

Onions

Garlic is ready when a few leaves go brown. Dig up and leave to dry in the sun, or place in a shed if the weather is bad.

Leeks can be judged by the thickness, depending on variety. They can stay out all winter.

Onions are ripe when the leaves collapse and fall over.

Storing onions Hang up onions and garlic in an airy place. Cook leeks in various ways and freeze.

Roots

You can make an educated guess at the size of root crops by looking at the size of the 'shoulders' that appear at soil level.

Carrots can be harvested and eaten at any stage of their growth, according to your needs and desires.

Parsnips Leave until after the frosts for good flavour.

Turnips and radishes must not get too big as they will become woody.

Storing roots Parsnip and swede can be left in the ground in winter if the soil is free draining. Carrots are edible at every stage of their growth from the tiny thinnings to full size. In milder parts of the country they can be left in the ground. If the soil is cold and wet they will rot off. Pull up winter radishes (mouli and daikon) before the frosts. Brush off the soil but don't wash them as this may damage the skin. The winter roots can be stored in boxes separated from each other by old compost, straw or sand and kept in a cool place. Salad radishes spoil after a few days.

Beets

Beetroot is ready when you see the shoulders at soil level. You can choose how big you want it to grow – golf- or tennis-ball size. Take care to lift without damage as beetroot 'bleeds'. Cut the leaves around 7.5 cm (3 in) above the root for the same reason.

Spinach goes to seed quickly. Harvest by cutting off leaves at ground level. Pick the outer leaves of spinach beet and chard on a regular basis.

Storing beets Store beetroots in the same way as roots in boxes of sand or compost. Spinach can be frozen. Spinach beet and chard don't store.

Curcurbits

Courgettes and summer squash grow at great speed, are prolific and need to

left *Carrots stored in old compost.*

right *Harvesting the crop.*

harvested daily before they coarsen. Courgettes will turn into marrows with surprising speed.

Cucumbers Catch young as they get pithy before yellowing.

Winter squashes colour up when ripe and pumpkins need to be brought in before the frosts. They sound hollow when you tap them when they are ready. Cut them off with a long stalk as it will protect the fruit from rotting while it dries. Leave them to dry out of direct sunlight for several weeks.

END OF THE GROWING SEASON

Storing curcurbits Pumpkins and winter squash should store for up to three months in a cool, frost-free shed, packed in cardboard boxes in straw. Watch out for mice as pumpkins and squash are mouse heaven.

Fruiting vegetables

Aubergines and peppers should be picked when still shiny. They become bitter when they dull down.

Sweetcorn The signal that sweetcorn is ripe is when the 'silks' turn brown. Test by sticking your nail into a kernel. If the juice is milky, it is ready to eat.

Tomatoes are picked daily as they ripen. At the end of the season they will need to be ripened before the frosts. If there is time, untie tall varieties and lay them down on straw, where they are growing. Take off the last flowers and put cloches on for extra warmth. If the weather turns and the tomatoes need to come inside, they will ripen on a sunny windowsill or, more effectively, in a brown bag with a browning banana.

Storing fruiting vegetables Make sauces from tomatoes, peppers or aubergines, and freeze. Tomatoes and chillies can be sundried by leaving them in outside in a heatwave (Mexicans dry them on the roofs of their pickup trucks) or in an oven set on its minimum temperature, overnight.

Salads

Lettuce and other salad leaves are eaten at an immature stage.

Saladini is picked from the outside to encourage more to come. Cut off the entire head, always leaving four leaves at the bottom to resprout. When cut back like this, most salads will put out fresh growth three times before giving up the ghost.

Perennial vegetables

Artichokes In their second year, artichoke plants are ready to be harvested. Cut off the top (terminal) bud first with a little stem. You want to catch the bud at the point just before the scales start to open.

Asparagus Start to harvest in its third year. Do this in May, when the spears are about 13 cm (5 in) long. Cut them below soil level. Stop harvesting in late June, to let the plants build up strength for next year.

Cardoons, unlike artichokes, are grown for their stems. Dig up the entire plant. Trim off the leaves and roots.

Seakale is eaten like asparagus. It is ready to harvest in spring, when the fresh, young shoots reach around 20 cm (8 in). Each plant should give you three harvests before being left to restore itself for following year.

Storing perennial vegetables Only by cooking and freezing. Artichoke hearts can be bottled.

fruit

Generally fruit is picked when ripe. One exception is the late-season pear, which starts to rot from the middle if left on the tree, so they are picked when hard and ripened indoors. Early pears that ripen in midsummer, however, are eaten off the tree. Apples are ripe when they come off with a twist of the wrist. The berries – gooseberries, raspberries, blackberries

Plums left on the table to share.

and hybrids – are picked individually. They don't ripen all at once so, if you need a good quantity freeze them and add more as they ripen. Currants – red, black or white – are picked by the bunch, or 'strig'.

Storing fruit Most fruit doesn't keep unless it is dried, preserved, cooked and/or frozen. The late varieties of apples are the exception. Wrap them individually and store in airy crates in the cool. If you are buying an apple tree, the storage time could be a consideration as it varies considerably. A Gala apple will store for three months, whereas a Granny Smith will keep going for around five months.

Artichoke harvest. Leave one or two to flower for the birds and the bees.

Chives (Allium schoenoprasum).

herbs

Herbs are at their best when fresh. Thyme and winter savory can be picked all year outside. Some herbs can be kept going in winter if they are potted up and brought indoors or else grown outside under protective covers. Parsley is a perennial, though generally treated as an annual. However, given some cover in winter, it will carry on until spring when you can sow new seed. The same goes for a late crop of chervil, sown in midsummer. Chives and French tarragon are herbaceous, so will die back in winter and re-emerge in spring, but the leaves can be picked and frozen. Coriander and marjoram are annuals so the only way to preserve them is to freeze the leaves. Basil doesn't dry or freeze well, so harvest it all and make it into pesto sauce.

The flowers of camomile, lavender, rosemary and thyme dry well for pot-pourri, teas or tisanes and culinary purposes. If you are collecting the leaves, do so just before the flowers open. Choose a dry day and collect the herbs in late morning, when the dew has dried off but the essential oils have not yet evaporated in the sunshine. Flowers should be picked at their peak. Either hang the herbs up in bunches or lay them out on racks to dry. Keep them out of the sun. When dried, strip them off the stems and store them in airtight containers. Keep them in a dark, cool place such as a cupboard.

Mint (Mentha spp).

Sage (Salvia officinalis).

saving seed

Seed saving has become so high tech amongst seed merchants that to an amateur it might well seem to be a daunting skill, full of mystique and difficulty. Keep in mind though that until the 20th century all gardeners saved their own seed.

Once you get the hang of it and if you are willing to accept the odd loss from time to time, saving seed is hugely rewarding. It costs nothing and you may be able to develop strains that are tailor-made for your particular conditions. Many of the old varieties and those local to an area have been lost or can only be found in seed libraries. The interests of the commercial growers, who are aiming to please the supermarkets, can differ greatly from those of the allotment gardener. Speed of harvesting mechanically, long shelf life, uniformity and good looks can be at the cost of taste.

First, however, you need to gather a few facts about the plant that you want to collect seed from.

Annuals and biennials

Annuals
These are sown, flower and set seed in one year.

Biennials
Biennials grow in the first year, then flower and set seed in the second. Carrots, parsnips, onions, beetroot and brassicas are all biennial. To get them to flower and set seed they will need to be kept going through winter. Hardy biennials such as parsnips and kale can stay in the ground. Other biennials such as beetroot and carrots may need to be lifted in cold areas and stored over winter. They can be kept in the cool and dark, stacked in boxes of slightly damp leaf-mould or of seed and potting compost. Make sure that they don't touch each other. In spring, biennials are replanted and brought into flower for seed.

how is seed pollinated?

Inbreeders

These are plants with flowers that contain both parents of the seed and so pollinate themselves. Peas and French beans self-pollinate before the flowers have even opened. Along with other inbreeders such as lettuce and tomatoes, they are the easiest type of vegetable from which to save seed. The likelihood of them taking up an unsuitable partner is practically nil. The seed will come true to type year in and year out. You need to keep only one or two plants for saving seed from inbreeders.

Outbreeders

The vast majority of plants are pollinated by insects, particularly bees, collecting pollen as they fly from flower to flower. The brassicas are outbreeders. They cannot pollinate themselves but need to crossed by a different plant of the same species. To breed successfully from outbreeders, it is recommended that you grow quite a few plants – 20 or more – to have a wide enough choice for a healthy diversity.

Both outbreeders and inbreeders

Other vegetables such as peppers can inbreed and outbreed.

Wind-pollinated seed

Some vegetables such as sweetcorn, beetroot, chard and spinach are wind-pollinated and are best planted in a block for successful germination.

Male and female flowers

Squashes and sweetcorn have male and female flowers on the same plant, but spinach and asparagus have separate plants.

FI hybrids

This type of seed does not come true, that is does not reproduce itself exactly. F1 stands for first filial generation. For each generation, the same two particular, carefully chosen parents need to be crossed to get the same result.

Pure strains

Some outbreeders are highly promiscuous and will cross-pollinate with a wide variety of genetically compatible partners. Many of our vegetables have been bred from one or two of their wild ancestors. Sprouts and cauliflowers are descendants of the wild cabbage, so are related. The way to check on this is to look at the Latin names. Vegetables with the same surname can interbreed. Cabbage, broccoli, cauliflower, kohlrabi and kale are all *Brassica oleracea*, so they can interbreed with each other. They cannot cross with a turnip (*Brassica rapa*), because it is a different variety. However, the turnip can cross with Chinese cabbage as it is another member of the *Brassica rapa* group.

Globe and bulb onions, shallots, spring onions and bunching onions are all *Allium cepa* and can cross-pollinate amongst themselves. However, they cannot cross with a leek, which is *Allium porrum*. Broad beans will cross with field beans grown as a green manure in a neighbouring plot as they are both *Vicia faba*. Maize and sweetcorn are both *Zea mays* and will cross. The wild carrot, the familiar pretty Queen Anne's lace in our hedgerows, has the same varietal name as the carrot – *Daucus carota*. A cross-pollination between them, however, would produce a bitter-tasting root.

how to keep varieties pure

Professional growers use isolation distances up to 1,000m (1,000 yd). In an allotment situation, where everyone is growing close to each other, this is not feasible. Physical barriers are, therefore, the best method. If you want just a few seeds, tie bags made out of fleece or mesh over individual flowers. Wrap cotton wool round the stems first to make them absolutely insect proof and tie the bag up. When the flowers drop off and the fruits begin to form, the bags can come off too. Mark the stem with a piece of tape or string, so you remember which ones have been bagged. If you want to save lots of seed, cover the whole plant with fine mesh or make a cage in which several plants can cross-pollinate. Insects can get through the tiniest holes, so make sure you close all gaps.

Hand pollinating

If you are planning to bag or isolate an outbreeder, you will need to arrange for its pollination. Professionals keep beehives or introduce blowflies into their isolation cages or greenhouses. The amateur can hand pollinate them. Once you have worked out which are the male and which are the female flowers, then you need to find flowers of each sex that is ready to open on different plants of the same species. Bag these up on the point of opening and seal carefully. The perforated, see-through cellophane bags that supermarkets sell bread in are ideal as you can see what is going on. When the male flower has opened, remove the bag, pull off the petals and, with a small paintbrush, move the pollen onto the stigma of the female flower. Bag it up again and leave it until the flower drops off.

which plant is best for seed?

'Positive selection' is the art of choosing and perpetuating the most desirable characteristics of a given plant. You might be looking for plants that grow well in your particular conditions, have the most disease resistance, taste the best, or have a good variation of colour, shape or form. However, it is important not to get carried away. You want to keep the new generations true to type. The idea is to weed out the 'rogues' and remove the weak. For example, should a plant run to seed, don't be tempted to leave it and keep for seed as a shortcut This would be considered a mistake because that plant is showing a tendency to bolt – not a desirable characteristic. Collect seed only from plants that are in the peak of health. Disease can be carried in the seed.

harvesting seed

Most seeds need to be grown on and left on the plant until they would release themselves spontaneously. Peas and bean should be rattling in their pods. Catching them at the ultimate moment can be a dicey business or a race against time. When you feel that the moment is imminent, it is best to cover the seedhead with a brown paper bag securely tied. If wet weather threatens before the ultimate moment, you can pull up the whole plant and hang it upside down in an airy, warm, dry place to carry on maturing.

There are always exceptions when it comes to seeds and a few types such as tomatoes and melons will be ready to harvest when the crop is ready to eat.

cleaning seed

Dry seed

Most seed is harvested dry and can easily be cleaned by hand. To separate the seed from the chaff, rub tiny seeds of lettuce between finger and thumb or shake them through a fine sieve. Alternatively, blow the chaff off with a hair-drier (start off cautiously on a low speed). Pick through and throw out any dud seeds, for quality control.

Drying large seed Larger seeds such as peas and beans just need to be shucked. Then put the dried beans into an airtight freezer bag and freeze them for 48 hours, to kill any bean weevils. Let the bag come back to room temperature before opening it so that the seeds don't get damp from condensation.

Drying lettuce seed Growing seedling crops all year round can be expensive in terms of seed, so saving lettuce seed is a good idea. It is one of the easiest ones to do. It is an annual and an inbreeder, being largely self-pollinating. The one hitch is that lettuce takes a long time to set seed – ten weeks to grow and a further ten to set seed. By week 20, when you want it to become as dry as a bone, it can be a race against bad weather. The way to get round this is precise timing. Sow overwintering lettuce in autumn in the greenhouse or cold frame for it to flower in summer. Sow summer lettuce in earliest spring. Space them far apart for good air circulation in a block. Loose-leaf types are less likely to get rots or grey mould (Botrytis). Each lettuce will produce literally thousands of seeds, but sow some extras in case of disasters. When the seeds are ripe over a period of weeks they form little white puffballs. These can be shaken off and collected every two or three days. If bad weather threatens the whole plant can be lifted, put into a big brown bag and hung up to dry in the warmth.

Wet seed

The seed of a few vegetables such as tomatoes and melons are harvested wet and when only slightly overripe. These need to have the gelatinous pulp, which is a germination inhibitor, removed before they can be dried.

Tomatoes are inbreeders, which make them an easy choice for saving seed. Grow normally. If you are cultivating different types together, bag the flowers for safety's sake. When the tomatoes are fully ripe, their seed will be ready. Cut the ripe tomato in half and scoop out the seeds. To get the gelatinous coating off drop them into a jar of water. Put the lid on, and then leave the jar in a warm place such as the kitchen. It will start to ferment. Though not necessary you can add a little washing soda – a teaspoonful dissolved in hot water, topped up with cold, speeds up the process. After some days the coating will float to the top and the seeds will stay at the bottom. Filter them off quickly as you don't the fermentation to go any further.

Drying wet seed The dryer the seeds, the better. Spread them out in a warm place out of sunlight to dry off further, for a couple of weeks. Large seeds should be so dry that they shatter into smithereens if tapped with a hammer.

Storing seed

Keep in a cool, dark, dry place. The fridge is ideal. Otherwise in a cool cupboard or drawer. Small, brown envelopes or bags (don't forget to label them with the name and the date) tucked into an airtight

1 *Lettuce seed is fine. Pull up the plant when the flowers reach puff ball stage. Hang it upside-down, covering the flowerheads with a brown paper bag, so that the seeds will release themselves into it.*

3 *Gather up the seed on the paper, dry further and store in the envelope in a cool dark place. Label and date.*

Collecting dry seed

You will need: paper bags to catch the seed, a fine sieve, a piece of paper to catch the seed when winnowing, a brown envelope to store it, label and pen.

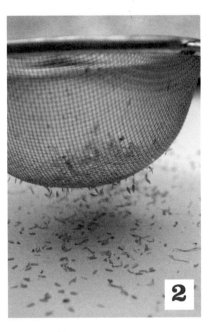

2 *Shake the seed through a fine sieve to remove the chaff.*

1 Select a really ripe tomato.

2 Scoop out seeds of the ripe tomato.

Collecting wet seed

You will need a jar, water, brown envelope to store the seeds, label and pen.

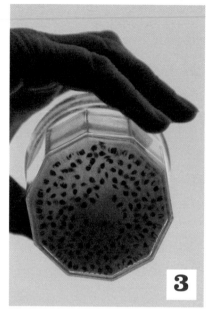

3 Put them in the jar. Add an equal level of water. Cover and keep in a warm place. Check daily. In a few days it will begin to ferment and a layer of scum will form on the top.

containers such as a kilner jar or a tupperware box with a tight lid will keep them dry. The addition of a little packet of silica gel (these come in shoe boxes and the like) will keep the seeds super dry. If you don't have any silica gel, put some dried rice in the oven for a few minutes, and put this in a little bag to mop up any last vestiges of moisture.

Seed storage times

These vary according to the particular seed and how it has been saved and stored. Parsnip seeds lasts only a year, whereas peas and beans will keep for three years, lettuce for 6–8 years and brassicas up to ten years in home conditions. To check the viability of some seeds, you can pregerminate them indoors.

4 Strain off and dry before storing in the dark in a brown envelope. Label and date.

wildlife

Allotments have an important role to play for wildlife. Many have natural features such as water and woodland, scrub, native hedgerows and trees. They are particularly invaluable in and around towns, where they make wildlife corridors and are calculated to have 30 per cent higher species diversity than urban parks.

If you can, encourage the management to put in a big pond. It will attract wildlife in droves. Get them to put in a native hedge with plenty of hawthorn in it. This will provide a wonderful safe habitats and a wildlife larder loaded with nectar, nuts, fruit and seeds. If there is space, try to persuade them to plant some native trees – oak, silver birch, crab apple, rowan, holly or hazel.

On your own plot, there are many simple things that you can do to encourage wildlife, which in turn will help you. When given time for things to settle down, together you can create a good balance of nature that will cut down the pest problem.

Let some meadow grasses grow long in a sunny place for meadow birds and butterflies. Have a little log pile and leave it to rot down undisturbed as a dead-wood habitat for beetles and such. Leave some stones unturned for reptiles. Keep

up with your compost heap – an invaluable habitat for many. Put in a little water. Even the smallest pond is a useful resource for wildlife.

Grow plants that offer fruit and nectar all year round, particularly when there isn't much else about in winter. Holly, ivy and dog rose are great sources of winter food.

Adopt a liberal attitude to the big autumn tidy up. Leave a few nettles in corners, seedheads for the birds, sweep some dead leaves under the hedge. Some creature will appreciate them for a winter nest.

Put up bird and bat boxes and feeders and make some insect hotels. Make your plot bird friendly. With their sharp eyes, the birds will assess the dangers and weigh up facilities that are on offer for water, shelter and food. Once they have come to trust you, it is important to keep up the service all year round so as not to let them down.

seven steps for biodiversity

Biodiversity, or biological diversity, is the total variety of life on earth. Flora and fauna diversity depends on climate, altitude, soil and the presence of other species. By following these seven steps you will be well on the way to creating a biodiverse environment on your allotment plot.

1. build a wildlife pond

Water is staff of life. Provide it, sit back and watch. Wildlife will swarm in without you having to lift a finger. Ponds attract a colourful population. Birds and mammals will visit ponds to drink, bathe and hunt while insects and other invertebrates, frogs, toads and newts will use ponds as breeding sites. Bats hunt over water. Ponds are essential to dragonflies and damselflies as they lay their eggs just below the surface of the water. The larvae spend between two and five years in the pond before climbing out of the water to shed their skin and emerge as adult insects. The adults feed on midges by swooping over water to catch them in flight.

Many insects need rotting vegetation or water for their larvae but live elsewhere as adults. Visitors will include mayfly nymphs, water beetles and the aquatic larvae of hoverflies and crane flies, snails, water skaters and tiny crustaceans (known as ostracods) as well as water boatsmen and pond skaters.

Beetles will assemble where there are bugs to eat and they like to hunt in the shallow margins. The water scorpion, the water measurer and the water stick insect are fearsome predators, though even they cannot measure up to the truly lethal Great Diving Beetle. Whirly gig beetles zip around the surface in a seemingly random manner searching for dead insects and fish. They are the pond vultures. The water spider cleverly spins a web into a diving bell. Water fleas, hoglice and water snails, purify the water by breaking down dead leaves, and eating up bacteria and algae.

Swallows, swifts, house martins and the spotted flycatcher take insects on the wing. The pond will provide a good source of food as many of the craneflies, mosquitoes, and midges that these birds eat have aquatic larvae.

2. grow plants for the birds

As we all know, many birds would starve in winter when there is snow and ice if we didn't provide food. Small birds like robins and blue tits need to eat almost half their body weight every day to survive. In the breeding season the parents are under huge pressure to get hold of enough to feed their broods. A pair of blue tits, themselves seed eaters as adults, need to find 10,000 caterpillars for each brood. Their young only weigh one gram when they hatch and need to gain 15 times that weight before they can be fully fledged.

Some species are found more in gardens and allotments in towns than in any other habitat. The woodland birds – tits, robins, blackbirds, song thrushes, sparrows, finches and buntings, rely heavily on gardens and allotments. Birds are drawn in to places where they feel safe and where there is food, water and shelter. They will wisely weigh it up and assess it carefully before trying it out.

Apart from putting up an assortment of food and feeders at different heights to suit different birds, grow plants for fruit, berry, seed and also to attract caterpillars as live food for birds. Provide water well out of the way of cats.

Chaffinches eat the seeds of over 200 different plants. Though in the wild, they find seed in invasive weeds like docks, fat hen and knotgrass, there are plenty garden worthy plants that will provide bird seed, for example, teasel, *Dipsacus fullonum*, sunflowers, *Helianthus annuus* and evening primrose, *Oenothera biennis* (which brings in the night moths as well), goldenrod, Solidago and Michaelmas daisies, *Aster novi-belgii* (particularly useful as they flower in autumn).

Other birds love fruit. The blackbird, song thrush, mistlethrush (so called as it adores mistletoe – not easy to provide), redwing and fieldfare. The warblers – whitethroat, lesser whitethroat, garden warbler and the blackcap like fruit especially in autumn before flying south. Robins, starlings, woodpigeons and finches also eat berries. In winter the common ivy and holly are rich in berries and provide

A simple birdhouse such as this one is an attractive addition to the allotment.

nesting cover as well. Honeysuckle, *Lonicera periclymenum*, produces masses of luscious red berries and roses provide hips through winter.

For habitats add in some evergreens and some thorny plants for safe nesting.

3. leave the compost heap over winter

Make a generous compost heap and leave it alone over winter so that hibernating creatures remain undisturbed.

Fortunately, most of the activity (mass murder) within the compost heap is too minute for us to see. Of the creatures that are visible, brandling worms, *Eisena foetida* help to recycle the rotting vegetation. Woodlice eat the detritus. Hedgehogs and toads hibernate in the dry areas of the heap and enjoy the ready supply of live food. Slugs and snails are particularly taken by the damper parts of the heap. When conditions are not to their liking they keep still and wait for things to improve.

Earwig, *Forficula auricularia*, is a scavenger. It comes out at night and eats decaying animal and vegetable matter as well as live food. Soldier flies, *Microschrysa polita*, are perfectly adapted to the compost heap. They look like wasps but are true flies. They like plenty of heat and are excellent decomposers. The larvae however are voracious feeders on worms. The worms will retreat to the bottom of the heap when the soldier flies are around.

Spiders and centipedes, which have poison claws, catch live prey. The vegetarian millipedes emit cyanide to put off their predators. It doesn't worry the birds however. Grass snakes (which are harmless to people) like to lay their eggs in compost heaps. The heat helps the eggs to

mature and there are plenty of invertebrates for them to eat when they hatch out. They generally lay 30 – 40 eggs. Slow worms look like silvery snakes but are in fact legless lizards. They are harmless and quite shy, hiding in the day and emerging at night to eat spiders, slugs, snails and earthworms. They like the damp warm conditions of the compost heap and are a protected species.

The kings of the compost heap though are beetles out on the hunt. The ground beetles, *Trechus quadristriatus* and *Pterostichus madidus*, or black clock, a black beetle sometimes with port coloured legs, eat slugs and snails in quantity. The devil's coach horse, *Ocypus olens*, is a rove beetle, easily identified by its habit when

An 'insect hotel' – an ideal environment for attracting wildlife to your plot.

threatened of standing up and opening its jaws like a scorpion while releasing a foul smell. Its descriptive Latin name 'olens' refers to the smell. It has been associated with the devil since the Middle Ages. Another rove beetle is *Hister quadrimaculatus*. Its party trick is to act dead when disturbed.

Robins and blackbirds are likely to appear if you are turning over your compost heap and will be looking out with a sharp eye out for a tasty snack.

4. make a log pile

The saying goes that there is more life in a dead tree than a living one. Studies in temperate forests reveal that a third of the woody biomass, or biological material, in the primeval forest would have been dead and decaying wood. As it dies, wood releases nitrogen crucial to the health of the forest. The dead and dying wood provides microhabitats for many creatures. These include fungi, lichens, many invertebrates, mosses and birds. It is reckoned that 1,700 species in Britain are dependent in some way on the decaying wood habitat, if not the wood itself the associated fungi. Some 40% of these are nationally scarce if not listed in the British Red Data Book as species whose continued existence is threatened.

When a tree dies, wood boring insects move into the sapwood and fungi follow down the holes that they leave. Predators and parasites, spiders, false scorpions and wasps, come after the wood boring insects. Different creatures like different levels of decay. Scavenging beetles, hoverflies, millipedes and mites join the party. Woodland birds make nests. Twelve out of 16 species of British bats use existing holes and the cavities of dead trees as roosts as they can't excavate or build one for themselves. They often squeeze out of sight behind loose bark to hide during the day while feeding on the insect population.

How to make a log pile

Find a cool shady spot. Bury the bottom logs to keep the pile chilly and damp – the ideal conditions for dead wood species. Make the log pile on the low side as you don't want it to dry out. Logs from a mixture of broad leaved trees – beech, oak, ash, apple or pear in different shapes and sizes would be ideal. If you are literally piling them one on top of the other horizontally, a post banged in each side will keep them in place. Alternatively you could make a pyramid of a few logs half buried vertically or even just one to imitate the monolith. Ivy growing over it will help to keep it moist and shady. In the wild, hollow trees and rot holes naturally fill up with leaves and bird droppings and other organic debris. You can get something of the same effect by making holes in the top and filling them with leaf mould and manure.

Pile on leaf litter to draw in any passing toads and hedgehogs. Other visitors might

include young frogs and newts, slug eating centipedes and beetles of various sorts. The regal stag beetle, lays its eggs underground near rotting wood so that the larvae can live and feed there before hatching. This can take several years, so don't disturb the log pile other than to add to it.

5. make a pile of stones and leave them unturned

Stones provide refuges for spiders, woodlice, millipedes, solitary bees and wasps over winter. Wrens, wagtails, wheatears, house and tree sparrows, stonechats, robins, redstarts, rock pipits, spotted fly catchers feast on them. Nut hatches, blue and great tits sometimes use crevices in walls for nesting and enjoy the built in larder. The Black Redstart, a bird of scree and crags, particularly favours old stone walls for nesting. Frogs and toads will hide away in cool damp recesses of stones. Nocturnal creatures will lodge in them unseen in daylight. Hedgerow animals - voles, shrews, field mice, hares and hedgehogs may find refuge in the wall. Rabbits and rats may tunnel under it. Squirrels store nuts under the stones. Weasels and stoats hunt for food in the nooks and crannies. Foxes will sniff out the inhabitants for their dinner.

6. relax a little

Adopt a slightly carefree attitude. Putting the garden "to bed" in autumn is an outdated concept. Leave the seed heads and hollow stems in winter for insects to hibernate in and lay their eggs. Don't be a good housekeeper. Tuck your prunings under the hedge out of view. Fret not if a few plants are nibbled

7. grow some long grass and meadow flowers

Grasses and meadow flowers provide nectar and pollen for a grassland community of bees, butterflies and many other insects that feed on grasses. Orange tips, ringlets, common blues, large whites, small whites, green-veined whites, brimstones, small tortoiseshells, speckled woods, peacocks, red admirals, painted ladies, the meadow brown and commas feed on grassland nectar, particularly on the field margins. The small skipper is particular and will feed on only a couple of tall meadow-grass species.

In Nature's way, the meadow insects in turn provide food for insectivores – bats, frogs, toads, voles, shrews, hedgehogs and birds, including swallows and wagtails. Rough grass offers cover for small mammals and large insects, and this makes it a more profitable hunting ground for predators such as kestrels, barn owls and stoats. Even a small verge on the edge of the lawn in a sunny spot can provide a few nectar plants for the meadow creatures.

the allotment year

january

In the bitter weather of January, visits to the allotment are inclined to be brief and purposeful. It is a good time to get on with structural improvements and general maintenance. Get ahead by cleaning the greenhouse. Repair and clean your tools. Clear out the shed. Plant new fruit trees and winter prune older ones. Order seeds. Don't attempt to dig when the ground is frozen or waterlogged. Turning over freezing soil moves the cold soil from top to bottom so that it will take longer to warm up in spring. Draw up an action plan for the coming months.

in season

- Artichokes (Chinese and Jerusalem)
- Beet (leaf)
- Broccoli (sprouting)
- Brussels sprouts,
- Cabbage (winter)
- Cauliflower (winter)
- Celeriac
- Chicory (red and sugarloaf)
- Corn salad
- Cress (American land)
- Endive
- Hamburg parsley
- Kale
- Komatsuna
- Leeks
- Oriental mustards
- Parsnip
- Radish (winter)
- Salsify
- Scorzonera
- Spinach (winter)
- Swiss chard

under protection

- Corn salad
- Endive
- Lettuce (winter)
- Mibuna and mizuna greens
- Oriental saladini
- Pak choi
- Radish (summer)
- Rocket
- Sorrel

general maintenance

Tools

To clean tools, scrape off any dried mud with a stiff brush. Fill a capacious bucket with coarse sand and mix in a small amount of oil – any oil type will do. Dip the tool heads into this several times until they come out transformed. If still rusty, rub them down with emery paper or wire wool.

Sharpen blades with a file. Wipe with an oily rag before hanging them up. To keep your tools in tiptop condition thereafter, it's good practice to wipe them off and spray them with oil at the end of the day. Send any machinery off for service.

Shred prunings
Persuade a few neighbours, or your allotment committee, to share the cost and hire a shredder. Wear goggles and protective clothing. The shredded prunings make a luxuriant carpet for paths.

other january tasks

• make sure that mulches and covers put on in autumn stay securely in place;
• check stakes are firm and ties not too tight;
• shake snow off branches;
• hoe out winter weeds such as chickweed and groundsel while at the seedling stage as they can harbour disease. Put healthy annual weeds on the compost heap and throw out perennial weeds;
• make leaf-mould;
• check your stores and remove anything less than perfect;
• clean the greenhouse. On sunny days open the doors for ventilation to prevent fungal diseases, particularly grey mould (Botrytis);
• make sure the birds have food and water.

vegetables

• order seed potatoes or look for them in the garden centres. Make sure they are certified virus free. This is one area where recycling is not a good idea;
• force chicory. If you planted chicory outside last May, you can force it for winter salads or cooking;

• force rhubarb and seakale for early, tender, young stems;
• clear any decaying leaves off the crowns of rhubarb, artichokes and asparagus to prevent them rotting in damp conditions;
• bend the leaves over the heads of cauliflowers to protect the developing curds. If they don't reach across, snap off a few outer leaves and tie them around with string.

Sowing
• unless you live in a warm microclimate, it is wiser to hold off sowing seed outside, even under cover, until next month;
• keep up seedling salads with radishes, chicory, mizuna and mibuna greens, oriental saladini and rocket, which will grow happily on the windowsill;
• exhibition onions are usually sown in January under cover.

fruit

• fruit trees, ordered earlier, may arrive any time from November. If the weather is not right for planting, heel them in or cover with wet sacking and keep in the shed. Plant them as soon as possible but not if the ground is frozen or waterlogged;
• winter prune apples and pears, blackcurrants, red- and whitecurrants, blackberries and hybrids, raspberries and gooseberries on days without hard frost. Wait until summer to prune plum trees, to avoid silver leaf disease.

herbs and flowers

• protect young perennial herbs such as French tarragon, sage and rosemary against the frosts with a mulch of straw or leaf-mould around the base. Continue to grow chervil, parsley and chives inside in cold areas and outside under cloches in warmer ones.

watch out for

• cold-weather damage. Have fleece, netting and cloches to hand to throw over vulnerable plants. Protect plants from icy winds by earthing up, mulching and windbreaks.

last chance

• insulate garden taps or put a ball in the pond, to prevent it freezing over.

getting ahead

• take advantage of icy conditions to make piles of organic matter at strategic points ready to spread later. The wheelbarrow should move effortlessly over frozen ground;
• make new beds but not if soil is frozen or waterlogged. If the mud sticks to your boots, it's too wet to work;
• cover newly dug ground with poly-thene. This will help to prevent nutrients leaching out and warm the soil up ready for sowing later;
• order seeds well ahead while there is plenty of choice.

february

In February the days are longer. The sap is already beginning to rise. It is time to finish winter pruning and planting barerooted trees and soft fruit before they start to grow. Dig the beds in fair weather, warm them with polythene, check the pH and lime if necessary. Put down slow-release fertilizers. Make your planting plans and be ready for the first joyous signs of spring next month.

in season

- Artichokes (Chinese and Jerusalem),
- Beet (leaf),
- Broccoli (calabrese and sprouting)
- Brussels sprouts
- Cabbage (winter)
- Cauliflower (winter)
- Celeriac
- Chicory (red, sugarloaf and forced witloof)
- Corn salad
- Cress (American land)
- Endive
- Hamburg parsley
- Kale
- Komatsuna
- Leeks
- Oriental mustards
- Parsnip
- Radish (winter)
- Salsify
- Scorzonera
- Spinach (winter)
- Swiss chard

under protection

- Corn salad
- Endive
- Lettuce (winter)
- Mibuna and mizuna greens
- Oriental saladini
- Pak choi
- Radish (summer)
- Rocket
- Sorrel

general maintenance

Prepare the seedbed
This will be in full use over the next few months. Rake the soil to a fine tilth. Cover the bed with polythene to warm the soil.

Make a bean trench
If you haven't already done so, dig out a trench about 45 cm (18 in) wide and the

depth of a spade for runner beans. If you want to grow them up a wigwam, make it circular, and if you want a double row make it twice as wide. Pile in plenty of organic matter and fork it in.

Prepare the asparagus bed

As it will last for 20 years, take trouble to eliminate perennial weeds. Dig well and mix in plenty of top-quality manure or garden compost.

Check soil temperatures

Push a soil thermometer 5–10 cm (2–4 in) into the soil to take a reading. The soil should be above 7°C (45°F) consistently for a week before sowing the seeds of the hardiest plants under cloches.

Check the pH of your soil and lime if necessary

Lime should be added at least two months ahead ready for planting out in May. Choose a still day and wear goggles and a mask.

Fertilize

Feed overwintering plants and the soil with organic fertilizers such as seaweed meal or blood, fish and bone. These are slow release and so will benefit the plants when they begin to shoot in spring.

other february tasks

• put up nesting boxes so that birds get used to them before the breeding season;
• feed the birds;
• protect plants against cold weather;
• make sure covers and mulches stay in place;
• clear decaying leaves and other debris;
• check stakes and ties;
• check stores;
• hoe off weeds when the soil is dry enough;
• keep the greenhouse aired.

vegetables

• Jerusalem artichokes can be planted. Site them carefully as they grow to 1.8 m (6 ft) at speed.

Sowing

• in the cold greenhouse or warmed soil outside, you can sow under cloche cover vegetables such as early summer cabbage, spinach, early carrots (e.g. 'Amsterdam Forcing'), the hardiest broad beans (Longpods), leaf beet (perpetual spinach), parsnips and swedes;
• sow early peas (e.g. 'Kelvenden Wonder', 'Little Marvel' or 'Early Onward') in sections of guttering in the greenhouse or cold frame;
• make successional sowings of chicory seedling crop, spring onions, beetroot and salad rocket;
• sow tomato seed in a propagator in gentle heat of 18°C (64°F) and aubergine seed at 21°C (70°F);
• bulb onions and shallots can also be sown from seed at home in February, at 10°C (50°F), or else grown from 'sets' later on. In cold areas, wait until the end of the month.

fruit

• make sure that new young trees stay firmly planted. The freezing and thawing action of icy conditions causes shrinkage and expansion, with the result that the roots can get pushed out of the ground. Tread to firm the soil around the rootball;
• finish winter pruning apples and pears, black-, red- and whitecurrants, blackberries and hybrids, raspberries and gooseberries;
• sprinkle potash around fruit trees and bushes to boost the fruit;
• mulch young trees after a good rain;
• protect flowers of soft fruit (if not emerging now, then soon) from frost by covering with horticultural fleece or netting on cold nights;
• hand pollinate fruit trees if they begin to flower before the insects are out;
• plant rhubarb;
• tidy up outdoor strawberries and cover with cloches for an early crop;
• plant barerooted fruit trees when the weather allows.

herbs and flowers

• sow parsley and chervil in biodegradable modules as they have taproots and don't transplant well. Grow with heat or wait until next month to sow in the cold greenhouse;
• to get a good supply of mint, dig up existing plants. You will find that the roots have put out runners. Cut them into sections, making sure that each has some healthy root and shoot. Mint is invasive, so plant the cuttings in an old bucket with drainage holes sunk into the soil. Keep a few potted up in the house for daily use;
• divide chives. Once they start to grow, dig up, pull apart the clumps and replant.

watch out for

• big bud on currants. You will spot it by the unnaturally swollen buds on blackcurrants and the withered ones on red- and whitecurrants. Pick off infected buds;
• deal with slugs and snails as you come across them to reduce later infestations;
• net fruit to protect it from the birds.

last chance

• winter prune fruit before the sap rises.

getting ahead

• on finer days, finish digging and making new borders ready for spring planting;
• warm the prepared beds with polythene or cloches ready for sowing and planting next month.

march

Though spring is just round the corner, March weather is notoriously treacherous. Careful timing is recommended. Clear away the last of the winter crops and prepare for sowing. Aim to get your seedlings to emerge or be ready to plant out at the optimum moment when the frosts are reliably over in May or even June. Bear in mind that the minimum temperature for the hardiest vegetables to germinate is 7°C (45°F). For tender plants, such as French beans, it's 16°C (61°F). When in doubt, wait.

in season

- Artichokes (Chinese and Jerusalem),
- Beet (leaf/perpetual spinach)
- Broccoli (calabrese, perpetual and sprouting)
- Brussels sprouts
- Cabbage (winter)
- Cauliflower (spring and winter)
- Celeriac
- Chicory (red and forced witloof)
- Corn salad
- Cress (American land)
- Hamburg parsley
- Kale
- Komatsuna
- Leek
- Oriental mustards
- Parsnip
- Radish (summer and winter)
- Red orache
- Rhubarb (forced)
- Salsify
- Scorzonera
- Spinach (winter)
- Spring onion
- Swiss chard

under protection

- Corn salad
- Endive
- Lettuce (winter)
- Oriental saladini
- Radish (summer)
- Rocket
- Sorrel

general maintenance

Continue to
- protect plants against cold weather;
- check stores;
- hoe off weeds;
- feed the birds.

other march tasks

- warm areas of soil by covering with polythene for plantings in April;
- apply general fertilizer to beds;
- feed plants that are tired after the winter with seaweed, comfrey or nettle liquid feed Gather nettles to make liquid fertilizer. They are at their most potent in spring;
- make 'stale seedbeds' to induce weeds to show themselves so you can hoe them off before sowing or planting your crops next month;
- cover weed-infested beds with black polythene;
- mulch beds with organic matter after rain, to retain moisture and black out weeds;
- harvest the last of the winter brassicas;
- clear winter crops as they go over;
- put healthy debris on the compost heap;
- sow green manures on empty beds. Crimson clover is a nitrogen fixer grown for only 2–3 months;
- move covers and cloches off plants outside on sunny days but replace them at night;
- clean the greenhouse windows for maximum light;
- open the doors and windows on bright days to get air through;
- shade young seedlings under glass on bright days;
- thin seedlings planted in February before they become overcrowded;
- prick out and pot on cuttings, seedlings and young plants as they outgrow their containers;
- harden off young vegetables for planting outside. Err on the cautious side.

vegetables

- plant asparagus crowns, Jerusalem artichokes, seakale offsets, onion and shallot sets;
- plant early, second early and maincrop potatoes chitted in January or February;
- dig a trench a spade's depth and half fill it with organic matter for trenching celery.

Sowing

- in the cold greenhouse or warmed soil outside, you can sow under cloche cover seeds of early brussels sprouts (e.g. 'Peter Gynt') for autumn eating, summer cabbage, salsify, scorzonera, spinach, spinach beet and chard, maincrop broad beans, calabrese, early carrots, swedes and leeks, early and second early peas. Hamburg parsley and texcel greens can either be sown in modules for transplanting, or in the seedbed with cover, from the middle of the month;
- make successional sowings of Japanese bunching onions, kohlrabi, summer radishes, early carrots, lettuce, rocket, mizuna greens and oriental saladini and salad leaves;
- at home, sow celery, globe onions and pickling onions at 10–15°C (50–59°F), either indoors or outside with cover;
- with heat, sow aubergine at 21°C (70°F) and tomatoes 18–20°C (64–68°F). Alternatively, wait and buy young plants to go straight out in June.

fruit

- if not done last month, clear weeds and give soft fruit a dressing of potash, to help fruiting;
- mulch with well-rotted manure or garden compost;
- spray with nettle, comfrey or seaweed if they need a boost;
- continue to prevent frost damage by covering fruit trees and bushes;
- hand pollinate flowers if they come out before the insects;
- prune away any winter damage. Tie in soft fruits as they grow, before they get into a tangle.

watch out for

- aphid eggs, which hatch out into wingless female nymphs. This first generation don't fly so this is a good time to catch them before the second generation fly off and start to breed. Crush them between finger and thumb and cut off the tops of broad beans where they congregate;
- wage war on slugs and snails.

last chance

- plant barerooted fruit trees. Once the leaves start to appear, they will dehydrate fast.

getting ahead

- put in stakes in readiness for young plants to grow up;
- place growbags in the greenhouse and polythene on beds to warm them up for spring sowing and planting.

april

April is a month of non-stop propagation. The vast majority of produce will be sown, transplanted or need some attention in the next few weeks. The birds are singing and nesting. Frogs, toads and hedgehogs are coming out of hibernation – just as well, as pests are on the move too. Spring is in the air and there is not a minute to waste.

in season

- Artichokes (Jerusalem)
- Asparagus
- Beet (leaf/perpetual spinach)
- Broccoli (perennial and sprouting)
- Cabbage (spring)
- Cauliflower (spring)
- Celeriac
- Chicory (red)
- Corn salad
- Cress (American land)
- Endive
- Leeks
- Lettuce
- Radish (summer)
- Red orache
- Rhubarb
- Rocket
- Spring onion
- Saladini (oriental)
- Salsify
- Scorzonera
- Seakale (forced)
- Sorrel
- Spinach (winter)
- Swiss chard

general maintenance

- make 'stale seedbeds' to encourage weeds to show themselves so you can hoe them off before sowing or planting your crops next month;
- cover any weed-infested beds with black polythene;
- mulch beds with organic matter after a good rain, to retain moisture and black out weeds;
- have a hoe to hand to pick up weeds as soon as they appear. They will be growing apace now;
- sow green manures on empty beds;
- remove cloches from hardy vegetables planted last month if conditions are right.

The cloches will be needed for the next batch of plantings;

• thin out seedlings. If you thin carefully without harming the roots, sometimes you can transplant the seedlings. They will crop a little later than the rest having been 'checked'.

other april tasks

• check stores;
• feed the birds;
• water regularly when the weather is dry;
• put up sturdy supports for climbing peas and beans.

vegetables

• finish planting early, second early and maincrop potatoes, or earth up potatoes planted last month;
• finish planting Jerusalem and globe artichokes, onion and shallot sets and asparagus crowns;
• harden off and transplant last month's vegetables sown from seed that are ready to go out to their final positions;
• shade young plants under glass with newspaper against bright sunlight.

Sowing

• sow the last summer cabbages;
• start sowing winter cabbage, sprouting and perennial broccoli in the seedbed;
• sow calabrese in biodegradable modules as it resents root disturbance;
• move from sowing early to late sprouts (e.g. 'Braveheart') for eating in the new year;
• sow maincrop broad beans for summer eating;
• sow autumn and mini-cauliflowers from mid-April to early May, when the soil temperature has reached min. 7°C (45°F);
• sow celeriac, kohlrabi, Hamburg parsley, leeks, mizuna greens, salsify, scorzonera,

seakale, spinach, spinach beet, Swiss chard and early bunching turnips;

• sow fenugreek and good King Henry;

• continue small sowings of hardy peas (e.g. 'Early Onward');

• carry on with successional crops of Japanese bunching onions, kohlrabi, summer radishes, early carrots, lettuce, rocket, mizuna greens and oriental saladini and salad leaves;

• sow rocket, komatsuna, Florence fennel, radicchio and sugar loaf chicories, texel greens and red orache;

• sow celery under cover in gentle heat, timing it eight or nine weeks before the last frosts;

• under glass, with heat or at home (min. temperature 16°C/61°F) sow French and runner beans, chillies, aubergine, sweetcorn and tomatoes. Remember that you can sow tender beans outside next month and buy tomatoes, aubergines and sweetcorn as plants ready to go out if you don't have time.

fruit

• protect fruit against the birds with netting. If you use a gauge of about 2 cm (¾ in) the bees will have access to pollinate;

• continue to give frost protection when necessary;

• pick off the flowers of newly planted early and late varieties of strawberry, to hold them back for a bumper crop next year;

• prune stone fruit trees – peaches, plums and nectarines – if weather allows. These were left unpruned through winter to avoid silver leaf disease. Now that the weather is milder, wounds will heal before the disease can take hold;

• if you have missed out on barerooted fruit trees, you can still buy container-grown trees, which can be planted at any time of year.

herbs and flowers

• sow annual flowers such as nasturtiums, marigolds, flax and the poached egg plant to attract friendly predators;

• sow basil indoors for planting out after the frosts. Pinch out the tip when there are three sets of leaves. Stop it from sprawling by trimming off the side branches. Feed once a week and water in the daytime so that the leaves are dry by nightfall;

• sow fennel in well-drained, loamy soil in the cold greenhouse, or plant a piece of root outside from an established plant;

• sow summer savory in the cold frame;

• sow parsley seed in deep soil outside with plenty of organic matter added, as it doesn't take to transplanting;

• divide established chives. Replant in rich moist soil in a sunny spot;

• dig up and divide creeping thymes, mint and French tarragon. Tarragon and mint are spreaders, so need to be curtailed by being planted in a bottomless bucket;

• take softwood cuttings from rosemary, sage and thyme;

• trim back lavender without cutting into the old wood. Let rosemary grow freely but cut away lanky and damaged growth completely. Cut off weak and damaged shoots on other established herbs.

watch out for

• vine weevil. The tell-tale signs are irregular holes around the edges of leaves. The larvae, which hatch out in spring, do the most damage having fed on the plant roots all winter;

• net or put a 60 cm (24 in) barrier round carrots to protect them against the carrot fly;

• catch aphids early;

• flea beetles are active from April till midsummer;

• deal with slugs and snails on encounter.

last chance

• sow sweet peas.

getting ahead

• keep warming the soil and have beds ready for the next batch of transplants.

may

By May, the frosts should be behind you. The countryside is full of fresh young growth and there is a new mellowness in the air. Take off covers in the daytime. The propagation boom from last month continues almost unabated. This month you move from early to late varieties of broad bean, carrots and cabbage for autumn and winter eating. If you have missed out on sowing seed or need more plants, you'll find starter packs of vegetables in the garden centres. Enjoy the first of the new season crops – early peas, young broad beans, salads, radishes and, most delicious of all, home-grown asparagus.

in season

- Artichokes (Jerusalem)
- Asparagus
- Beans (broad, both autumn and spring sown)
- Beet (leaf/perpetual spinach)
- Broccoli (perennial)
- Cabbage (spring)
- Cauliflower (spring)
- Celeriac
- Corn salad
- Cress (American land)
- Endive
- Gooseberry thinnings
- Lettuce
- Peas (autumn sown)
- Potatoes (early)
- Radish (summer)
- Red orache
- Rhubarb
- Rocket
- Saladini (all types)
- Sorrel
- Spinach (summer)
- Spring onion
- Strawberries (grown under cover)
- Swiss chard
- Turnip

general maintenance

- introduce fast-growing French marigolds (*Calendula*) or English marigolds (*Tagetes*), poached egg plant (*Limnanthes douglasii*) and many other annuals to brighten up your plot, provide flowers for the house and bring in friendly predators. They may seed themselves around every year but are no trouble to pull up if you don't want them.

other may tasks

- keep on hoeing;
- thin seedlings as they grow;
- keep potting on, hardening off and transplanting, warming the soil ready for new sowings, making stale seedbeds to get ahead of the weeds;
- water young plants regularly and feed when necessary;
- feed the birds as they will need it for their young.

vegetables

- keep earthing up potatoes. Never let the tubers get near the light or they will develop poisonous, green patches;
- transplant self-blanching celery at the end of the month. To save space, interplant with fast crops – beetroot, early carrots, salad onions, lettuce, radishes and early bunching turnips;
- plant globe artichokes, either bought as small plants or grown from seed;
- plant offsets or 'thongs' of seakale;
- if you have been raising tomatoes, peppers and aubergines under cover and the weather is still too cold for them to go out, transplant into bigger containers;
- harden off and transplant seedlings sown last month. Water well before and after transplanting and over the next few days.

Sowing

- outside sow maincrop beetroot, winter cabbage, sprouting broccoli and perennial broccoli, kale and swedes, mini-, autumn and late winter/early spring cauliflowers and the last of the early and maincrop leeks;
- parsnips need to be sown in situ. Try pregerminating them and fluid sowing;
- carry on sowing salsify, scorzonera and Swiss chard;
- switch from sowing early varieties to maincrop types of broad bean and carrot;
- amaranthus and fenugreek can be sown outside when the soil temperature is above 10°C (50°F);
- courgettes, marrows, squashes, pumpkins and outdoor cucumbers can be sown either outdoors on warmed soil under cloches in mild areas or, safer and faster, under cover in modules for planting out next month;
- sweetcorn, French beans and runner beans can be sown outside at the end of the month in mild areas. By the time the seeds have germinated, all threat of frost should be over. Or, safer, they can be raised in modules;
- under cover, sow the tender asparagus pea.

fruit

- net developing fruits to protect them from birds;
- give fruit a good watering when in flower;
- remove blossom from new trees to give them every chance to establish before bearing fruit;
- tuck straw under your strawberries to prevent rain splash and slugs. Fluff it up to let in air. Barley straw is the best. Remove runners so the plants put all their energy into the fruits;
- prune out any unwanted shoots of raspberries to give the fruits good air circulation, to get sunshine on the berries and to avoid a tangle later;
- prune and tie in fans and cordons. Tie in canes as they grow on blackberries and their hybrids;
- remove alternate berries on gooseberry bushes for big fruits. The pickings can be used for cooking;
- continue to prune stone fruit trees – peaches, plums and nectarines.

herbs and flowers

- keep picking and cutting coriander, chives, fennel and dill to encourage new fresh growth, but always leave two-thirds of the leaves;
- sow seed of marjoram under cover at 16°C (61°F);
- carry on sowing parsley;
- sow chervil in light but moist soil in partial shade. Check the sell-by date and make sure that the seed is less than a year old;
- sow coriander seed outside in situ as it doesn't like being moved. Cover thinly with soil;
- thin out seedlings sown last month. Layer creeping thyme by burying the runners with hairpins of wire around the parent plant. When the little plants start to grow, cut them free.

watch out for

- battle on with aphids, slugs and snails;
- if you have had trouble from the codling moth maggots, put up pheromone traps;
- check broad beans for black fly and pinch out the flowering tops where they congregate;
- check for signs of mildew;
- pick off any sawfly caterpillars;
- watch for capsid bugs and scab;
- put up a screen of fine netting or completely cover carrots to protect them from carrot fly.

last chance

- plant out onion sets for autumn;
- plant potatoes;
- sow spinach before late summer.

getting ahead

- nip problems in the bud.

june

In June, the first month of real summer, there should be plenty of delicious produce in season, including the first of the summer fruits. As you harvest the early potatoes, the tender vegetables can go in – tomatoes, aubergines, marrows, courgettes, sweetcorn and peppers. As gaps appear, think ahead to winter and to getting the winter greens, sprouts, leeks and carrots transplanted into their permanent positions.

in season

- Asparagus
- Asparagus pea
- Beans (broad, autumn and spring sown)
- Beet (leaf/perpetual spinach)
- Beetroot
- Broccoli (calabrese and perennial),
- Cabbage (spring and summer)
- Carrot (early)
- Cauliflower (summer)
- Cherries
- Corn salad
- Cress (American land)
- Endive
- Gooseberries
- Kohlrabi
- Lettuce
- Onions (bulbs autumn planted; spring and bunching onions)
- Peas (autumn sown)
- Potatoes (early)
- Radish (summer)
- Raspberries
- Redcurrants
- Red orache
- Rhubarb
- Rocket
- Saladini (all types)
- Sorrel
- Spinach (summer)
- Strawberries
- Swiss chard
- Turnip
- Whitecurrants

general maintenance

- water plants thoroughly and according to their needs. A good soaking less often is better than frequent light sprinkling;
- conserve moisture by applying and renewing mulches.

other june tasks

- carry on weeding;
- make sure the birds have water.

vegetables

- plant out your tender crops such as tomatoes, aubergines, outdoor cucumbers and peppers in a sunny, sheltered spot outside. Make a little moat around the plants to keep them moist. Feed with a high-potash fertilizer every week. Tomato cordons will need staking;
- remove sideshoots from cordon tomatoes, cucumbers and melons;
- marrows, courgettes, pumpkins and winter squashes will be ready to plant out now. They are 'greedy feeders' and like nothing better than being planted in the compost heap. Make sure they have masses of organic material incorporated in the soil and plunge sections of pipe or inverted water bottles with the bottom sawn off alongside the plants to get plenty of water to the roots;
- plant sweetcorn in square blocks as they are wind-pollinated,
- transplant leeks and late brussels sprouts, for harvesting from January to March, to their permanent positions;
- stop cropping asparagus at the end of June until next year so the plants can build up strength;
- earth up potatoes;
- fill gaps in beds. Drop in quick-growing vegetables such as salad greens and radishes in empty spaces;
- stop sowing texel greens and rocket for a few weeks as they bolt in hot weather.

Sowing

- sow runner beans and climbing French beans outside;
- sow New Zealand spinach and maincrop 'wrinkled' peas;
- continue to sow maincrop carrots (e.g. 'Autumn King') for winter storage and fast-growers (e.g. 'Nantes 2') for autumn eating;
- sow Witloof chicory this month for forcing in winter;
- continue to sow saladini every 2–3 weeks. Lettuce doesn't germinate in high temperatures so find it a spot in dappled shade.

fruit

- trim off strawberry runners as they take energy from the plant;
- pinch out sideshoots on trained fruit. Tie in the ones you want as they grow;
- thin gooseberries, apples and pears for larger fruits and so the fruits won't touch each other when fully grown;
- thin plum fruits and pears if they are growing too close together. Apples thin themselves in the 'June drop';
- continue to net fruits against birds;
- summer prune red- and whitecurrants at the end of the month;
- tie in new canes of blackberries and blackberry hybrids.

herbs and flowers

- sow a few seeds of coriander every few weeks in well-drained soil in full sun. You need quite a few plants to get a good bunch of leaves;
- make a second sowing of parsley. It prefers part shade in summer;
- keep chervil, coriander, fennel, dill and parsley well watered in dry spells;
- remove flowers regularly to keep the leaf supply, unless you want to take seed;
- give mint a trim to perk it up;
- trim sage after it flowers;
- basil can go out into the allotment now in a sunny place;
- take softwood cuttings of rosemary and sage if you want more plants;
- build up your collection of shrubby herbs – thymes, sage, rosemary, bay and lavender. There will be a good selection on offer in June.

watch out for

- cabbage white butterfly by checking undersides of leaves for small clusters of yellow eggs;
- gooseberry sawfly caterpillar can also be a problem at this time of year;
- put up pheromone traps against codling moth – one trap protects five apple trees;
- if you see grey mould (Botrytis) on strawberries, remove the affected leaves. Put straw or mats under them so the fungus is not spread by rain splashing on them;
- big bud in blackcurrants. Pick off any unnaturally large buds and distorted leaves. If the infection is serious, destroy the bush.

last chance

- plant out tomatoes, runner beans and sweetcorn in time to get a first-class crop;
- sow winter brassicas and turnips, carrots, summer beetroot, fast-growing peas and radicchio for autumn eating.

getting ahead

- sow chicory to force for winter salads.

july

July is high summer, a month of barbecues and good living on the allotment. There should be masses of vegetables to harvest from French beans to tomatoes. Gooseberries, raspberries, blackberries and their hybrids are all in season. Carry on sowing the winter vegetables – maincrop turnips, leeks, late Brussels sprouts, sprouting broccoli and winter peas. If you are quick, you can get one more sowing of runner beans and peas in before autumn.

in season

- Artichoke (globe)
- Asparagus pea
- Bean (broad; spring sown)
- Bean (French)
- Bean (runner)
- Beet (leaf/perpetual spinach)
- Beetroot
- Blackberries and hybrids
- Blackcurrants
- Blueberries
- Broccoli (calabrese)
- Cabbage (spring)
- Carrot (early)
- Cauliflower (spring and summer)
- Celery (self-blanching)
- Corn salad
- Courgette and marrow
- Cress (American land)
- Cucumber (outdoor)
- Endive
- Florence fennel
- Garlic
- Gooseberries
- Kohlrabi
- Lettuce
- Onions (bulbs from spring sets; spring and bunching onions)
- Peas (autumn sown)
- Potatoes (early)
- Pumpkins and squash
- Radish (summer)
- Raspberries
- Redcurrants
- Red orache
- Rhubarb
- Rocket
- Saladini (all types)
- Shallots
- Sorrel
- Spinach (summer and New Zealand)
- Strawberries
- Sweetcorn
- Swiss chard
- Tomatoes (outdoor)
- Turnip

general maintenance

• conserve water. Only water the plants that need it. Young vegetables such as tomatoes, aubergines and courgettes will need watering daily in hot weather. A light sprinkling achieves little. Give a good soaking less often;
• feeding. Plants become tired in high summer. Organic compost and manure applied in spring should see you through but keep an eye out for any signs of flagging and have some fertilizer to hand;
• start to collect seed. If you are planning a holiday, find someone to take over.

other july tasks

• keep up regular hoeing and weeding;
• keep a ball of string in your pocket for tying in and secateurs to hand for deadheading;
• top up ponds in hot weather;
• make sure the birds have water for drinking and bathing.

vegetables

• carry on harvesting early and mid-early potatoes. Lift one plant to check that they are ready. Water well once a week to encourage the tubers to grow;
• lift garlic, onions and shallots carefully with a fork when the leaves turn yellow. Lay out in the sun to cure. Bring them in if wet weather strikes and put in a light airy place to dry even further;
• keep harvesting beans and courgettes while young and tender;
• give texel greens and rocket a rest as they may bolt in hot weather;
• stop climbing beans when they reach the top of their supports to encourage them to

make more sideshoots and more beans;
• pinch out the tips of the trailing stems of pumpkins and squashes;
• earth up (or put sections of pipe or wrap newspaper round) hearting celery when the stems are 30cm (12in) high, leaving the top leaves exposed;
• cover cauliflowers over with their leaves, to slow down the curds from opening too soon;
• if you see white roots appearing on cucumbers, cover with a topdressing of well-rotted manure;
• spray runner beans with a fine jet of water every evening to help the flowers 'set';
• finish planting out winter brassicas sown in April and May, putting collars and fleece or netting over them to protect against the cabbage root fly laying its eggs.

Sowing

• make several sowings of spring cabbage a couple of weeks apart. Your aim is for them to be big enough to survive the winter but not so large as to make them bolt when the frosts arrive;
• sow maincrop turnips, winter leeks, late brussels sprouts, sprouting broccoli, spring broccoli and headed Chinese cabbage;
• sow winter peas, choosing mildew-resistant varieties;
• sow maincrop carrots and fast carrots for an autumn crop;
• sow runner beans in situ until the end of the month;
• in cooler areas, sow mustard greens.

fruit

• pick and store summer-fruiting raspberries, black-, red- and whitecurrants;
• summer prune and train red- and whitecurrants (blackcurrants are grown as bushes and pruned in winter);
• summer prune gooseberries, blackberries and their hybrids and fan-trained fruits;
• cut down the old canes of summer raspberries as soon as they have finished fruiting and tie in the new;
• thin out fruit on apples and pears;
• protect the ripening fruit of plums from birds and wasps;
• layer blackberries and hybrids if you want more plants;
• shear off old foliage from strawberries once they have finished fruiting. Peg down runners for new crops. Clear away the straw and hoe around the plants carefully. Discard strawberries when three years old. Start anew with the runners or buy certified, virus-free plants.

herbs and flowers

• cut lavender, sage, rosemary and thyme and other herbs and flowers for drying. Tie into bunches and hang them in an airy place upside-down or freeze the culinary ones;
• take cuttings of sage and thyme. When they root in 4–6 weeks, pot up individually;
• pick herbs regularly, to keep up a supply of young shoots and to prevent them from becoming spindly. If they are looking tired, give the bushy types a light trim all over with shears;
• trim sweet marjoram after it flowers.

watch out for

• high heat and humidity as it can spread diseases;
• leaf spot and rust can also be a problem in hot weather especially following a damp spell;
• raspberry beetles;
• blossom end rot in tomatoes (sunken patches); this is caused by a calcium deficiency due to an erratic water supply;
• tomato and potato blight is most likely to strike in hot, humid weather. If you get blight, destroy affected tomatoes. Potatoes can pull through, with luck, if you remove the foliage.

last chance

• sow fast-growing carrots, beetroot, salad onions, young turnips and runner beans to eat this autumn.

getting ahead

• sow winter salads and vegetables.

august

In August, just at the height of the holiday month, harvesting reaches its peak, as does the need for watering. Picking the tomatoes, courgettes and beans when they reach perfection, and before they coarsen, becomes a daily task. Delicious freshly picked sweetcorn will be ready for the barbecue. The stone fruits – plums, damsons and peaches – will be ripening. As the summer cabbages go over, fill the gaps with fast-growing orientals for autumn and winter. Start to collect seed while enjoying the sunshine.

in season

- Apples
- Artichoke (globe)
- Asparagus pea
- Aubergine
- Bean (broad; spring sown)
- Bean (French)
- Bean (runner)
- Beet (leaf/perpetual spinach)
- Beetroot
- Broccoli (calabrese)
- Cabbage (summer)
- Carrot (maincrop)
- Cauliflower (late and mini)
- Celery (self-blanching)
- Corn salad
- Cress (American land)
- Courgette and marrow
- Cucumber and gherkin (outdoor)
- Damsons
- Endive
- Florence fennel
- Garlic
- Kohlrabi
- Leek
- Lettuce
- Melon
- Onions (bulbs, from spring sets; spring and bunching onions)
- Peaches
- Pears
- Peas (autumn-sown and maincrop)
- Peppers and chillis
- Plums
- Potatoes (early, maincrop and lates)
- Pumpkins and squash
- Radish (summer and winter)
- Red orache
- Rhubarb
- Rocket
- Saladini (all types)
- Shallots
- Sorrel
- Spinach (summer and New Zealand)
- Sweetcorn

- Swiss chard
- Tomatoes (outdoor)
- Turnip

general maintenance

- sow green manure crops on vacant ground. Mustard is a good choice for the potato patch as it inhibits eelworm. It can be sown now and dug in during autumn. Other overwintering green manures, alfalfa, crimson clover, winter tare, grazing rye, or Italian rye grass can be sown at the end of August through to autumn. Broadcast the seed and level with a rake;
- trim hedges. They won't be growing much after this month;
- collect seed.

other august tasks

- hoe and weed. Watch out for desirable, self-sown seedlings while doing so;
- water well in dry spells;
- top up ponds in hot weather;
- provide water for the birds.

vegetables

- harvest cabbages, cauliflowers, carrots, peas, young turnips, beetroot and globe artichokes. Tomatoes, courgettes and beans will need picking almost daily. Pick cucumbers before they go yellow, and aubergines and peppers while still shiny. Pick sweetcorn when the silks go brown and the juice is milky;
- continue to lift and dry onions;
- clear away the last of the mid-early potatoes. Start to dig up maincrop ones;
- collect seed. Tomatoes, peas, French beans and lettuce are a safe bet.

Sowing

- sow a few seeds of winter spinach, spring cabbage and Japanese onions. Timing is a gamble. If they are too small when the first frosts come they may not survive winter. If too large they may bolt. To hedge your bets, sow a few a week or so apart. Spring cabbage and early greens will be ready and will heart up afterwards;
- sow Welsh onions, pak choi, Chinese cabbage, mizuna and mibuna greens, headed Chinese cabbage, komatusna and rocket;
- sow mustard greens in the south of England;
- sow winter radish (mooli or daikon) for autumn eating and winter storage;
- sow winter spinach, winter radish (mooli), and turnips;
- sow maincrop turnips under collars. Turnips resent transplanting, so sow in situ in cool, damp soil in partial shade. Thin when only 2.5cm (1in) high so they can get their roots down in time for winter. They can be harvested when they are the size of a tennis ball, up until the new year. The tops can be used as greens;
- sow corn salad to grow under cover for eating in autumn. It will carry on through winter if given fleece or cloche protection.

fruit

- continue to summer prune raspberries, gooseberries, cherries, redcurrants, damsons, cordons and espaliers;
- prune plums and damsons immediately after fruiting. Cut out any dead wood and broken branches;
- strawberry runners, pegged down last month, can be severed from the parent plant. Prepare a new strawberry bed and plant them out or buy and plant new, certified stock;
- test apples and pears for ripeness. Cup the fruit in one hand and twist the stem. When ready it will come off easily with the stalk intact. Apples are picked when perfectly ripe but pears when still hard;
- continue tying in and pruning the cane fruits. Leave the autumn raspberries;
- keep harvesting stone fruit and all the berries and currants;
- blueberries ripen over the weeks so, if you don't have too many, freeze them and keep adding until you have enough for a good serving.

herbs and flowers

- sow parsley and chervil for winter use under cloches. Net against carrot fly as it is attracted by parsley, too;
- pot up chives for winter. Cut off old foliage and water;
- take semi-ripe cuttings from shrubby herbs such as rosemary, lavender and sage;
- trim lavender after flowering, without cutting into the old wood;
- collect seed from dill, fennel and coriander as it ripens. It can be resown at once outside, stored or used for flavouring.

watch out for

- mildew, which thrives in warm, dry weather;
- fungal diseases, including rust and leaf spot, may strike with the warmth and humidity of August thunderstorms following hot weather. Keep plants well watered;
- as last month, watch for tomato and potato blight and blossom end rot in tomatoes;
- take precautions against the second generation of carrot fly;
- if you get pear and apple scab, remove all affected fruits and prune back.

last chance

- sow maincrop turnips for winter and spring onions, lettuce, red-leaved chicory, turnip, radish and parsley outside for eating in autumn.

getting ahead

- as crops go over, sow a green manure;
- there is still time for a catch crop of fodder radish or mustard to dig in late October.

september

September is a great month for earth works. The weather is generally mild and the ground easy to work, so conditions are ideal for digging and for making new beds. As you harvest, build up a fine compost heap to rot down in winter. Gather up falling leaves for leaf-mould. Keep harvesting and get your crops preserved, frozen or stored. The hedgerows are laden with elderberries, damsons and sloes. Fruit on the plot is full swing. Plums are in top production and apples and pears are coming into season along with autumn raspberries.

in season

- Apples
- Artichoke (globe)
- Aubergine
- Bean (broad)
- Bean (French)
- Bean (runner)
- Beet (leaf/perpetual spinach)
- Beetroot
- Blackberries
- Blueberries
- Brussels sprouts
- Cabbage (Chinese)
- Cabbage (summer)
- Carrot (maincrop)
- Cauliflower (late and mini)
- Celeriac
- Celery (self-blanching)
- Chicory (red)
- Corn salad
- Courgette and marrow
- Cress (American land)
- Damsons
- Endive
- Florence fennel
- Hamburg parsley
- Kohlrabi
- Komatsuna
- Leek
- Lettuce
- Melon
- Mustards (oriental)
- Onions (bulbs, from spring sets; spring and bunching onions, pickling)
- Parsnip
- Peaches
- Pears
- Peas (maincrop)
- Peppers and chillis
- Plums
- Potatoes (maincrop and lates)
- Pumpkins and squash
- Radish (summer, winter and mouli)
- Raspberries
- Red orache

- Rocket
- Saladini (all types)
- Sorrel
- Spinach (summer)
- Strawberries (perpetual)
- Sweetcorn
- Swiss chard
- Tomatoes (outdoor)
- Turnip

general maintenance

- clear autumn debris and falling leaves. Collect leaves for leaf-mould;
- start a new compost heap;
- dig heavy clay before the rains make it harder work. Incorporate pea shingle and compost to help drainage and get air through if necessary;
- cover light soils for winter so they don't get leached. Black polythene will deal with bad weeds or else sow some green manures. Winter beans, Italian rye grass or grazing rye are good for autumn sowing and spring digging;
- slow down on feeding. You don't want plants outside to put out soft growth now as they can be knocked back by frost;
- collect seed as it ripens.

other september tasks

- hoe and weed;
- provide water and food for the birds.

vegetables

- harvest maincrop potatoes on a warm, sunny day. Dry out. Keep in the dark at room temperature. Store in paper sacks in a frost-free place. Bin the leaves for the council to collect as they may carry disease;

- lift root vegetables – beetroot, maincrop carrots and turnips. Store in boxes with sand or in clamps. Leave parsnips in the ground as the frost improves the taste;
- dig out any onions still in the ground and leave to dry in the sun. Bring under cover if necessary;
- take out the stakes and lay cordon tomato plants down on straw. Cover with cloches to speed ripening in the sunshine. You are now in a race to maximize the crop before the frosts;
- leave marrows, pumpkins and winter squashes to grow on as long as possible. Ripen and dry under cover. Store in a cool dry place;
- start to harvest autumn brassicas – Brussels sprouts, Hamburg parsley, cauliflowers and young leeks;
- when the leaves of Jerusalem artichokes go black after the first frost, cut them down. Mark the spot for harvesting later;
- continue to earth up trench celery or to blanch it with sections of pipe or newspaper collars. If frost is forecast, throw fleece over the tops of the plants. They should be ready next month;
- protect Chinese and spring cabbages from cold with cloches;
- cut down asparagus foliage when it goes brown. Wear gloves as the stems have sharp spines. Pile plenty of garden compost or well-rotted manure onto the beds;
- stake tall brussels sprouts plants for overwintering in exposed areas;
- plant garlic. It needs a period of cold weather to grow well. If starting fresh, buy bulbs especially cultivated for planting. Pull the bulb apart, remove the papery skin and plant the cloves individually with the tip pointing up;
- plant Japanese onion sets and autumn-sown onions;
- transplant spring cabbages sown last month. Cover with netting or fleece against the birds. Pigeons are particularly partial to them;
- start to force chicory.

Sowing
- sow hardy winter lettuce (e.g 'Winter Density') outside covered with cloches or in the cold greenhouse. It will be ready to harvest in January;
- make a final sowing of mizuna, mibuna and mustard greens;
- sow summer cauliflowers;
- sow forcing carrots in the cold frame and spinach for spring eating. Make several small sowings a few weeks apart. Choose the sturdiest to overwinter under cover.

fruit

- plant young strawberries and keep well watered;
- plant new blackberries, or increase your stock by pegging down the tip of a new shoot into the soil. It will be ready to be severed from the parent in spring. Freeze the fruits as they ripen individually and keep adding until you have enough. After fruiting, cut out the old canes and tie in the new;
- autumn-fruiting raspberries should be ready now. Leave the canes unpruned until late winter or early spring.

herbs and flowers

- sow fennel;
- protect parsley and chervil with cloches to carry on through autumn;
- split large clumps of chives, making sure that each division has plenty of roots. They die back in winter but if you pot them up you can keep them going inside on a sunny windowsill;
- dig up mint plants, pot them up and bring inside for winter use;
- divide and replant established plants of sweet marjoram;
- trim back lavender, sage, thyme and other shrubby herbs to tidy them up for winter;
- harvest all the basil or pot it up for growing on the kitchen windowsill, as it won't survive a frost.

watch out for

- aphids, slugs and snails as always;
- fix grease bands on the trunks of fruit trees, to trap the female winter moths as they crawl up the trunks to lay their eggs;
- protect ripening fruit from birds and wasps;
- prune mildew-infected shoots of apples and pears, and destroy.

last chance

- for a final sowing of coriander;
- planting strawberries;
- harvesting tender crops before the frosts.

getting ahead

- have protection to hand, fleece or netting, in case of frost;
- clean old bird boxes as they might harbour parasites;
- put out insect hotels and new bird boxes;
- while clearing up, make cosy habitats for wildlife – piles of leaves under hedges, a wood pile left to rot down undisturbed, stones and water.

october

The autumn work becomes more urgent with the arrival of the first frosts. Protect your plants from winter weather where necessary by covering them with cloches, fleece, nets or polytunnels. Earth up or stake vegetables such as Brussels sprouts that can take the cold but may suffer from windrock. Any crops not hardy enough to stay out in winter need to be harvested, even if they are not ready. Bring them in to ripen. Cut down the Hallowe'en pumpkin with a long stalk and let it cure in the dry, ready for its big day at the end of the month. Provide shelter and food for wildlife.

in season

- Apples
- Bean (French)
- Bean (runner)
- Beet (leaf/perpetual spinach)
- Beetroot
- Blackberries
- Brussels sprouts
- Cabbage (Chinese)
- Cabbage (summer and autumn)
- Carrot (maincrop)
- Cauliflower (autumn and mini)
- Celeriac
- Celery (trench)
- Chicory (red)
- Corn salad
- Cress (American land)
- Courgette and marrow
- Endive
- Florence fennel
- Hamburg parsley
- Kohlrabi

- Komatsuna
- Leek
- Lettuce
- Mustards (oriental)
- Onions (bulbs, from spring sets; spring, bunching and pickling onions)
- Pak choi
- Parsnip
- Pears
- Peas (maincrop)
- Peppers and chillis
- Plums
- Potatoes (lates)
- Pumpkins and squash
- Radish (summer)
- Raspberries (autumn)
- Red orache
- Rocket
- Saladini (all types)
- Salsify
- Scorzonera
- Sorrel
- Spinach (summer and winter)

- Strawberries (perpetual)
- Swede
- Sweetcorn
- Swiss chard
- Tomatoes (outdoor)
- Turnip

general maintenance

- clear the garden of debris and use it to make a big compost heap. Get anything that is affected by pests and disease off site;
- rake up falling leaves and pile them up for leaf-mould;
- try to get hold of a big heap of horse manure to rot down through winter;
- dig borders while the soil is not too sticky. Break up heavy soils before the onset of winter when it becomes much harder work;
- cover ground with polythene on light soils, to prevent nutrients leaching from winter rains;
- sow green manures;
- feed the birds. In October there should be plenty of seeds, nuts and berries on the allotment but put out extra food and water. Oily seeds are nourishing. The seeds of sunflower, flax and rape will be enjoyed by the insect eaters as well as the seed eaters when there is ice on the ground. Make sure the feeders can be washed out and have a little roof to keep them dry;
- check stores.

other october tasks

• keep weeding and hoeing but don't be too tidy. Leave seedheads for the birds to eat and some cover where useful insects can hibernate.

vegetables

• clear away tomato, aubergine and pepper plants. Harvest any remaining French or runner beans still on the plants and clear topgrowth too;
• store winter root vegetables. In mild areas you can leave carrots, parsnips, beetroot, swedes and turnips in the ground for many weeks with extra protection in the form of a mulch;
• harvest trenching celery. If frost is forecast, cover the tops with straw kept in place with chicken or plastic netting, or with fleece pegged into the ground;
• cut down the foliage of Jerusalem artichokes, if you didn't last month;
• protect globe artichokes with straw or bracken, leaving the crowns of the plants exposed;
• force seakale from now until January;
• plant garlic, spring cabbage, Japanese and autumn onion sets;
• collect seed.

Sowing

• sow winter lettuces (e.g. 'All Year Round', 'Arctic King' or 'Winter Density') in the cold greenhouse. Water sparingly at the base, rather than from overhead, as they are prone to grey mould (Botrytis) and rotting off;
• sow radishes and winter salads. You can plant them in the grow bags formerly used for tomatoes. Give them a regular liquid feed and protect with cloches;
• sow broad beans outside and cover with cloches. The seeds will germinate quickly but grow slowly through the winter for harvesting in early summer.

fruit

• finish picking maincrop apples and pears;
• freeze or make jam with the last of the soft fruits;
• prune blackberries and their hybrids when the fruit has been harvested;
• take hardwood cuttings of black-, red- and whitecurrants and gooseberries;
• you can prune blackcurrants now but the job is more easily done when the foliage has dropped off, in December;
• order fruit trees and soft fruit bushes and canes. Plant as soon as possible while the soil is warm. If the weather isn't right for planting when they arrive, heel them in or cover with wet sacking;
• clean up strawberry beds, removing yellow foliage and any remaining runners. Keep young plants well watered so they can develop well before winter.

herbs and flowers

• lift parsley, chives and some mint, if you haven't already. Pot up and keep on the kitchen windowsill for winter use;
• tidy up winter savory and mulch the soil;
• clear away annual herbs now – dill, coriander, summer savory and sweet marjoram.

watch out for

• grey mould (Botrytis) and mildew are common in damp weather. Cut off and bin affected parts of plants as soon as you spot them. Courgettes and marrows are particularly prone;
• cut off yellowing leaves of brussels sprouts, cabbages, cauliflowers and broccoli;
• practise good hygiene. Check for viral infections, particularly on fruit;
• put on grease bands around the trunks of fruit trees, to protect against the winter moth.

last chance

• get your onions in;
• harvest apples and pears.

getting ahead

• now there is space, clean out the greenhouse;
• sow winter green manures – grazing rye or field beans.

november

Batten your hatches. Lag down pipes. Float a ball in the pond. Carry on digging on fine days, planting green manures and enriching the soil with the last of the old compost and manure. Plant garlic and overwintering broad beans. Winter vegetables will be coming in now – kale, cabbage, spinach, leeks, oriental mustards, chards, beets and Jerusalem artichokes, scorzonera, salsify and trench celery. Parsnips and sprouts will be sweeter after the first frosts.

in season

- Artichokes (Chinese and Jerusalem)
- Beet (leaf/perpetual spinach)
- Brussels sprouts
- Cabbage (Chinese)
- Cabbage (autumn and winter)
- Cardoon
- Carrot (maincrop)
- Cauliflower (winter)
- Celeriac
- Chicory (red)
- Corn salad
- Cress (American land)
- Endive
- Hamburg parsley
- Kale (borecole)
- Kohlrabi
- Komatsuna
- Leek
- Lettuce
- Mustards (oriental)
- Pak choi
- Parsnip
- Peas (maincrop)
- Radish (summer and winter)
- Red orache
- Rocket
- Saladini (oriental)
- Salsify
- Scorzonera
- Sorrel
- Spinach (summer and winter)
- Swede
- Swiss chard
- Turnip

general maintenance

- dig heavy soils when the conditions are right;
- cover light soils with polythene to prevent leaching and leave digging until spring, or sow green manures on bare ground to replenish the soil before spring planting;

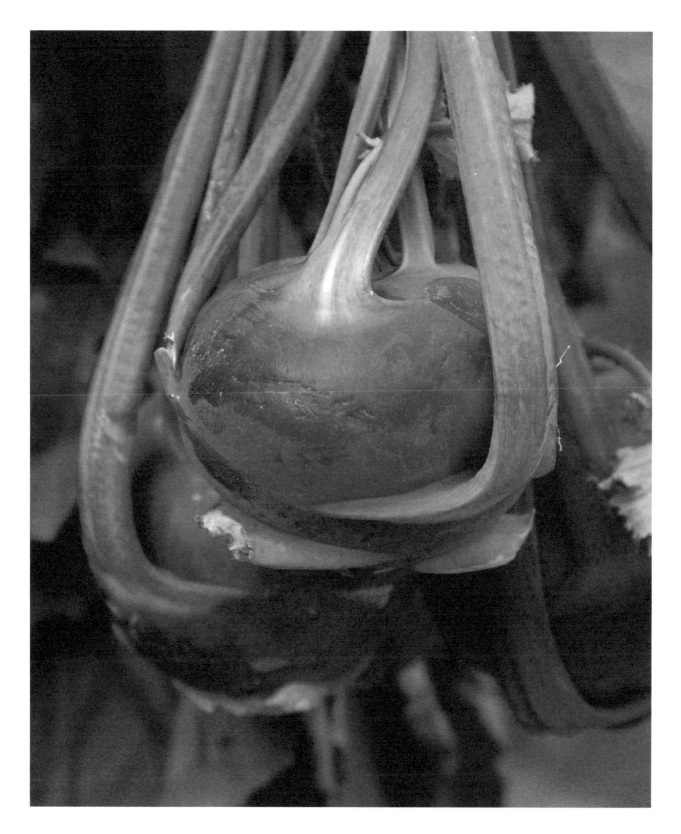

- tidy beds. Clear away old foliage;
- cover compost bins;
- clear leaves and stack them up for leaf-mould;
- protect vulnerable plants from frost and wind with netting or fleece;
- lag downpipes from the shed to the water butt;
- check stakes and ties, as winter weather is imminent;
- in cold areas, insulate cold frames with polystyrene. With bubble wrap on top, this will keep out several degrees of frost. On bitter nights put a piece of carpet or an old blanket on top of that. Take it off during the day to let light in;
- check the shed for leaks before winter;
- float a ball in the pond, to prevent freezing;
- if you are on a windy site, put up windbreaks;
- check your stores. Use up or dispose of anything that looks less than perfect;
- clear out old bird boxes as they can harbour parasites. The birds will be looking for cosy winter roosts any time now. Put food and water out for them.

other november tasks

- keep going on the compost heap.

vegetables

- net brassicas against pigeons;
- pick brussels sprouts, starting from the bottom, and remove old leaves;
- harvest parsnips after the first frosts in cold areas. Store them in the same way as the other root vegetables;
- lift a few leeks if there is frost about. They are impossible to dig out in icy conditions. Bury them horizontally with the tops

sticking out in a sheltered spot;
- protect the curds of cauliflowers by tying the leaves over them;
- force chicory and seakale;
- cut down globe artichokes and pack straw around them in cold areas;
- it is not too late to plant Japanese and autumn onion sets.

Sowing
- sow broad beans and winter peas outside under cloches in mild areas.

fruit

- begin winter pruning apple and pear trees, gooseberries and currants when the leaves have dropped off. Weed carefully and topdress all soft fruit with a layer of organic matter;
- if you haven't already done so, put grease bands around the trunks of fruit trees, to protect against the winter moth;
- propagate rhubarb by digging up and splitting into smaller pieces. Repeat every four years. Start to plant newly bought crowns;
- take hardwood cuttings of redcurrants, blackcurrants and gooseberries;
- plant new fruit trees while there is still some warmth in the soil;
- check stored fruit.

herbs and flowers

- put cloches over parsley, winter savory and chervil;
- dig up mint and chives and grow them on in containers at home or in the cold greenhouse;
- protect young plants of French tarragon, sage and rosemary with straw or leaf-mould around the roots.

watch out for

- canker on apple trees;
- renew sticky bands if necessary against the winter moth;
- continue to remove yellowing leaves on brassicas as they may harbour disease;
- pests lurking in old containers and trays, so clean them out.

getting ahead

- make sure you have a good supply of horticultural fleece or mesh fabrics to protect your plants;
- start to save newspapers, netting, old plastic bottles and blankets. They may be useful in the months ahead;
- prepare the onion bed. Let it settle over winter as onions like firm soil;
- order seeds.

december

Work on the allotment tails off in winter. You can get on with winter pruning and DIY projects – construction, cleaning your tools or scrubbing out the greenhouse. Check your crops. Look through the seed catalogues as there are always new and interesting varieties to try. If you have had a problem with particular pests and disease during the last year, look for cultivars that are resistant. Order your seeds and seed potatoes. Make plans for the new year. Enjoy the fruit of your well-earned labours, your winter produce and your stores.

in season

- Artichokes (Chinese and Jerusalem)
- Beet (leaf/perpetual spinach)
- Brussels sprouts
- Cabbage (Chinese)
- Cabbage (autumn and winter)
- Cardoon
- Carrot (maincrop)
- Cauliflower (autumn)
- Celeriac
- Chicory (red)
- Corn salad
- Cress (American land)
- Endive
- Hamburg parsley
- Kale (borecole)
- Kohlrabi
- Komatsuna
- Leek
- Lettuce (with protection)
- Mustards (oriental)
- Pak choi
- Parsnip
- Radish (summer and winter)
- Red orache
- Rocket
- Saladini (oriental)
- Salsify
- Scorzonera
- Sorrel
- Spinach (summer and winter)
- Swede
- Swiss chard
- Turnip

general maintenance

- protect plants against severe cold and strong winds. Cover with polytunnels and cloches. Insulate cold frames and the greenhouse with bubble wrap if you are planning to use them through winter;
- rig up a polystyrene box in which to raise seed in the cold greenhouse. Glue sheets

together and cover the top with a piece of glass or see-through plastic;

• put sheets of polystyrene under winter salads and other plants in pots or trays in the cold greenhouse;

• when the soil is not frozen or waterlogged, move plants that are in the wrong place, taking as much soil as possible with the rootball;

• check existing stakes and ties and put in new ones where necessary;

• test the soil pH. Apply lime if necessary. Don't use it at the same time as manure as they react against each other;

• tackle DIY projects. Make a cold frame. Repair fences and sheds;

• on mild days, open up the cold frame or cold greenhouse to let air circulate for an hour or two;

• feed the birds but don't let them get at your brassicas. Don't trim down any ornamental plants that provide food for the birds in the depth of winter. The seedheads of asters, teasel and thistles and the berries of cotoneaster and honeysuckle will be greatly appreciated. Leave newly dug soil in large lumps for birds to pick through. Make sure the birds have water. Provide bird feeders and nesting boxes.

other December tasks

• continue to winter dig when conditions are right. Clear debris but leave a few hidey holes for beneficial creatures – small piles of leaves, stones and logs;

• carry on collecting leaves for leaf-mould. Use planks, hands or a 'gripper' to pick up leaves rather than a fork, to avoid harming dormant creatures;

• check on stores.

vegetables

• earth up spring cabbages and winter brassicas, to avoid windrock. Keep removing yellowing leaves which could harbour disease;

• pick brussels sprouts regularly from the bottom up;

• cut leaves from the crowns of kale, to encourage sideshoots to grow for harvesting in late winter;

• put straw or bracken around perennials such as globe artichokes, but leave the crowns clear;

• mulch maincrop carrots, parsnips, beetroot, turnips and swedes that have been left in the ground, to keep the worst of the frost off. In cold areas, lift and store;

• harvest celery and leeks. If severe frost threatens, lift some and heel them in where you can get to them easily;

• harvest Jerusalem artichokes as you want them;

• continue to force seakale and chicory. After the first frosts, start forcing rhubarb.

Sowing

• sow early crops of lettuce, summer cabbage, radishes, round varieties of carrot, spinach, salad onions and turnips. They don't need a high temperature – 13°C (55°F) is sufficient. If started on a windowsill in good light, they can go outside under cloches or fleece in February.

fruit

• check tree stakes, supports and ties;

• winter prune apples, pears, gooseberries and currants on days without hard frost;

• force rhubarb for harvesting in January;

• carry on inspecting your stores.

herbs and flowers

• cut down on watering indoor herbs to a minimal level;

• protect young plants of French tarragon, sage and rosemary with a straw or leaf-mould around the base in cold areas.

watch out for

• canker in apples;

• hibernating colonies of pests lurking in corners of the greenhouse or cold frame as you clean.

last chance

• protect plants from January frost.

getting ahead

• clean your tools;

• scrub flowerpots and seed trays ready for next spring;

• clean the glass of greenhouse and cold-frame glass, for extra light in winter;

• order seed potatoes;

• make a review of failures and successes and make plans for the year to come. One of the delights about gardening is that you never, ever, finish learning.

vegetable directory

Amaranthus, Calaloo

Amaranthus gangeticus
AMARANTHACEAE

Vigorous and easy to grow, amaranthus is a tender plant widely grown in the Far East, Africa and the Americas as a cereal crop – a striking one with magnificent, magenta, feathery plumes. In the UK, it is usually harvested young for its leaves.

Types
Large and small leaved. Greens, red, variegated.

Seed to harvest
10–12 weeks.

Min. germination temp.
10°C (50°F). Better warmer.

Situation
Hot as possible, sheltered.

Soil
Fertile for best crops.

Ideal pH
7

Sowing and planting
The seed is fine, so mix with a sand or sieved soil. Sow in situ 2 cm (¾ in) deep. Provide extra warmth with crop covers

Spacing
Thin to 10 cm (4 in).

Cultivation
Keep watered and feed every two weeks. Pinch out the growing tips when 20 cm (8 in) high, to encourage the plants to bush out. Don't let the plants flower as they self-seed prolifically.

Harvesting
Pick off outer leaves or pull up the entire plant when 20–25 cm (8–10 in) high, before it coarsens.

Problems
Damping off, bolting, red spider mite, flea beetle, leaf hopper.

Cooking
An accompaniment to salt fish in West Indian cuisine. Callaloo is a hot Carribean stew made with okra and many variants including sea food and coconut milk. Seedling crop for salads.

Varieties
• 'Red Leaf'
• 'Large leaf Chinese'
• 'Small Leaf Indian'
• 'Tampala'.

American land cress

Barbarea vulgaris
BRASSICACEAE

Peppery salad leaf like watercress. Easy to grow. All-year-round crop, it comes into its own in winter.

Types
No cultivars.

Seed to harvest
Saladini: eight weeks.

Min. germination temp.
10°C (50°F).

Situation
Light shade in summer.

Soil
Moist, fertile.

Ideal pH
7.5

Sowing and planting
Sow seed in July or August for harvesting in autumn. Cover for winter crops. Sow in spring for summer crops.

Spacing
Thin to 15 cm (6 in) apart.

Cultivation
Keep well watered in dry spells to prevent coarsening. Leave a few to flower the following spring, to self-seed for a midsummer crop.

Harvesting
Pick outer leaves as you want them.

Problems
Generally trouble free. Flea beetle.

Cooking
Salads, soup, garnishes.

Artichoke, Chinese

Stachys affinis
LAMIACEAE

The root of Chinese artichoke resembles white jade. It has sage-like leaves, pink flowers and grows to about 45 cm (18 in). The tubers are segmented like a caterpillar. They grow in strings at the ends of the roots. They are about 5 cm (2 in) long and as thick as a fountain pen. They taste like water chestnut and artichoke combined. They are easy to grow, though you need to plant quite a few for a decent helping. After flowering, and when the first frosts have blackened the leaves, dig them out as you want them, as they don't store for long. In spring, clear the ground thoroughly as they can take over. Keep a few back for the next crop.

Artichoke, globe

Cynara scolymus
ASTERACEAE

A statuesque plant from the thistle family growing to 1.5 m (5 ft). The heart of flower buds and flesh inside the bracts are a delicacy that has been enjoyed since Greek and Roman times.

Types
Green to purple.

Offset to harvest
A full season, then harvest annually. Sowing from seed has variable results.

Situation
Sunny and sheltered.

Soil
Light, free draining.

Ideal pH
7

Plant
Set the crown just below the surface.

Spacing
90 cm (3 ft) apart.

Cultivation
Keep watered until established.

Harvesting
Cut flowerheads off with some stem.

Problems
Aphids.

Cooking
Steamed and served with butter or hollandaise sauce.

Varieties
- 'Green Globe' – popular.
- 'Purple Globe'
- 'Romanesco' – purple.
- 'Vert de Lyon' – hardy; good flavour.
- 'Violetta di Chioggia' A decorative variety with purple heads. Not very hardy.

Artichoke, Jerusalem

Helianthus tuberosus
ASTERACEAE

The Jerusalem artichoke is a relative of the sunflower and, like it, grows at speed to a great height, sometimes reaching 3 m (10 ft) in a single summer. It makes an excellent temporary screen, windbreak and cover for wildlife. The tuberous roots taste of artichoke.

Types
Yellow or red. Less knobbly and no-peel cultivars.

Plant to harvest
4–5 months.

Situation
Sun or part shade.

Soil
Fertile soil. Not soggy.

Ideal pH
6–7.5

Sowing and planting
Buy plump, egg-sized tubers, from the greengrocer to plant in early spring, 10–15cm (4–6in) deep. Large tubers can be cut into sections with one or two eyes. Subsequent years you can use your own.

Spacing
30 cm (12 in) apart. Rows 60 cm (2 ft) apart.

Cultivation
Stake and earth up if you are on a windy site. Water in dry spells. Remove any flowers, to improve the crop.

Harvesting
Cut right down after frost has killed off the tops. Spread the tops over the patch for winter protection. Dig the tubers up as you want them through winter. They will store for a week in the fridge. Clear the ground thoroughly in early spring.

Problems
Generally trouble free. Can become rampant if left in the ground too long.

Cooking
Treat as potatoes. Cook before peeling as they discolour when exposed to the air when raw. Substitute for water chestnuts in Chinese cookery. Delicious in soups.

Varieties
- 'Dwarf Sunray' – no need to peel.
- 'Fuseau' – old variety; smooth tubers.

Asparagus

Asparagus officinalis
ASPARAGACEAE

Asparagus, the food of kings, is easy to grow given the right conditions and will produce for 20 years. It needs its own bed.

Types
All-male F1 cultivars are recommended. The female plants are less vigorous and inclined to self-seed. White asparagus is grown in the dark.

Seed to harvest
3–4 years.

Crown to harvest
1–2 years.

Min. germination temp.
10°C (50°F).

Situation
Sunny, sheltered.

Soil
Well drained.

Ideal pH
7

Sowing and planting
Dig a trench a spit deep and eliminate perennial weeds. The traditional bed is 1.2 m (4 ft) wide. Seed takes three years, so it saves time to buy one- to three-year-old crowns. The one year olds are said to establish better in the long run. In spring, build ridges in the prepared trenches and place the crowns in two staggered rows. Straddle them across the ridges with the roots going downwards. When you fill the trench, the crowns should be 15 cm (6 in) below ground.

Spacing
45 cm (18 in) apart.

Cultivation
Hand weed regularly. In autumn, when the leaves turn yellow, cut them down to the ground. Apply a thick mulch of well-rotted manure or compost. Feed with some fertilizer the following spring. Watch out for late frosts.

Harvesting
From its third year onwards, asparagus can be harvested for six weeks in May and June. Use a sharp knife to cut the spears just below the ground, taking care not to damage the crown.

Problems
None usually. Slugs and snails, asparagus beetle, violet root rot. Late frosts.

Cooking
Steamed with hollandaise sauce or butter. Soups, stir-fries, quiches, salads.

Varieties
- 'Backlim' F1 (AGM) and 'Gijnlim' F1 (AGM) – large spears; high yields; all-male hybrids.
- 'Connover's Colossal' (AGM) – 19th-century favourite.
- 'Giant Mammouth' – Similar to 'Connover's Colossal' but tolerates heavy soil.
- 'Gijnlim' F1 (AGM) – All-male hybrid.
- 'Jersey Giant' – All-male hybrid.
- 'Lucullus' F1 (AGM) – Late but high yielding.

Asparagus pea

Lotus tetragonolobus
PAPILIONAECEAE

The asparagus pea is something of a rarity – not really a pea at all but a small creeping vetch, no higher than 15 cm (6 in) and 60 cm (24 in) wide. It's not a great cropper but it has enchanting, red flowers. The winged pods are a delicacy as long as they are picked when young.

Seed to harvest
12 weeks.

Min. germination temp.
19°C (65°F).

Situation
Sunny.

Soil
Fertile, light, well drained.

Ideal pH
6–7

Sowing and planting
Sow seeds under cover in April or May, barely covering them. Or sow in situ after frosts.

Spacing
2 cm (¾ in deep), 15 cm (6 in) apart.

Harvesting
Pick regularly when 2.5 cm (1 in) as they toughen quickly.

Problems
Birds, mildew.

Cooking
Steam briefly.

Varieties
No cultivars.

Aubergine / Eggplant

Solanum melongena
SOLANACEAE

Aubergines are grown in the same way as tomatoes, though they are more cold-sensitive and take longer to develop. Their ideal ripening temperature is 25–30°C (77–86°F). They can be grown outside in hot summers if bought as young plants or started off with heat at home.

Types
Purple, white, pink, pink flecked, violet, green, orange and striped. From large to egg sized. Long, thin Chinese types. Fast-growing cultivars. Minis.

Seed to harvest
16–24 weeks.

Min. germination temp.
21°C (70°F).

Situation
Warm and sheltered.

Soil
Well drained. Fertile.

Ideal pH
6.5

Sowing and planting
Soak seed overnight. Sow in spring in a propagator. Pot on individually when there are three true leaves. Warm the soil for two weeks before planting out under cover, when the minimum soil temperature at night is above 15°C (59°F). Taller varieties will need staking.

Spacing
45 cm (18 in) apart.

Cultivation
For sizeable fruits, restrict each plant to five buds by nipping off the others. Give a liquid feed weekly, switching to a high-potash (tomato) feed when the fruits are forming. Keep well watered and mulched.

Harvesting
Harvest before fruit lose their shine.

Problems
Aphids, whitefly and red spider mite in the cold frame. Grey mould (Botrytis) in wet weather.

Cooking
Aubergine combines with tomatoes and garlic for many Mediterranean dishes, tempura (Japan), imam bayeldi – the fainting imam – (Turkey).

Varieties
- 'Adona' F1 (AGM) – big shiny black fruits; prolific.
- 'Black Beauty' F1 – old stager with big, purple fruits; high yields.
- 'Easter Egg' – quick grower with small, white fruits.
- 'Galine' F1 (AGM) – Big shiny fruits.
- 'Mohican' F1 (AGM) – Compact with white fruits.
- 'Moneymaker' – bred to withstand cooler conditions.
- 'Rima' (AGM) – Suitable for growing outside under cover. Good flavour. Purple fruits.
- 'Vernal' (AGM) – Good for cold frame or cloche. Good-quality, vigorous plant.
- 'Violetta di Firenze' – violet fruits, occasionally striped; sensitive to cold.

Beetroot

Beta vulgaris subsp. *vulgaris*
CHENOPODIACEAE

Beetroot is a quick grower. Generally care free.

Types
Red, gold, stripy. White, pink and white and golden cultivars, which don't stain. Long and round. Summer and maincrop.

Seed to harvest
7–13 weeks.

Min. germination temp.
7°C (45°F).

Situation
Sunny, open.

Soil
Fertile from previous crop. A good depth of stone-free topsoil.

Ideal pH
7 or above.

Sowing and planting
Seed usually comes in clusters. Monogerm, or single-seed types, are popular as they avoid thinning out. Soak to soften the coating for half an hour. Use bolt-resistant cultivars for spring sowings. Sow a few seeds every fortnight, for continuous crops. Switch to maincrop types in June.

Spacing
2.5 cm (1 in) apart, thin to 10 cm (4 in). Rows 20 cm (8 in) apart.

Cultivation
Water carefully. Too much will make them produce more leaf than root. Too dry and the roots will toughen. If suddenly soaked when dry, the roots may fork. Keep mulched. Weed carefully as the roots 'bleed' when damaged.

Harvesting
Twist off the leaves about 5 cm (2 in) above the root to avoid bleeding. Loosen the soil with a fork and pull up the roots carefully. Harvest earlies when golf-ball sized, and

maincrops when no bigger than a tennis ball. Lift the remaining late crops in autumn and store in moist sand in a cool shed. In mild areas, the late ones can be left in the ground until wanted covered with straw or bracken.

Problems
Bolting.

Cooking
Salads, boiled, raw and grated. Baked in its skin. Sildesalat with herring (Scandinavia). Puréed with apples, onions and nutmeg (Holland). Borscht with sour cream (Russia). Curried, chutneyed, pickled.

Varieties
- 'Boltardy' (AGM) – popular; bolt-resistant; good for early sowings.
- 'Bonel' (AGM) – Bolt resistant, early cropper. High yields of round, red, tasty roots.
- 'Bulls Blood' – old variety with dramatic, red foliage; Victorian favourite for bedding out; young leaves good in salads.
- 'Burpees Golden' – yellow with orange skin; doesn't stain.
- 'Cheltenham Green Top' (AGM) – old variety; tapered root.
- 'Cheltenham Mono' – Monogerm and resistant to bolting.
- 'Chioggia' – Roots are red with white stripes.
- 'Detroit 2 Little Ball' and 'Pronto' – baby beet.
- 'Moneta', 'Monopoly' and *'Monogram' – All monogerm types. Saves thinning.
- 'Regala' (AGM) – Good resistance to bolting.

Broad bean / Fava bean
Vicia faba
PAPILIONACEAE

The broad bean is easy to grow and is the hardiest of the legumes. Sow in autumn for spring eating or in spring for summer eating. The flowers are sweetly scented and appreciated by bees.

Types
Dwarf to tall. Beans kidney shaped, round. Green, almost white to red. Longpod types with eight seeds are hardier, more prolific and are best for early crops. Shorter Windsors with four seeds are finer type and are generally grown later in the season. New cultivars have the merits of both. Dwarf varieties are usually sown for late summer harvest.

Seed to harvest
Spring sown: 12–16 weeks. Autumn sown: 28–35 weeks.

Min. germination temp.
5°C (41°F).

Situation
Open, sunny. Sheltered in winter.

Soil
Heavy, yet not too heavy for the big taproots to penetrate. Avoid waterlogged or dry soil.

Ideal pH
7

Sowing and planting
When sowing is done under cover, this deals with the mouse problem and can speed things up for an early crop. Sow in biodegradable tubes and transplant when the plants have four true leaves. Alternatively, sow hardy cultivars in a sunny, sheltered spot outside in autumn or between February and March under cloches.

Spacing
In double rows 15–20 cm (6–9 in) between plants. 60 cm (2 ft) between double rows.

Cultivation
Tall varieties may need supports. When the first flowers open, pinch out the growing tip to deter black fly.

Harvesting
Do this before the beans toughen, when you can feel the young beans in the pods.

Problems
Mice, pea and bean weevil, black bean aphid, broad bean chocolate spot, rust, foot and root rot.

Cooking
If picked when tiny, broad beans can be eaten whole in their shells. Mature beans slow cooked with savory (France). Puréed with other pulses (Morocco). Mashed with olive oil for ful medames (Egypt). Dried and ground into flour.

Varieties
- 'Aquadulce Claudia' (AGM) – longpod suitable for autumn planting; favourite since 1844. The Aquadulce series, including 'Super Aquadulce', are the hardiest type of broad bean.
- 'Express' (AGM) – strong, hardy with mild-tasting beans good for freezing; quickest for spring planting.
- 'Imperial Green Longpod' (AGM) – Good for freezing. Noted for flavour.
- 'Red Epicure' – crimson seeds and flowers.
- 'The Sutton' (AGM) – dwarf variety, up to 45 cm (18 in); good for windy sites.
- 'Witkiem Manita' (AGM) and 'Witkiem Major' (AGM) – two of the earliest for spring sowing.

Broccoli

Brassica oleracea Italica Group
BRASSICACEAE

Sprouting broccoli is a slow-growing, overwintering plant that needs space but crops in the hungry gap of winter. It produces masses of small florets for up to two months and is easy to grow. Calabrese (the more usual type sold in the shops with a single head) is a summer crop. When the main head or 'curd' is harvested, the plants send up succulent sideshoots, each with a small head and some leaves, for weeks afterwards. Romanesco, another late summer or early autumn vegetable, is a large, attractive, cone-shaped cross between a calabrese and a cauliflower. It has attractive, spiralling, lime-green curds. Along with calabrese, however, it is a challenge to grow well, having the bolting tendencies of its close relative, the cauliflower. Perennial broccoli, or Nine Star, comes up every year, producing loose, white heads for harvesting in spring. It is usually replaced every three years.

Types

Sprouting broccoli – green, purple and white. The purple forms are hardier and more prolific than the white ones. Calabrese – early, midseason and late. Romanesco – different greens, some can be harvested into late autumn. Perennial broccoli – few cultivars, 'Nine Star' is the best.

Seed to harvest

Sprouting broccoli 8–10 months. Calabrese 12–14 weeks. Romanesco 4–5 months. Perennial broccoli 10 months, then harvested annually.

Min. germination temp.

7°C (45°F).

Situation

Open and airy but sheltered, especially for sprouting and perennial broccoli as they can become top-heavy. Romanesco Partial shade in summer.

Soil

Fertile and well drained.

Ideal pH

6–7.5. Romanesco 7 or higher.

Sowing and planting

Sprouting broccoli – Sow in spring or early summer, either in modules or the seedbed. When transplanting, plant up to the first leaves to reduce the danger of cabbage root fly and to encourage a good rooting system for winter. Calabrese – Earliest crops can be sown in modules in late autumn under cloches and transplanted to a cold greenhouse or frame in winter. Otherwise sow in May in situ. Calabrese doesn't transplant well, especially in the heat of summer. Romanesco – Start off in modules in May. Pot on and transplant outside early, to avoid bolting. Perennial broccoli Sow in midspring and transplant in early autumn into good-quality soil. Firm well to avoid windrock in winter. All types Cover plants with fleece or insect-proof mesh, to protect them from pests.

Spacing

Sprouting broccoli 2.5 cm (1 in) deep, 60 cm (24 in) apart, and 75 cm (30 in) between rows. Calabrese 20 x 45 cm (8 x 18 in). Romanesco 45 x 60 cm (18 x 24 in). Perennial broccoli 90 cm (3 ft) apart.

Cultivation

Keep sprouting broccoli weed free, watered in dry spells, earthed up and firmly staked against winter gales. Avoid cosseting it with too much fertilizer or water, as it needs to be tough enough to cope with winter. Earth up through summer to encourage a strong rooting system. Keep calabrese and romanesco well watered throughout the growing season to prevent them bolting. Perennial broccoli is best grown against a fence or support. Feed each spring.

Harvesting

Cut the central stem first, to encourage sideshoots to grow. Keep picking sprigs, a few at a time when the buds form. This will encourage new shoots to form. Don't let the plants flower or production will halt.

Problems

Mealy aphids, cabbage root fly, cabbage aphids, cabbage caterpillars, flea beetle, cabbage whitefly, birds, club-root, downy mildew.

Cooking

Like cauliflower. Soups or stir-fries.

Varieties

Sprouting broccoli

- 'Bordeaux' (AGM) – Early. Quite compact and stands well over winter.
- 'Claret' F1 (AGM) – Tall with a heavy yield of dark purple spears from March to April.
- 'Express Corona' – Good for resistance to downy mildew.
- 'Early Purple Sprouting Improved' – Ready to harvest in February or early March.
- 'Late Purple Sprouting' (AGM) – For April picking. It's a good over-winterer.
- 'Red Arrow' F1 (AGM) – Early mid-season, long cropping.

Calabrese

- 'Corvet' F1 (AGM) – good summer crop.
- 'Decathlon' (AGM) – does well on poor soils.
- 'Flash' F1 (AGM) – Crops over a long period.
- 'Hydra' F1 (AGM) – Mid to late vigorous variety; uniform.
- 'Tenderstem' – abundant crop of delicious spears.
- 'Tiara' F1 (AGM) – Sow in May for early medium-sized heads.
- 'Trixie' F1 (AGM) – Early mid-season

- 'Red Arrow' F1 (AGM) – Early mid-season, long cropping.

Romanesco
- 'Emeraude' F1 Hybrid – Emerald-green heads; can be harvested into early autumn.
- 'Veronica' – particularly attractive cultivar that can be harvested into early autumn.

Perennial broccoli
- 'Nine Star' – reliable.

Broccoli, Chinese

Brassica rapa var. *alboglabra*
BRASSICACEAE

Chinese broccoli looks like a smaller version of calabrese, growing to about half the height, 45cm (18in). The young, white or yellow, flowering stems in bud are a delicacy and crop over a long period. The thick stems are also good to eat. Chinese broccoli is probably the easiest of the oriental brassicas. It can take some heat and even mild frost.

Types
White and yellow flowering.
Seed to harvest
Maturity: 9–10 weeks. Harvest the whole plant young: six weeks.
Min. germination temp.
10°C (50°F).
Situation
Sunny and sheltered.
Soil
Fertile.
Ideal pH
6.5–7
Sowing and planting
Sow any time through summer, although midsummer for autumn eating is the best time. An early autumn sowing under cover should bring a spring crop unless the winter is severe. Alternatively, broadcast seed baby leaves.

Spacing
Thin to 30 cm (12 in) apart. To harvest the whole plants young, space 10 cm (4 in) apart.
Cultivation
Keep watered to prevent bolting. Earth up to protect from winter winds.
Harvesting
Harvest the top shoot of full-sized plants to encourage sideshoots to form. They should produce two more crops. Also pick bits and pieces as they grow for salads and stir-fries. Alternatively, lift the whole plant when young.
Problems
Usually trouble free. Their waxy leaves give them some protection. Cabbage root fly, mealy cabbage aphid, flea beetle, cabbage whitefly, club-root, brassica white blister, pigeons.
Cooking
The shoots and flowering heads for stir-fries. Any stems accidentally left to toughen can be peeled and parboiled first.
Varieties
- 'Green Lance' F1 – vigorous and fast maturing.
- 'Tenderstem' – cross with calabrese.
- 'White Flowered' – tall with blue-green leaves and white flowers.

Brussels sprouts

Brassica oleracea Gemmifera Group
BRASSICACEAE

Sprouts are extremely hardy. The toughest can withstand -10°C (14°F). They take nearly five months to grow, but they can be picked fresh over a period of 2–3 months in the depths of winter, when fresh, home-grown vegetables are scarce. They are usually started in the seedbed or in modules for a more controlled, pest-free start and to save space.

Types
Sprouts are classified according to season – early, mid and late. The F1 hybrids have been bred to avoid traditional problems, especially the habit of producing 'leafy blowers' instead of tight sprouts. The newer varieties produce good quantities of uniformly tightly packed 'buttons'. They are also stockier plants, so are less likely to get blown over, and are sweeter tasting. Red or purple.
Seed to harvest
20 weeks.
Min. germination temp.
7°C (45°F).
Situation
Best in sun, though they can take a little shade and even do well on a north-facing slope.
Soil
Fertile, well drained but moisture retentive, manured for the previous crop and firm. Prepare the soil ahead so that it can settle down. Secure the sprouts from windrock in winter.
Ideal pH
6.5–7.5
Sowing and planting
For sprouts at Christmas, sow thinly, 1.3 cm (½ in) deep, in late March or early April outside. Cover with a cloche mounted on tiles or stones. to let in air. Keep the seeds in the dark until they germinate. After that take the cloche off on sunny days, replacing it at night, when it rains heavily or if the weather turns cold. When big enough to handle, thin out to 15 cm (6 in) apart. Transplant in May, when plants are about 23 cm (9 in) high.

Earlier sprouts for autumn can be germinated with bottom heat of 18°C (64°F)

in a propagator in late winter. Remove them from the propagator after about a week and keep them at a cool 10°C (50°F) to prevent them getting leggy. Transplant into modules when big enough to handle, to encourage a strong taproot to form. Plant out in spring under netting. Sprouts ready in the new year and onwards are started off in April and grown in the same way as earlies – without the weather worries.

Spacing
60 cm (24 in) apart both ways.

Cultivation
Once in their final positions, sprouts need little attention. Keep them weed free, watered in dry spells and staked on the windward side as they get bigger. In autumn, stabilize the plants further by earthing them up to the level of the first set of leaves.

Harvesting
Remove yellowing or diseased leaves regularly. Harvest from the bottom upwards. Dig out entirely at the end of the season but wait until the plants have made one final departing gesture by throwing out a tasty top shoot.

Problems
Mealy aphids, cabbage root fly, flea beetle, cabbage whitefly, birds, club-root, downy mildew, brassica white blister.

Cooking
If you put the freshly picked sprouts in salted water, any hidden insect life will emerge. Sprouts should generally be boiled quickly.

Varieties
Early
- 'Diablo' (AGM) – good-quality, clean, round sprout.
- 'Icarus' (AGM) – large, smooth, solid sprouts; stands well.

Mid Season
- 'Cavalier' F1 – Dark green, well-spaced sprouts.

- 'Clodius' (AGM) – good-quality; stands and yields well.
- 'Igor' (AGM) – Midseason to late. Small smooth sprouts.
- 'Lunet' F1 – Tall plants. High yielding.
- 'Patent' (AGM) – Large, round, dark green solid sprouts.
- 'Roger' (AGM) – Large smooth, good-quality pale green sprouts. Plants stand well.
- 'Wellington' (AGM) – Good-quality, smooth, dark green, round, solid sprouts.

Late
- 'Bosworth' (AGM) solid, closely spaced sprouts.
- 'Noisette' – nutty. Both crop into February.
- 'Cascade' (AGM) – Smooth, clean, well-spaced, dark green button sprouts.
- 'Millenium' – Recommended by GW for sprouts into the New Year.

Mini
- 'Peter Gynt' – tried-and-tested, F1 dwarf.
- 'Rubine' – red.

Cabbage
Brassica oleracea Capitata Group
BRASSICACEAE

Cabbages are hardy and happy growing in cool conditions. There are eight main types and myriad introductions and crosses. They are easy to grow as long as they are given good soil, continuous moisture and protection against pests and diseases.

Types
The main types are classified by harvesting times – spring, summer and autumn. Spring cabbages can be eaten as 'greens' or can be left to 'heart up'. The winter ones are divided into winter whites, January King cultivars, savoys, savoy hybrids and red cabbage. The winter whites are mild tasting

and store throughout winter. The savoys and the January King cultivars are bred to stand out all winter. The savoy hybrids, a cross between the savoy and the winter white, have the hardiness of one parent and the milder taste of the second. The red cabbage is harvested in late autumn and can be stored for a couple of months.

Seed to harvest
Average 20 weeks.

Min. germination temperature
7°C (45°F).

Situation
Open and sunny.

Soil
Fertile, well drained.

Ideal pH
6.5–7.5

Sowing and planting
Generally sown in modules or in the seedbed and transplanted six weeks later. To help their roots to get a good hold, use a dibber to plant them out and firm the soil round them well. If your soil is light, make a shallow drill and earth the young cabbages up as they grow. Use collars and netting. Spring cabbage will provide spring greens in March or April and hearted cabbage in April, May and June. Make two sowings a couple of weeks apart in autumn, to cover your bets. Summer cabbage can carry on right through summer if you start with early varieties and move onto maincrop types. Earliest crops are sown in March outside under fleece for June eating. For even earlier crops, start them off in a propagator at 16°C (61°F) in February. Harden them off well before transplanting on a cool day, at around 20°C (68°F) to prevent bolting. For a succession of summer cabbage, sow more seeds every couple of weeks through April. A final sowing at the end of April will give you cabbages for September. For autumn to early winter eating, change varieties and sow outside from May onwards.

Spacing

Full-grown cabbage: 45 cm (18 in) all round. Spring cabbage: first set 60 cm (24 in) apart, the second set can be slotted in between.

Cultivation

Keep watered in dry spells. Don't fertilize overwintering cabbage in winter as it will encourage a flush of soft growth susceptible to frosts.

Harvesting

Spring, summer and most autumn cabbages are eaten freshly harvested. Some of the autumn cabbages do store for a while. Spring cabbages are picked as greens while the others are harvested when they have a solid heart. If the stumps are left in the ground, they may produce some tasty top shoots, especially if you make a cross cut on them.

Winter cabbages

Winter whites, as well as some red cabbages, store for up to five months. Dig them up carefully to avoid damage before the frosts and hang (either with all the roots or a good-sized stump) in nets or pack loosely in straw. Check from time to time and remove any damaged, outer leaves. Savoys and the January King cultivars are cropped as needed into the new year. At the end of the season, completely clear the ground.

Problems

Cabbage root fly, mealy cabbage aphid, flea beetle, cabbage whitefly, club-root, brassica white blister, pigeons.

Cooking

The winter whites are used for coleslaw. Red cabbage is usually cooked with apple and the other cabbage types are used as greens – steamed, braised, boiled, pickled, stir-fried or wrapped around fillings in the Greek way for dolmades.

Varieties

Spring cabbage

- 'Duncan' F1 (AGM) – Spring greens and hearted cabbage.
- 'First Early Market 218' (AGM). Hearts up slowly to produce large, quite loose heads.
- 'First Early Market 218 – Mastercut' (AGM) – Well filled hearts.
- 'Offenham 1 Myatt's Offenham Compacta' (AGM) – Big-hearted cabbage.
- 'Offenham 3 – Mastergreen' (AGM) – Uniform, bright green spring greens.

Summer cabbage

- 'Augustor' F1 (AGM) – Bright green. Mid-season.
- 'Charmont' F1 (AGM) – Round type, bright green.
- 'Derby Day' F1 (AGM) – Early, bright mid-green and round.
- 'First of June' F1 (AGM) – Early, round and mid-green.
- 'Greyhound' F1 (AGM) – Early, pointed type.
- 'Hispi' F1 (AGM) – Smooth and pointed with a solid heart.
- 'Stonehead' F1 (AGM) – Round type, mid-green. Can be cropped into autumn.

Early reds

These varieties are not for storing.
- 'Lanfgedijker Red Early' (AGM) – Good solid heads.
- 'Rodeo' F1 (AGM) – Good colour.
- 'Rondy' F1 (AGM) – Ready early autumn.
- 'Ruby Ball' F1 (AGM) – Uniform round heads.

Winter white

- 'Marathon' F1 (AGM) – Stores well but needs to be harvested before the frosts.

Savoy

- 'Alaska' F1 (AGM) – Mid-season to late. Dark green, good blistering.
- 'Clarissa' F1 (AGM) – Early. Peppery taste.
- 'Famosa' F1 (AGM) – Very early. Bright green.
- 'Midvoy' F1 (AGM) – Dark green blistered outer leaves, solid round hearts.
- 'Primavoy' F1 (AGM) – is earlier and 'Protovoy' F1 (AGM) is earlier still.
- 'Tarvoy' F1 (AGM) – Mid-season to late and 'Wivoy' F1 (AGM) is late.

Savoy hybrids

- 'Beretta' (AGM) – Dark green and blistered with mild-tasting hearts.
- 'Celtic' (AGM) – Large and leafy with solid heads.
- 'Embassy' (AGM) – Lightly blistered, bright green, sweet tasting.
- 'Renton' (AGM) – Early.

January King

- 'Flagship' F1 AGM – Pronounced purple colour. Stands well.
- 'Holly' F1 – Dark green with purplish tinge. Winters well.
- 'Marabel' F1 – Round heads, reddish, stands well.

Mini varieties

- 'Golden Cross' F1 (AGM) – Small, round, uniform, bright green summer cabbage.
- 'Gonzales' F1 (AGM) – Compact round summer cabbage with pale leaves.
- 'Pixie' (AGM) – Very early hearted cabbage for spring.

Cabbage, Chinese

Brassica rapa var. *pekinensis*
BRASSICACEAE

Chinese headed cabbage is the familiar, crisp, mild-tasting vegetable that looks like a tightly packed, pale green cos lettuce. It is a challenge to grow well in the European climate as any hiccup in the smooth running of its growth will make it bolt. It is good for baby leaves.

Types
Cylindrical, barrel-shaped and loose-headed types. Also ornamental varieties with frilly leaves. The loose-headed types are the easiest. The Japanese F1 hybrids with built-in disease and bolt resistance are the safest.

Seed to harvest
Maturity: 8–10 weeks. Baby leaf: three weeks.

Min. germination temp.
10°C (50°F).

Situation
Open and sunny, part shade in summer.

Soil
Top-quality, moist, fertile loam.

Ideal pH
6.5–7

Sowing and planting
Sow in situ. Safest time to sow headed Chinese cabbage is in July–August, to crop in September–October. Sow a few seeds of loose-leaf varieties every couple of weeks, starting in late spring using fleece or cloches for protection.

Spacing
1.3 cm (½ in) deep, 30 cm (12 in) apart.

Cultivation
Water regularly and keep soil weed free. If you are attempting headed cabbage, tie the leaves together with soft twine in late summer, to blanch them.

Harvesting
When the heads are solid and before the frosts, cut them off at the stalk. They may sprout again. Once harvested, they will stay fresh for a week or two in a cool, frost-free shed or in the fridge.

Problems
Cabbage root fly, mealy cabbage aphid, flea beetle, cabbage whitefly, club-root, brassica white blister, slugs, pigeons.

Cooking
Headed cabbage is used in stir-fries or sliced as a salad green. Loose-headed types can be used as ornamental salad leaves, depending on variety.

Varieties
- 'Early Jade Pagoda' F1 (AGM) and 'One Kilo SB' (AGM) – solid, cylinder shaped; slow to bolt.
- 'Ruffles' – loose-headed type, green with a white heart.
- 'Santo Serrated Leaved' – pretty leaves for saladini.

Cardoon

Cynara cardunculus
ASTERACEAE

Closely related to the globe artichoke, with a similar taste, cardoons grown for eating are treated as annuals. If left, they produce dramatic flowerheads attractive to wildlife. It is the stem not the flower bud that is eaten. They are a high-maintenance vegetable and quite a bother to prepare.

Seed to harvest
Maturity: 36 weeks.

Min. germination temp.
13°C (55°F).

Situation
Sunny and sheltered.

Soil
Light, free draining.

Ideal pH
7

Sowing and planting
Sow seed in gentle heat in spring. Transplant after frosts with four or five leaves or station sow outside in April.

Spacing
90cm (3ft) apart.

Cultivation
Keep well watered and fed for succulent stems. In early autumn, tie collars of cardboard, newspaper or plastic guttering around the stems, to blanch them.

Harvesting
After a month of blanching, dig up the plant. Wear gloves. Cut off the roots. Pull apart the stalks.

Problems
Aphids.

Cooking
Peel off leaves and thorns with a vegetable peeler. Cut the stalks into short lengths and soak in water with a little vinegar to prevent them from oxidizing (going brown). Cardoons are usually parboiled before cooking and being made into creamy gratins (Lyon) or savory tagines (Morocco).

Carrot

Daucus carota
UMBELLIFERAE

There is a very wide range of Britain's most popular vegetable, not only in shape, size and colour but also in cultivars bred to suit different seasons. Carrots can be grown all year and eaten at any stage of their development.

Types
Long, round or short, and yellow, white or purple as well as orange. Types to suit different seasons.

Seed to harvest
Earlies 9 weeks. Maincrop 20 weeks.

Min. germination temp.
7°C (45°F)

Situation
Earlies – Sheltered and sunny for earlies. Maincrop – Open and sunny.

Soil
Stone free. Sandy loam manured from the previous crop – new manuring can make carrots fork.

Ideal pH
6.5–7.5

Sowing and planting
Carrots are best sown in situ as they don't like to be moved. Earlies – sow earliest spring varieties (Amsterdam Forcing types) outside under cover in February or March, when the soil is warm enough. Carry on with these and the Round and Nantes varieties. Maincrop – sow between April and June. For summer eating and winter storage sow Chantenay, Berlicum and Autumn King cultivars in late May or early June. Sow in September with protection for the following spring. Paris Market carrots have small, round or square roots and are the best bet for heavier soil. All types – make drills 1.3 cm (½ in) deep. Scatter carefully as seed is fine. Sift a very thin covering of compost over the seed. Protect the seedlings from carrot fly with a low barrier or cover completely with fine netting. Sow a few seeds outdoors every two weeks from April onwards for a succession of carrots until early winter. For winter storage, sow in May or June to harvest in October.

Spacing
Sow as thinly as possible. For full-sized carrots thin to 4 cm (1½ in) for earlies and 7.5 cm (3 in) for maincrop. Rows 15 cm (6 in) apart. For smaller carrots give less space.

Cultivation
Firm the soil well after thinning and weeding. Keep carrots on the dry side for sweetness of flavour but not so dry that they will fork. Try to maintain a low but constant level of moisture. Mulching between rows helps.

Harvesting
Pull them up by hand if the soil is light, otherwise water the ground well before easing them out with a fork. Try to make minimum disturbance and damage as the smell will alert the carrot fly. If you have light, sandy loam, maincrop carrots can be left in the ground until needed. Protect them with straw before the onset of frost. Otherwise lift the crop, twist off the foliage and store in a cool, dry shed in boxes of sand.

Problems
Carrot fly.

Cooking
Carrots are widely eaten raw, or cooked in stews and soups. They can be used in sweet dishes – for carrot cake and charlottes. In India they make carrot halva to be eaten with cream.

Varieties
Earlies
'Amsterdam Forcing' – traditional, tried-and-tested, first carrot of the year.
- 'Autumn King 2' (AGM) – fine quality, cylindrical, deep orange roots; stores well; can be left in the ground without losing flavour.
- 'Bangor' F1 (AGM) – cylindrical roots and heavy yields; stores well.
- 'Danvers' – Victorian carrot for successional summer crops.
- 'Early Nantes' – old favourite for successional planting.

Maincrop
- 'Nantes 2' – an early maincrop; virtually coreless.
- 'Kingston' (AGM) – Autumn King type; a handsome carrot, long and pointed; good for showing and autumn storage.
- 'New Red Intermediate' and 'Sutton's Red Intermediate' – fine, exhibiting carrots.
- 'Resistafly', 'Sytan' (AGM) and 'Flyaway' (AGM) are repugnant to the carrot fly.
- 'Giganta' – A large Autumn King type. Good show carrots.
- 'Kingston' (AGM) – Autumn King type. Good for showing and autumn storage.
- 'New Red Intermediate' – A fine carrot for exhibiting. Stores well.

- 'Panther' F1 (AGM) – A stumpy, quick-growing maincrop. Recommended for successional plantings.
- 'Parabel' (AGM) – Sweet round roots. Early French Market type. Good flavour.
- 'Sutton's Red Intermediate' – Large. Favourite for showing.

Cauliflower

Brassica oleracea Botrytis Group
BRASSICACEAE

Cauliflowers are a challenge. They are classified by season, though some of the newer varieties can be grown at any time of year. As they need constant moisture, the spring varieties, sown in autumn or winter and ready before the full heat of summer, are the easier ones to grow. Easiest of all are the new mini-cauliflowers and the new cultivars. Summer and autumn cauliflowers are grown in one season, while over wintering types take the best part of a year.

Types
Purple, green and orange varieties amongst the summer types. Pyramid and round. A novelty is the pale green 'Floccoli', a cross between cauliflower and broccoli. Mini-cauliflowers.

Seed to harvest
Summer and autumn and mini-cauliflowers 15–16 weeks. Winter and early spring 40 weeks.

Min. germination temp.
7°C (45°F).

Situation
Sunny and sheltered.

Soil
Top-quality, moisture-retentive soil. Cauliflowers are sensitive to acidity and generally don't thrive in acid soil even when it has been limed. Acidity can cause 'whiptail' (which shows as narrowing, mottling and yellowing of the leaves) and also chlorosis (yellowing of the leaves). The curds sometimes turn brown from tipburn if the soil lacks sufficient calcium – a characteristic of acid soils. The autumn before planting, dig the soil over and tread it down well.

Ideal pH
6.5–7.5

Sowing and planting
Sow extras as cauliflower seeds can come up 'blind', without a central bud. Spring cauliflower Sow seed in winter over a couple of weeks, to hedge your bets. Use modules in the propagator set to 21°C (70°F). Harden off and transplant in early spring. Water the evening before you move them and firm them in thoroughly. Protect with cloches or fleece. Alternatively, sow seed in autumn in the seedbed or in situ. Autumn cauliflower is sown in the same way in mid- to late spring and transplanted in early summer. Winter and early spring cauliflower – sow in May in the seedbed and transplant in July to a spot with frost protection in winter. The curds are not frost hardy, so they are not worth trying unless your allotment is in a very mild, frost-free part of the country. Mini-cauliflower – sow in April in situ for July eating. Sow a few seeds every couple of weeks for a succession. Net against pests.

Spacing
Summer types 45 cm (18 in) apart, with rows 60 cm (24 in) apart. Overwintering types 60 cm (2 ft) apart both ways. Mini-cauliflower 15 cm (6 in) apart both ways.

Cultivation
Try to grow them smoothly, without any checks in growth. Keep them mulched and watered so that the level of moisture is constant. Cauliflowers develop in two stages – juvenile and mature. The juvenile stage is leaf growth. A period of cold weather triggers the mature stage, when the curds are formed. If the plants suffer any stress – lack of water or a sharp frost when the curds are forming – 'buttoning' or 'riciness' may occur in the form of small curds poking out above the leaves or growing taller than the others. Cover the curd with the leaves in summer to prevent it going yellow and in winter to protect it from harsh weather. Don't give the overwintering types too much nitrogen, as it encourages lush growth that may collapse in the cold.

Harvesting
Harvest as soon as the cauliflowers are ready, before the curds start to turn brown or separate. Don't cut off all the leaves as they will help to protect the curd. Cauliflowers can be stored for a couple of weeks if suspended by the roots and kept in a cool, frost-free place. Mini-cauliflowers should be eaten soon after harvesting.

Problems
Cabbage root fly, whitefly, caterpillars, clubroot, pigeons.

Cooking
Cauliflowers are partnered with cheese and other creamy sauces. Raw or blanched as crudités and in salads.

Varieties
Summer cauliflower
- 'Nautilus' F1 (AGM) – vigorous.
- 'Perfection' F1 (AGM) – Very early. Large curds.
- 'Plana' F1 (AGM) – midseason, uniform and vigorous.
- 'White Rock' F1 (AGM) – late; white, well-protected curds.

Autumn cauliflower
- 'Alverdo' F1 (AGM) and Esmeraldo' F1 (AGM) – green curds.
- 'Aviso' F1 (AGM) – Early. Short cropping

season but first-class, smooth white curds.

- 'Minaret' F1 (AGM) – pyramid shape; green curd.
- 'Marmalade' F1 (AGM) – orange curds; very early.
- 'Violet Queen' F1 (AGM) and 'Violetta Italia' F1 (AGM) – early purple to violet curds.
- 'Violetta Italia' F1 (AGM) – Very early with violet curds.

Winter and spring cauliflowers
- 'Christingle' (AGM), 'Galleon' (AGM), 'Jerome' F1 (AGM) – white curds; high quality.
- 'Galleon' (AGM) – Early mid-season. Medium to large curds. Good leaf protection.

Mini-cauliflower
- 'Red Lion' F1 (AGM) – purple heads in summer.

Celeriac
Apium graveolens var. *rapaceum*
APIACEAE

Celeriac is grown for its bulbous stem. A relative of celery but hardier and less temperamental. If protected, it can stay in the ground right through winter. It is slower growing than celery, and you may not achieve the size you find in the shops.

Types
Some are easier to peel.
Seed to harvest
26 weeks.
Min. germination temp.
10°C (50° F).
Situation
Open, damp. Copes with part shade.
Soil
Moist soil, high in organic matter.

Ideal pH
7
Sowing and planting
Start seed off in a propagator at 18°C (64°F) in midspring or outside under glass in late spring. Harden off before planting outside after the last frosts. If the temperature drops, delay by clipping off the tops. Plant so the crown is just above soil level.
Spacing
30 cm (12 in) apart.
Cultivation
Keep mulched and watered. Feed liquid seaweed every fortnight. In midsummer, remove sideshoots and growing buds, leaving just one. Snip off the outer leaves so the sun can get to the crown and ripen it.
Harvesting
Usually ready by autumn. In mild areas, celeriac can be left in the ground covered with cloches or straw through winter and be harvested as needed. Otherwise, dig up and store in damp sand in a cool shed. Remove most of the leaves but don't take out the central tuft as the root will waste away trying to produce more leaves.
Problems
Slugs, celery crown rot, celery leaf miner, carrot root fly, celery fly, celery leaf spot, calcium deficiency.
Cooking
For salads, use blanched cut into julienne strips and mixed with mayonnaise. Sautéed or boiled and mashed like potato. The leaves as flavouring in stews and soups.
Varieties
- 'Diamant' (AGM) – medium-sized bulbs with clean, white skin.
- 'Ibis' (AGM) – small, round balls.
- 'Kojak' (AGM) – smooth, flattened shape.
- 'Marble Ball' – good storer.
- 'Monarch' (AGM) – popular; succulent, firm, white flesh and smooth skins.

- 'Prinz' (AGM) – early variety with big bulbs; slow to bolt.

Celery
Apium graveolens var. *dulce*
APIACEAE

Growing celery from seed represents a challenge. If its growth is not smooth, celery is inclined to bolt.

Types
Self-blanching or summer celery does not need earthing up but is not frost hardy. Pale yellow, pink flushed, as well as green. Trench celery is the traditional British celery and has the best flavour. It can take a mild frost, and some varieties can stand out in winter. The pink- and red-stemmed varieties are hardier than the green. Large and small types.
Seed to harvest
11–16 weeks.
Min. germination temp.
10°C (50° F).
Situation
Open.
Soil
Rich and damp.
Ideal pH
7
Sowing and planting
Self-blanching – sow treated seed in modules in midspring in a propagator set to 16°C (61°F). Celery seed is fine, so mix it with sand or vermiculite to make it more manageable. It germinates in the light. Scatter seed thinly on dampened compost. When big enough to handle, thin to one per module. Transfer into boxes with glass on top, at 13–16°C (55–61°F). When they have five or six true leaves in early summer, seedlings can be hardened off and

transplanted outside in May or June. If it's still cold when they are ready to go out, trim the young plants down to hold them back. Plant them with the base, or crown, at soil level. Plant the closely in a square block so they shade each other, to help blanching. Cover with fleece or cloches for a few weeks and protect against slugs. Put collars (strips of cardboard or newspaper, covered in black plastic and tied with string) around the outer ones of the square. Trench celery – sow in the same way and at the same time as the self-blanching types. The winter before, dig a trench about 30 cm (12 in) deep and wide and partially fill it with well-rotted manure or compost. The remaining soil is left on the side for earthing up. Let them grow about 30 cm (12 in) high, then tie the tops loosely together with soft string and begin to earth up. Water well before adding soil at the rate of 7.5 cm (3 in) every three weeks. Take care to avoid getting soil into the hearts, as it could cause them to rot, and don't pack it around the plants. The easier method is to grow them on the flat with collars. When the plants are about 30 cm (12 in) high, place loose collars of cardboard or brown paper around them, tied with string. Cover this with polythene, to prevent the paper disintegrating in the rain, or else use roofing felt or small sections of plastic pipe. Always leave the top third of the plant out in the open. Lift the covers from time to time, to check for slugs.

Spacing
Self-blanching 20 cm (8 in) apart. Trench celery 30 cm (12 in) apart.

Cultivation
Constantly supply water and give a weekly liquid feed from early summer until the frosts. Mulch with straw in winter.

Harvesting
Self-blanching Test for readiness by snapping off an inner stalk between the end of July and September. Lift before the stems become stringy and tough. Water well first. Clear the crops before the frosts. Trench celery is ready in autumn and early winter. If you have grown it using the trench method, carefully remove the soil that you used for earthing up before lifting the plant with a spade. Wash off and remove unnecessary leaves before storing upright in boxes with dampened sand at the roots. Store in a cool, frost-free shed.

Problems
Celery leaf miner, carrot root fly, celery fly, celery leaf spot, slugs and snails, and calcium deficiency.

Cooking
With cheese, Waldorf salad, stewed or braised as a side vegetable. Soup.

Varieties
Self-blanching celery
• 'Celebrity' (AGM) – self-blanching; early, nutty and crisp; bolt resistance.
• 'Ivory Tower' (AGM) – nearly stringless. 'Lathom Self Blanching' (AGM) – vigorous early variety popular.
• 'Pink Champagne' – ornamental, pink variety.
• 'Tango' (AGM) and 'Victoria' F1 (AGM) – reliable, green types with good flavour.

Trench celery
• 'Giant Pink – Mammouth Pink' (AGM) – green with a pink tinge; harvest in early winter.
• 'Giant Red' – known for its hardiness, as is 'Solid Pink', introduced in 1894.

Chard
(Swiss chard, ruby chard, seakale beet)
Beta vulgaris Cicla Group
CHENOPODIACEAE

Chards are the glamorous members of the beet family. They produce over a long period, are easy to grow and generally trouble free.

Types
Leaves smooth or crinkly. White, crimson, yellow or purplish stems and green, reddish or rainbow-coloured leaves.

Seed to harvest
8–12 weeks.

Min. germination temp.
8°C (47°F).

Situation
Open and sunny. Can take seaside conditions – winds.

Soil
Fertile.

Ideal pH
7

Sowing and planting
Sow in March or April outside under cover or indoors. Seed is multigermed and needs to be thinned. For a winter crop, sow in an unheated polytunnel or greenhouse in August.

Spacing
30 cm (12 in).

Cultivation
Water in dry spells. If the leaves coarsen, rejuvenate the plant by cutting it down almost to soil level.

Harvesting
Pick off outer leaves as required.

Problems
Leaf beet miner.

Cooking

Cook as spinach. Provençal rice dishes, soups and tarts with nuts and fruits, lemon and cheese. Midribs are cooked separately and eaten with a vinaigrette dressing.

Varieties

- 'Bright Lights' (AGM) – the rainbow chard.
- 'Bright Yellow' (AGM) – yellow stems with a puckered, green leaf.
- 'Charlotte' (AGM) – bright red.
- 'Fordhook Giant' (AGM) – white ribs and green leaves.
- 'Lucullus' (AGM) – good flavour.
- 'Rhubarb Chard' (AGM) – scarlet ribs; purple, puckered leaves.

Chicory

Cichorium intybus
ASTERACEAE

The chicories provide good, bitter leaves to perk up cool-weather salads. The long-rooted types have been used roasted and ground as a coffee substitute since the Napoleonic wars.

Types

Witloof or Belgian chicory – 'white' chicory grown and blanched for winter eating. Radiccio – red chicory for autumn.

Sugarloaf – non-forcing types. The outer leaves are discarded and the heart, which is naturally blanched and mild tasting, is good to eat.

Seed to harvest

Seedling crop: four weeks.

Min. germination temp.

10°C (50°F).

Situation

Sunny or part shade.

Soil

Fertile and free-draining soil.

Ideal pH

6–7.5

Sowing and planting

Witloof – sow sparingly outside in May or June about 1.3 cm (½ in) deep. Water until the seeds come up, then leave them fairly dry, to encourage root growth. Radiccio – best sown in midsummer for autumn eating. Broadcast in situ. For a summer crop, start off in modules under cover. Use some for seedlings and others to hearten up. Sugarloaf – sow in midspring indoors, or outside through summer. For a mature crop, sow outside in midsummer for autumn eating. Sow a few seeds every two weeks for a seedling crop.

Spacing

Witloof and sugarloaf – thin to 20 cm (8 in) apart. Radiccio – thin to 30 cm (12 in) apart.

Cultivation

All types – keep weed free and water in dry weather. Witloof – in mild areas, blanch the plants outside. Cut leaves down to 5 cm (2 in). Cover the whole plant with soil, straw or leaf-mould and put a bucket on top. Or dig up in late autumn or early winter, cut the leaves off as before and trim the roots to 30 cm (12 in). Store them in moist sand in a frost-free shed. Plant in large pots of moist soil with the crowns just showing as you want them. Keep in the dark at a minimum of 10°C (50°F). The chicons will

grow within a month. Radiccio – can be grown on through winter in a polytunnel. Sugarloaf – if covered with cloches or fleece in autumn, they will continue to grow for some time. You can extend the season further by lifting them, and growing them on in pots indoors. They will keep in the ground for several weeks.

Harvesting

Witloof – break off carefully and more will form. Sugarloaf and radiccio Keep picking young, tender leaves for salads. Headed chicory is usually harvested by autumn. Leave the stump in the ground to resprout. Under cloches, the plants can be kept on as loose leaf through winter.

Problems

Slugs, but generally trouble free.

Cooking

Raw in salads or braised as a side vegetable.

Varieties

Witloof

- 'Zuckerhut – Witloof de Brussels' (AGM) – great traditional variety.

Radiccio

- 'Leonardo' (AGM) – hearty, red variety.
- 'Palla Rossa' (AGM) – dark red with white veins.

Sugarloaf

- 'Pan di Zucchero' (AGM) – dark leaves but blanches well.
- 'Sugarloaf' – cold resistant; good for winter under cloches.

Corn salad

(Lamb's lettuce, Mâche)

Valerianella locusta, Valerianella eriocarpa

VALERIANACEAE

Gourmet salad leaf. Grows prolifically. Happy in part shade and self-sows freely, if allowed. If kept covered, corn salad will carry on through winter.

Types

Compact French varieties and longer-leaved types.

Seed to harvest

6–12 weeks.

Min. germination temp.

8°C (47°F).

Situation

Sun or part shade.

Soil

Deep, fertile and free draining.

Ideal pH

7

Sowing and planting

Sowings before midsummer are likely to bolt. Sow a few seeds 1.3 cm (½ in) deep every couple of weeks after that for non-stop production. Give winter crops some cover.

Spacing

Thin to 15cm (6in).

Cultivation

Keep weed free and well watered in dry spells.

Harvesting

Pick as you want seedling crops.

Problems

Slugs and snails, but generally trouble free.

Cooking

Salads.

Varieties

• 'Cavallo' (AGM) and 'Verte de Cambrai' are traditional, small-leaved, neat, French types.

• 'Vit' – modern variety with dark green leaves vigorous; good for winter production.

Courgette and summer squash

(Zucchini)

Cucurbita pepo

CUCURBITACEAE

One or two plants will give you a plentiful supply. They are vigorous, bushy, trailing annuals, easy to grow and prolific. You need to keep picking courgettes as they will turn into marrows as soon as you turn your back.

Types

Summer squash: scallop, patty pan or 'custard', crookneck.

Seed to harvest

Ten weeks or more.

Ideal germination temp. 18°C (64°F).

Situation

Sun and shelter.

Soil

Warm and rich on the acid side. Put in plenty of organic matter or grow them on the compost heap.

Ideal pH

6–6.5

Sowing and planting

Soak the seeds overnight. Sow them about 2.5 cm (1 in) deep on their sides in individual pots indoors in late April or early May. Harden off carefully after all danger of frost and plant outside under a cold frame. Alternatively, sow outside in late May on prewarmed soil under cloches.

Spacing

Bush varieties 60 x 90 cm (2 x 3 ft). Trailers 1.2 x 1.8 m (4 x 6 ft).

Cultivation

Male and female flowers form on the same plant. So remove any covers when the plants are in flower so that the insects can pollinate them. To get a good enough supply of water down to the roots, which is essential until they establish, sink a piece of open-ended pipe or sawn-off plastic bottle into the ground. Squashes can be trained up a strong trellis or grown into a coil to save space. If you are letting them sprawl freely, put a stick near the middle to indicate where to water. Feed at least once a fortnight with liquid feed. Growing plants through black polythene will give them extra warmth and keep the fruits of the sprawling types clean. They rot quickly if in touch with the soil.

Harvesting

Courgette – cut the fruits off with a sharp knife when they are young and succulent, to encourage more to develop. Summer squash are ready when they are 7.5–10 cm (3–4 in) in diameter. This can be within four days of the flowers appearing.

Problems

Powdery mildew, cucumber mosaic virus, slugs and snails. In the cold frame, watch for red spider mite and whitefly.

Cooking

The whole plant is edible including the flowers and seeds. Summer squash can be steamed, roasted or sautéed. Courgettes are stuffed with rice, cous cous or meat fillings or made into courgette fritters with yoghurt (Middle East). They can be grilled or griddled on an open fire in slices. The flowers are an Italian delicacy, deep fried in batter.

Cucumber and gherkin

Cucumis sativus
CUCURBITACEAE

Cucumbers are tender. They come as swish greenhouse types and the ridged ones for outdoors. The indoor ones are more difficult to grow well. The introduction of Japanese and burpless cucumbers has made it possible to grow hothouse types out in the open. Gherkins are small cucumbers grown for pickling, though they can be eaten fresh.

Types
Climbing and bush types. Round, short and long. White- and yellow-skinned. Various greens.

Seed to harvest
12 weeks.

Min. germination temp.
20°C (68°F).

Situation
Sheltered and sunny position.

Soil
Rich with plenty of well-rotted manure or compost incorporated. A couple of weeks before the plants are ready to go out, dig a trench, half fill it with well-rotted manure or compost and pile back the soil on top to make a ridge (hence ridge cucumbers).

Ideal pH
6–7

Sowing and planting
Sow outdoor types indoors in biodegradable modules (two seeds per module) in a propagator in late spring, about 2.5 cm (1 in) deep. Time this to a month before the last frosts. Thin to the strongest. Keep the seedlings warm, a minimum 16°C (61°F) at night. Don't overwater at this stage as the seedlings are prone to damping off. Harden off carefully when they have about three leaves, before planting out under cloches. Plant a little less deeply than before, to avoid neck rot. Another option is to sow straight outside in June, or when the soil temperature is at least 20°C (68°F).

Spacing
Depending on cultivar.

Cultivation
Nip out the growing tip when it reaches the top of the support. Keep well watered, and mulched. When the plants are in flower, remove any covers so the insects can pollinate them. Give liquid feeds, particularly when the fruits form. Climbing types can be grown on the ground with straw under the fruits, or trained up a support. This is more practical as it has the double effect of keeping the fruits clean and protecting them (to some extent) from slugs.

Harvesting
Cut the fruits off with a sharp knife when ripe but before they start to yellow.

Problems
Cucumber mosaic virus, slugs, aphids, red spider mite in hot weather, powdery mildew, neck rot.

Cooking
Salad vegetable. Combined with yoghurt and mint for Indian raita and Turkish soup cacik.

Varieties
Outdoor cucumber
- 'Bush Champion' F1 (AGM) – compact; high yields resistant to cucumber mosaic virus.
- 'Burpless Tasty Green' F1 – mildew resistant; good cropper; possibly the best of the new outdoor varieties for glasshouse-quality fruits.
- 'Crystal Lemon' – lemon-shaped with a tangy taste; pickling or eating.
- 'Marketmore' (AGM) – ridge type, high yielding; resistant to cucumber mosaic

Varieties
Courgette
- 'Bambino' F1 (AGM) – bush type, with small fruits; popular; prolific.
- 'Defender' F1 (AGM) – lightly flecked; resistant to cucumber mosaic virus.
- 'Early Gem' F1 (AGM) – Dark green slim fruits. Prolific.
- 'El Greco' F1 (AGM) – Bush type with mid-green fruits.
- 'Jemmer' F1 (AGM) – yellow.
- 'Rondo di Nice' – An Italian round courgette.

Summer squash
- 'Early Golden Crookneck' – prolific fruiter; buttery flavour.
- 'Patty Pan' – pretty flying saucers in green or yellow with scalloped edges.
- 'Sunburst' – golden fruits in the same shape as 'Patty Pan'; harvests over many weeks.
- 'Vegetable Spaghetti' – Pale yellow. When cooked the flesh inside looks like spaghetti.

virus, powdery and downy mildew; good for cooler climates.

Gherkins

- 'Fortos' (AGM) – uniform fruits.
- 'Gherkin' – fast growing; masses of small, prickly fruits. 'Vert Petit de Paris' – prolific.

Endive

Cichorium endivia
ASTERACEAE

Endives are easy to grow and more tolerant of both heat and cold than lettuce. They can be grown to maturity or used as a seedling crop, making a lively addition to the salad bowl, and are particularly useful in winter.

Types

Frisée – frilly-leaved and the best for summer and autumn. They can survive a light frost. Batavian, endive or escarole are broad leaved and can go well into winter, given cloche protection.

Seed to harvest

Maturity: 12 weeks.

Min. germination temp.

20°C (68°F).

Situation

Open. A little shade in the heat of summer. Shelter in winter.

Soil

Light, free draining, Manured the year before.

Ideal pH

6–7

Sowing and planting

Sow outside or indoors. Sow thinly 1.3cm (1/2in) deep. Sow from June to July for autumn crops, and start hardier types in August for winter crops. Sow successively for seedling crops.

Spacing

30cm (1ft).

Cultivation

Keep weed free. Water in dry weather and mulch. To remove bitterness, blanch for 2–3 weeks before harvesting. Tie the leaves together with soft string or raffia, or cover with a bucket. To blanch just the centre, use an old plate. Make sure the leaves are completely dry and slug free first.

Harvesting

Pick individual leaves or cut the head off and leave the plant to resprout.

Problems

Slugs, lettuce root aphid, caterpillars, tip burn.

Cooking

Salads. Blanched and eaten hot.

Varieties

Batavian

- 'En Cornet de Bordeaux' – a hardy old French variety for saladini through winter.

Frisée

- 'Grosse Pancalieri' – self-blanching variety; curly with rosy midribs.
- 'Jeti' (AGM) – bright green plants with a curly leaf.

Florence fennel

Foeniculum vulgare var. dulce
APIACEAE

Florence fennel, which tastes of aniseed and has elegant, feathery foliage, is not the easiest vegetable to grow. Like its relation celery, it is prone to bolting.

Types

Some speedy growers with bolt resistance.

Seed to harvest

10–15 weeks.

Min. germination temp.

15°C (59°F).

Situation

Sunny.

Soil

Light, well drained, rich in organic matter, preferably, sandy.

Ideal pH

7

Sowing and planting

Buy fast-growing, bolt-resistant seed. To avoid transplanting shock, sow outside in May, when the soil is at least 10°C (50°F). Sow more in late summer for an autumn crop. Use fleece at each end of the season.

Spacing

30cm (12in) apart.

Cultivation

Water well and mulch. When the bulbs start to form, either earth up to half way up the bulb or tie cardboard collars around them to blanch the stems. Cover with fleece as the nights draw in.

Harvesting

Cut the bulbs off, leaving the roots in the ground, to throw out a few shoots. Even if the bulbs don't swell, you can eat the rest of the plant.

Problems

Bolting, slugs.

Cooking

Fennel is a classic, aniseed-tasting accompaniment to fish or chicken, parboiled and roasted with garlic or cooked with tomatoes. The heart of it can be eaten raw like celery.

Varieties

- 'Carmo' F1 (AGM) and 'Heracles' (AGM) – fine quality, fast maturing.
- 'Dover' (AGM) – early.
- 'Romanesco' – resistant to bolting; hefty, round bulbs up to 1kg (2lb)] in weight.
- 'Zefo Fino' (AGM) – good bolt-resistance; medium-sized, well-filled, white bulbs; ornamental.

French beans

(Flageolet, haricot beans)
Phaseolus vulgaris
PAPILIONACEAE

French beans are known in China as sandomame, or the 'three times bean', as they mature from French beans into flageolet beans and finally into haricot beans for drying and storing over winter. French beans are easy to grow, prolific and delicious.

Types

Climbing varieties will cling and can be grown up supports in the same way as runner beans. The dwarf types make low bushes, which have the advantage of fitting under cloches when you need to protect them from the cold. Pods come speckled, stripy, yellow, violet or green, flat or pencil-shaped. The flowers are purple, lilac or white. Modern cultivars are usually stringless. Some types are designed for drying.

Seed to harvest:

8–13 weeks. Haricot 17 weeks.

Min. germination temp.

13°C (55°F).

Situation

Sunny and sheltered.

Soil

Light and fertile.

Ideal pH

7.

Sowing and planting

For earliest beans start in April indoors. Harden off after the last frosts. For sowing outside, prepare the soil by covering it with polythene for a couple of weeks, before sowing in late spring. Keep undercloche protection until June. French beans are usually sown in staggered, double rows for extra warmth. Use bush types for the last sowings so they can be kept warm with cloches at the end of summer.

Spacing

15 cm (6 in) early crops. 23 cm (9 in) maincrops. 60 cm (24 in) between rows.

Cultivation

Make parallel drills 5 cm (2 in) deep and station sow two seeds, scar downwards. Sow a few extras as the germination rate of French beans is only 75 per cent. For a continuous supply, sow a few seeds every two or three weeks until July. Climbing French beans are self-twining and will scramble up twiggy peasticks, netting, a pole or even up sweetcorn. The bush types are earthed up to the first set of leaves to give them extra support. Protect against slugs, birds and particularly mice. Keep the plants moist and well mulched. Water well when in flower.

Harvesting

French beans will continue to produce if you keep gathering the beans when young. They are ready when they snap off. Flageolet beans have to be caught at the intermediate stage, when the seeds are quite small and still bright green. Haricot beans – pick each pod as it ripens. If the weather turns cold, pull out the entire plant at the end of the season and hang it out to dry in an airy place. Shell haricots when the skins are dry and crackly. Dry the beans further for a couple of days in a sunny room or in the airing cupboard and store in airtight jars.

Problems

Slugs, aphids, anthracnose, halo blight, bean seed fly, red spider mite, bean mosaic virus.

Cooking

French beans – young French beans are quickly cooked and served hot or cold in their entirety. As they mature the bean seeds are stewed in the Greek way with onions and tomatoes.

Flageolet beans – are shelled, cooked and eaten like peas.

Haricot beans – these dried beans are soaked overnight and simmered slowly until tender for stews, soups and bean salads.

Varieties

Climbers

- 'Algarve' (AGM) – stringless, slicing beans up to 25cm (10in) long.
- 'Eva' (AGM) and 'Diamont' (AGM) – early varieties with long, round pods and black seeds; resistant to bean mosaic virus.
- 'Hunter' (AGM) – strong-growing, heavy cropper with straight, stringless pods, some 23 cm (9 in) in length; white seeds; popular for exhibition.
- 'Kingston Gold' (AGM) – yellow.

Bush beans

- 'Cantare' (AGM) early, high-yielding, good flavour; resistant to bean mosaic virus.
- 'Cropper Tepee' (AGM) – pencil-shaped pods.
- 'Purple Tepee' – purple version.
- 'Mont d'Or' – yellow. 'Purple Queen' – purple.

- 'The Prince' (AGM) – masses of slender, flat pods; good for exhibition.

Haricot beans

- 'Barlotta Lingua di Fuocco' – the Italian 'Fire tongue' bean has bright green, flat pods with red markings (which disappear when cooked).
- 'Brown Dutch' – brown.
- 'Horsehead' – dark red.

Mini-haricot beans

- 'Barlotto Lingua di Fuocco Nana' – bright green, flat pods with red markings.

For drying

- 'Barlotta Lingua di Fuocco' – The Italian 'Fire tongue' bean has bright green, flat pods with red markings (which disappear when cooked). A classic.
- 'Brown Dutch' – Brown beans.
'Horsehead' – Dark red beans.

Mini varieties

- 'Aroza' – Resistant to mosaic virus.
- 'Purple Queen' – Purple pods.
- 'Sprite' (AGM) – Stringless Continental variety with dark green round pods. Heavy yields.

Disease-resistant

- 'Copper Tepee' – Resistant to anthracnose.
- 'Daisy' – Resistant to common bean mosaic virus.
- 'Forum' – Resistant to halo blight, anthracnose and common bean mosaic virus.

Garlic

Allium sativum
ALLIACEAE

Given sunshine, garlic is easy to grow. Start off with bulbs from a nursery or seed merchant (not a greengrocer), as they will be certified free of disease and should be suited to a UK climate. After that you can grow from your own stock.

Types

'Soft necked', the non-flowering type, is the most commonly grown. 'Hard-necked' garlic also produces good bulbs, especially if the flowering stem is cut back by half a couple of weeks before flowering. Bulbs come in pink, purple and white, and in various strengths of flavour. Some have a short dormancy but generally the best garlics are the slow types, which grow over winter. Elephant garlic (*Allium ampeloprasum*) is rather like a leek that produces a large, mild-tasting garlic bulb. Clove to harvest 16–36 weeks. Most bulbs need around two months at 0–10°C (32–50°F).

Situation

Sheltered, sunny spot. Waterlogging can be fatal.

Soil

Light and sandy.

Ideal pH

6–7.5

Planting

In the UK, garlic is planted in autumn in warmer areas or in late winter in colder ones. Choose plump, healthy-looking cloves. Split cloves up just before planting and discard weaklings. Plant with the basal plate (flat end) facing down, 7.5–10 cm (3–4 in) deep, using a dibber.

Spacing

30 cm (12 in) apart.

Cultivation

Keep weeded. Water in dry spells.

Harvesting

Dig up when the leaves go yellow but before they dry out too much. Dry outside in an airy shed for a week or so. Keep a few healthy bulbs back for replanting. Elephant garlic is harvested just before the flowers open.

Problems

Onion white rot, leek rust.

Cooking

Garlic is one of the most essential flavourings across all cultures.

Varieties

Soft-necked

- 'Cristo' – large bulbs with up to 15 cloves.
- 'Early Wight' – adapted to the British climate on the Isle of Wight; an early purple variety.
- 'Elephant' – giant, sweet-flavoured bulbs.
- 'Thermidrome' – selected for the UK climate.
- 'White Pearl' – strong resistance to virus, white rot and eelworm.

Hard-necked

- 'German White' – popular.
- 'Music' – giant bulbs, very hardy.

Good King Henry

Chenopodium bonus-henricus
CHENOPODIACEAE

Good King Henry is an old-fashioned perennial from the beetroot family. You won't find it in the shops as it wilts quickly after picking. It is an undemanding plant growing to 90 cm (3 ft) tall and is useful for salads early in the year.

Seed to harvest

Two years, then harvest every year.

Min. germination temp.

7°C (45°F).

Situation

Partial shade in summer.

Soil

Well drained and fertile.

Ideal pH

7

Sowing and planting
Sow seed in situ in spring 1.3 cm (½ in) deep. Or grow under cover without heat for earliest crops. Once you have established plants, divide in spring.

Spacing
Thin to 20 cm (8 in).

Cultivation
Water when dry.

Harvesting
The spring after sowing, snip off the flowering spikes and later in the year pick the outer leaves as you want them. Split the plants every third year.

Problems
Unlikely.

Cooking
Leaves are cooked like spinach and the flowering shoots like asparagus.

Hamburg parsley
Petroselinum crispum var. *tubersosum*
APIACEAE

Two vegetables in one, root and shoot. Hamburg parsley is widely grown in eastern Europe and is gaining popularity in the UK. Slow growing and hardy.

Types
Little choice.

Seed to harvest
30 weeks.

Min. germination temp.
7°C (45°F).

Situation
Open and sunny but will tolerate a little shade.

Soil
Sandy loam, stone free.

Ideal pH
7

Sowing and planting
Work the soil to a fine tilth and warm it in early spring. Sow thinly in rows 1.3 cm (½ in) deep or station sow three seeds at intervals, thinning to the strongest when they are 5 cm (2 in) high. Germination is slow, up to six weeks. Mark each end of the row with a radish seed. Sow in May or June for crops the following spring.

Spacing
25 cm (10 in) apart.

Cultivation
Keep well watered. Hoe carefully when young, to avoid damage. If leaving over winter, protect with straw or mulch.

Harvesting
Dig out in autumn or leave all winter to harvest fresh as wanted. The roots can be stored in a dry shed in sand, though they will gradually lose quality.

Problems
Erratic, slow germination. Parsnip canker.

Cooking
Winter stews, casseroles or soups. Roasted, boiled or mashed like parsnips. Use the tops like parsley.

Kale
Brassica oleracea Acephala Group
BRASSICACEAE

Kales are hardy winter greens and useful at the tail end of winter. They can also be grown for autumn. They are easy and fun. Some of the ornamental varieties are striking and full of personality.

Types
Four basic types: Siberian kales; collards (popular in the southern states of America); Scotch kale (or borecole); and ornamental. The ornamental kales have real character. 'Chou Palmier' (the palm tree cabbage) looks like a cartoon of a palm tree. Leaves come serrated, frilly, crumpled and smooth and white, pink, or deep purple and blue. There are types like 'Coral Queen' with its handsome, serrated, green leaves and coral-coloured veins and 'Cavalo Nero', with near-black tongues of blistered leaves. Heights vary from 30 cm (1 ft) to 1 m (3 ft). New cultivars have been bred for sweetness.

Seed to harvest
3–7 months to maturity. Can be harvested over many more weeks or eaten young.

Min. germination temp.
7°C (45°F).

Situation
Sunny, though kale can tolerate some shade and wind.

Soil
Fertile and well drained. Tolerant of poor soil.

Ideal pH
6.5–7.5

Sowing and planting
For a summer crop, sow in February in modules under cover. For a winter crop, station sow in threes outside in the seedbed in May and thin to the strongest. Use collars and net when transplanting.

Spacing
Small varieties 30–45 cm (12–18 in). Large varieties 45–60 cm (18–24 in).

Cultivation
Keep watered until established. Don't overwater or overfeed as you come to the end of summer, to avoid a late flush of growth, which could get cut back by the frosts. Earth up the taller types in autumn, to avoid windrock. Feed in early spring, to encourage sideshoots to grow.

Harvesting
Constantly cut off young leaves so that the plant doesn't have a chance to coarsen.

Problems
Cabbage whitefly, club-root, cabbage root fly, mealy cabbage aphid, birds.

Cooking
Use as greens. The flavour is said to improve after a frost.

Varieties
- 'Afro' (AGM) – Mid-green, very curly leaves. Compact. Stands well in winter.
- 'Jersey Kale' – The walking stick kale.
- 'Ragged Jack' – Pink in the leaves and mid ribs.
- 'Reflex' F1 (AGM) – Curly blue-green leaves. Sweet tasting.

Collards
- 'Florida' – quick to mature.
- 'Georgia' – a popular variety.

Scotch kale
- 'Dwarf Blue Curled Scotch' – manageable size, good as a salad leaf when young.
- 'Redbor' – fabulous colour, sweet flavour.

Siberian
- 'Ragged Jack' – pink in leaves and midribs.
- 'Red Russian' (AGM) – frilly, green-red leaves.
- 'True Siberian' – lives up to its name; blue-tinted, frilly leaves.

Kale, Chinese.
See Broccoli, Chinese.

Kohlrabi
Brassica oleracea Gongylodes Group
BRASSICACEAE

Kohlrabi translates as the cabbage-turnip, accurately describing the way it tastes, though it is crisp like a water chestnut. A fast grower, it produces swollen stems that sit just above the ground and look like little sputniks. Popular in continental Europe, it is catching on in the UK at last – with good reason. Apart from its amusing appearance, it has a spreading root system that helps it to cope well with dry spells.

Another bonus is that it rarely falls prey to cabbage diseases.

Types
Pale green, white or purple skin. The purple types are slower but hardier and are best for autumn eating. Mini varieties.

Seed to harvest
White and green 8–12 weeks. Purple 12–16 weeks.

Min. germination temp.
10°C (50°F).

Situation
Sunny and open.

Soil
Firm and ideally manured the autumn before. Limed where necessary.

Ideal pH
6–7

Sowing and planting
Under cloches from February onwards in mild areas, though safer to wait, to avoid bolting. Sow a few seeds outside every couple of weeks from spring onwards, starting with the white varieties. Station sow in threes, 2 cm (¾ in) deep. For winter crops, sow the hardier purple varieties until September.

Spacing

23 cm (9 in) apart. Space rows 30 cm (12 in) apart. Mini-kohlrabi Thin to 2.5 cm (1 in) apart.

Cultivation

Keep weeded and well watered in dry spells.

Harvesting

Dig up when each stem is no bigger than a tennis ball. Cut off the roots and trim back the leaves. In mild areas, kohlrabi can be left in the ground in early winter. Eat shortly after harvesting. Mini-kohlrabi Harvest when the size of a ping-pong ball.

Problems

Cabbage root fly, flea beetle, mealy cabbage aphids, club-root, although generally trouble free.

Cooking

Grated into salads when young. Can be treated like a potato – mashed, steamed, sautéed or made into chips.

Varieties

- 'Azur Star' – striking, blue-purple variety.
- 'Kongo' F1 (AGM)- large, green, fast-growing variety of exceptional quality; sweet, high yielding.
- 'Quickstar' F1 (AGM) – early, fast-growing, green type.
- 'Purple Danube' (AGM) – purple, sweet-tasting.
- 'White Danube' – white.
- 'White Vienna' and 'Purple Vienna' – traditional varieties.

Komatsuna

See Mustard spinach

Leek

Allium porrum
ALLIACEAE

Leeks are five-star allotment plants. Robust and easy to grow, they can stay in the ground to be harvested over many weeks in winter.

Types

Earlies are for harvesting in late summer. They are slimmer and less hardy than maincrop leeks for winter eating or the lates, which are ready in spring. Slim or stout types. Blue varieties.

Seed to harvest

16–20 weeks.

Min. germination temp.

7°C (45°F).

Situation

Open.

Soil

Fertile, well drained, light. Manured the previous autumn.

Ideal pH

7 or above. Lime if necessary.

Sowing and planting

Leeks are usually started off in modules so that they can be planted more deeply (to blanch the stems) than if sown in situ. Earlies Sow seed in a propagator set to 12°C (54°F) in late winter. Grow on until the young leeks are 20 cm (8 in) tall before hardening them off. Make holes, 15 cm

(6 in) deep, with a dibber where the leeks are to grow and drop the leeks in. Don't trim the roots. Water them in gently but don't backfill the hole. Maincrop Sow in spring in modules when the temperature is at least 7°C (45°F). Warm the soil if necessary beforehand, with polythene. Cover with cloches in cold weather. Lates These follow on from the maincrops. Sow a couple of weeks later.

Spacing

15 cm (6 in) apart. Increase the spacing for big leeks and maincrops.

Cultivation

The traditional way to keep the stems white was to earth them up. It is easier to put collars – small sections of plastic pipe or tubes of roofing felt, cardboard or newspaper – around the necks. Keep weeded and watered until established.

Harvesting

Dig up as you want them from late summer.

Problems

Leek moth, leek rust.

Cooking

The staple ingredient of many classic soups such as vichyssoise, soupe à la bonne femme and cock-a-leekie. Leeks go wonderfully with cheese sauce. Young

leeks can be eaten cold in the Greek style, with an olive-oil dressing.

Varieties

Earlies

- 'Carlton' F1 (AGM) – slow to bolt.
- 'Jolant' (AGM) – long cropping for an early type.
- 'King Richard' (AGM) – abundant cropper, mild taste; bolt resistant.

Maincrop

- 'Autumn Mammoth – Cobra' (AGM) – midseason to late; bolt resistant.
- 'Bleu de Solaise' – French variety; blue leaves and long cropping season.
- 'King Richard' – widely recommended for mini-leeks.
- 'Mammouth Blanche' (AGM) – high yields of big leeks; often used for showing.
- 'Swiss Giant – Jolant' (AGM) – December cropping. Good yields. Long, solid shafts. Few bolters or 'bulbers'.
- 'Toledo' (AGM) – Early winter to late spring. Uniform and smooth.
- 'Upton' F1 (AGM) – Has good rust resistance.

Lates

- 'Toledo' F1, 'Bandit' F1 and 'Atlanta' F1 – quality leeks through to March.

Lettuce

Lactuca sativa
ASTERACEAE

There is a wide array of lettuce available in the shops. The ones that store least well are the most expensive but also the easiest to grow. These are the loose-leaf types and the mixed batches of baby leaves. The hearting lettuces ('Iceberg' and the butterheads) are little more tricky.

Types

Butterhead, crisphead, Romaine (or Cos),

and loose-leaf. Bolt and disease resistance. Green, red and bronze. Many shapes.

Seed to harvest

Loose-leaf: four weeks. Over winter: 14 weeks.

Min. germination temp.

5°C (41°F). Over 25°C (77°F) the seed may go into dormancy.

Situation

Open. Sunny early in the season. Part shade in summer.

Soil

Light, sandy, fertile, moisture-retentive soil with free drainage, fertilized for a previous crop.

Ideal pH

6.5–7

Sowing and planting

Early and late lettuces are usually sown under cover and the midseason ones where they are to grow. If sowing indoors, use biodegradable modules as lettuces suffer from transplanting shock. Thin when about 5 cm (2 in) high. Transplant when they have six leaves, setting them so the leaves are just clear of the ground. If planted any deeper, they may rot off; if any higher, they may not grow to their full potential. Hardy lettuces planted in autumn will stand out through winter, under cloches or in the cold frame in mild areas. In colder places, they can be sown in February for spring eating. Loose-leaf – keep up a constant supply by sowing a few seeds every few weeks.

Spacing

Up to 30 cm (1 ft) apart, depending on cultivar.

Cultivation

Cover early sowings with cloches or fleece. Keep consistently moist throughout their growth.

Harvesting

Loose-leaf – pick outer leaves as you want them. If you cut the lettuce above the

roots, it may resprout from the base two or three times. Headed types Cut when the head feels solid and hearty. If you leave the root in it may resprout.

Problems

Bolting, slugs, lettuce root aphids, cutworm, downy mildew, grey mould, sensitivity to temperature.

Cooking

Raw as a prime salad ingredient. Soup, petits pois à la française. Braised.

Varieties

Butterhead, for summer

- 'Enya' (AGM) – good garden variety. 'Lillian' (AGM) – solid and round, well filled.
- 'Merveille de Quatre Saisons' – old French variety; dark bronze leaves.
- Webb's Wonderful' – introduced in 1890; popular and reliable.

Butterhead, for autumn under cover

- 'Avondefiance' (AGM) – large, midgreen heads.
- 'Sunny' (AGM) – early; quick to mature.

Crisphead

- 'Beatrice' (AGM) – small, quick growing and early.
- 'Iceberg' – well known and popular; crisp and tender.

Romaine/cos

- 'Bath Cos' – introduced in 1880; massive heads.
- 'Lobjoit's Green Cos' (AGM) – delicious, old variety with smooth, midgreen leaves.
- 'Winter Density' – tried and tested for winter growing under a cloche or cold frame.

Loose-leaf

- 'Delicato' (AGM), 'Lollo Rossa' (AGM), 'Lollo Blonda', Red Ruffles' (AGM), 'Oak Leaf', 'Salad Bowl' (AGM), Frillice' (AGM) – all pretty types.

Mini-lettuce

- 'Blush' (AGM) – baby iceberg with pink tinges.
- 'Little Gem' – famous cos type for early sowings.
- 'Minigreen' (AGM) – neat, little crisphead, just right for one person.

Marrow

(pumpkin and winter squash)
Cucurbita pepo, Cucurbita maxima and *Cucurbita moschata*
CUCURBITACEAE

Vigorous, bushy, trailing annuals. They can easily be grown outside to fruit in a British summer, especially if started off indoors using the new hardier varieties. Many shapes and sizes – some comic and full of character.

Types

Butternut, Spaghetti, Turban, Kabocha, Delicata. Pumpkins gigantic and small.

Seed to harvest

Ten weeks.

Ideal germination temp.

18°C (64°F).

Situation

Full sunshine, shelter.

Soil

Prewarmed, fertile, moist. Plenty of well-rotted compost, or grow on the compost heap.

Ideal pH

6–6.5

Sowing and planting

Soak seeds overnight. Sow them 2.5 cm (1 in) deep on their sides in individual pots indoors in late April or early May. Harden off after all danger of frost has passed. Plant outside under a cold frame or cloche.

Alternatively, sow outside in late May on prewarmed soil under cloches.

Spacing

Bush varieties 60 x 90 cm (2 x 3 ft). Trailers up to 1.8 m (6 ft) apart, depending on cultivar.

Cultivation

Male and female flowers form on the same plant. Remove any covers when the plants are in flower so that the insects can pollinate. To get enough water to the roots, sink a piece of open-ended pipe or sawn-off plastic bottle into the ground. Squashes can be trained up a strong trellis or grown into a coil to save space. If you are letting plants sprawl freely put a stick near the middle to remind you where to water. Feed at least once a fortnight with liquid feed. Growing through black polythene will give plants extra warmth and keep the fruits of the sprawling types clean. They rot quickly if in touch with the soil.

Harvesting

Marrow – harvest marrows before the skin hardens and they get too big and unappetizing. Pumpkin and winter squash – leave in the ground as long as possible before the frosts. The aim is to harden the skins so that they will store through winter.

Test them for readiness by tapping them. When ripe, they sound hollow and skins are hard. Test with a fingernail. Another sign of readiness is when the stalks start to split. With a sharp knife (and wearing gloves) cut the fruits off with a good length of stem, 12.5cm (5in), to protect the fruit from rotting. Leave in the sun (or dry shed) to harden further. Store in a cool, dry place at 10°C (50°F).

Cooking
Roasted, sautéed, mashed or puréed. Soups. Stuffed with savory fillings. Sweetened with maple syrup, American style. Big pumpkins are tasteless and best kept for Hallowe'en Jack o' lanterns.

Problems
Powdery mildew, cucumber mosaic virus, slugs and snails. In a cold frame, red spider mite and whitefly.

Varieties
Pumpkin
- 'Atlantic Giant' – worldwide record-breaking, exhibition pumpkin.
- 'Triple Treat' – ideal for Hallowe'en; round and orange with tasty flesh.
- 'Sugar Pie' for single portions.

Winter squash
- 'Butterball' – fast grower.
- 'Crown Prince' – nutty, orange flesh.

- 'Crown of Thorns' – spherical fruits with spikes.
- 'Turk's Turban' – fun shape.

Marrow
- 'Badger Cross' F1 (AGM) and 'Tiger Cross F1 (AGM) resistant to cucumber mosaic virus.
- 'Clarita' F1 (AGM) – high yields.

Mibuna and mizuna greens

Brassica rapa var. *nipposinica* and *Brassica rapa*
BRASSICACEAE

The name mizuna derives from the Japanese word for 'juicy' or 'water vegetable' – a characteristic of the leaf stalks of these plants. Mibuna and mizuna greens are easy to grow in Europe, being both hardy and heat-tolerant. Mibuna greens closely resemble mizuna, although they have different-shaped leaves – long and elegant. They have a stronger taste but are less resilient.

Types
Green and purple leaved.

Seed to harvest
Saladini: 2–3 weeks. Maturity: 8–10 weeks.

Min. germination temp.
7°C (45°F).

Situation
Open, sunny. Part shade in summer.

Soil
Fertile, moist.

Ideal pH
6.5–7

Sowing and planting
Sow April to August outside for seedling crops and inside from September for winter pickings. For mature-headed plants or seedling crops in winter and early spring, sow under protective cover in autumn. Full-headed crops can be sown in modules in March or April, for growing outside.

Spacing
Saladini 5 cm (2 in) apart. Small plants 10 cm (4 in) apart. Medium plants 20 cm (8 in) apart. Mature plants 30–45 cm (12–18 in) apart.

Cultivation
Keep weed free and well watered.

Harvesting
The first leaves can be harvested within three weeks. To keep up a supply of young leaves over many months, keep on picking.

Problems
Flea beetle, cabbage root fly, mealy cabbage aphids, club-root, although generally healthy.

Cooking
The young leaves are an ornamental addition to the salad bowl all year. The older leaves are peppery and can be cooked as greens. The leaf stalks take longer to cook than the leaves and are usually done separately.

Varieties
Mizuna
- 'Mizuna Greens' – popular.
- 'Tokyo Beau' – cold resistance.

Mibuna
- 'Green Spray' F1 – early.

Mustard greens

Brassica juncea
BRASSICACEAE

Hardy winter crop. Diverse group of leafy plants from China.

Types
Red-leaved varieties, including 'Red Giant', can be grown as seedling crops through summer. Giant and the curly-leaved

mustards are robust plants for winter. Green-in-snow types are fast growing, pungent and distasteful to pests.

Seed to harvest

6–13 weeks.

Min. germination temp.

7°C (45°F).

Situation

Open.

Soil

Fertile, well drained, manured for the previous crop.

Sowing and planting

Mustard seed is fine. Sow sparingly on the surface of the soil in situ and sieve over a thin layer of compost. As a rule of thumb, sow mid- to late summer for winter eating, from spring onwards for seedling crops.

Spacing

Seedling crops 15 cm (6 in) apart; gauge upwards according to the ultimate size of plants. Thin giant mustards to 60 cm (24 in).

Cultivation

Keep well watered.

Harvesting

Pick salad leaves as desired. Small plants are harvested whole when 15 cm (6 in) high. Large plants can be treated either way. By spring, most run to seed.

Problems

Flea beetle, cabbage root fly, aphids, slugs.

Cooking

Young leaves raw. Mature plants: stalks are removed and the leaves cut into ribbons before being cooked like any other spring green. The flowering shoots are eaten.

Varieties

- 'Art Green' – curly; good in both high and low temperatures.
- 'Green in the Snow' – jagged leaves.
- 'Red Giant' – large; wrinkly, red leaves.

Mustard spinach

(Komatsuna)

Brassica rapa var. *perviridis*
BRASSICACEAE

Cross between mustard greens and turnip, it can be eaten at any stage and sown from spring right through summer. A late-summer sowing will make for a winter or spring crop under cover. If left to mature, mustard spinach will grow up to 50 cm (20 in) in both width and height.

Seed to harvest

Loose-leaf: four weeks. Maturity: 8–10 weeks.

Min. germination temp.

10°C (50°F).

Situation

open, sunny, part shade in summer.

Soil

Moist, fertile loam. Manured the year before.

Ideal pH

6.5–7.

Sowing and planting

Sow in July for autumn and early winter harvesting, and late autumn for winter use for mature crops. Make both the first and last sowings for saladini under cloches or fleece in early spring and autumn. Late spring onwards, sow every two weeks in situ.

Spacing

45 cm (18 in) apart. Saladini Thin to 2.5 cm (1 in) apart.

Cultivation

Keep well watered, weed free.

Harvesting

Saladini Leave 2.5 cm (1 in) of the plant to regrow. Mature plants Cut whole or pick off leaves over a long period. Keep picking flowers for more flowering greens.

Problems

Cabbage root fly, flea beetle, mealy cabbage aphids, club-root, although generally healthy.

Cooking

Steamed, stir-fried or mixed with other greens such as spinach.

Varieties

- 'Big Top' F1 – greens plus turnip-like roots.
- 'Tendergreen' F1 – first pickings in 20 days.
- 'Tokisan' F1 – bred for heat tolerance.

New Zealand spinach

Tetragonia tetragonoides
TETRAGONACEAE

This type is easy and, unlike true spinach, New Zealand spinach enjoys the heat of summer. Not hardy, so grown as an annual in the UK. Self-seeds. Needs space.

Types

No cultivars.

Seed to harvest

6–7 weeks.

Min. germination temp.

13°C (55°F).

Situation

Sunny.

Soil

Damp and sandy. Tolerates poor conditions.

Ideal pH

7

Sowing and planting

After frosts, soak seed overnight. Station sow two or three seeds, 2 cm (¾ in) deep, in situ. Or grow under cover in midspring. Harden off before transplanting at the end of May or in June.

Spacing

75 cm (30 in) apart and between rows.

Cultivation

Keep watered, fertilized and mulched. Pinch out the growing tips, to encourage sideshoots. Weed until established.

Harvesting

Pick outer leaves regularly.

Problems

Usually trouble free.

Cooking

Cook as spinach. Midribs and seeds are not eaten. When it goes over, eat the tasty flowering shoots.

Onions, bunching and spring

Allium cepa
ALLIACEAE

Bunching onions are useful for salads and stir-fries. Spring onions are the most refined type. Some can stand out in winter.

Types

Red or white shank.

Seed to harvest

Eight weeks in summer.
Sowing Sow seed thinly in drills, 2.5 cm (1 in) apart, every 2–3 weeks for non-stop production. Start in early spring with crop covers and carry on until midsummer. The hardier types can be sown in late summer for the following spring.

Cultivation and harvest

Water in dry periods and pull them up as you need them.

Cooking

Generally eaten raw or used as a garnish. Also chopped into stir-fries or added to soup.

Varieties

• 'Deep Purple' – new cultivar with violet, torpedo-shaped bulbs.
• 'Ramrod' (AGM), 'White Lisbon' (AGM) and

• 'Winter White Bunching' (AGM) – good for frequent sowing; winter hardy.

Onions, globe and bulb

Allium cepa
ALLIACEAE

Onions are fairly easy to grow, particularly from sets. Some varieties will store for months and the Japanese onions (Allium fistulosum) will grow through winter to provide you with a supply all year.

Types

Globe, elongated (flattened) globe and spindle types. Skin: white, yellow, brown, purple. Different types for different seasons. For mini-onions plant close together. The maincrop types are sown in spring (seed or sets) and harvested in late summer or autumn. They can be stored through winter. Japanese onions (seed or sets) are sown or planted in late summer or early autumn to overwinter and provide onions the following summer. They don't store well but will keep you supplied until the maincrop ones are ready in autumn. Breeding has also brought in autumn sets of other globe onions. These are treated in the same way, and are harvested in June. Shallots are small bunching onions, which can tolerate more heat and cold than maincrop types and they store well. Shallots are always grown from sets, as seed will produce only a single bulb rather than a bunch. They are planted in winter (early or late depending on the area) and will be ready to eat between the end of the stored maincrop ones and the beginning of the Japanese and autumn types.
Seed/sets to harvest Spring-sown seed: 22 weeks. Spring-planted sets: 19 weeks. Autumn-sown seed: 42 weeks. Autumn-sown sets: 37 weeks.

Min. germination temp.

5°C (41°F).

Situation

Open and sunny. Good air circulation, to avoid downy mildew.

Soil

Free draining, fertile. Onions dislike acid soil so liming may be necessary. Mix in rotted compost the autumn before, as freshly manured soil can encourage bulb rots.

Ideal pH

7 or higher.

Sowing and planting

Certified sets of bulb onions are recommended for ease of cultivation, speed and a lesser tendency to disease. The heat-treated ones are bolt resistant. Growing from seed gives you a wider choice. It is important to get the sowing time right for seed, as onions are sensitive to day length and start to form bulbs only from midsummer onwards. Growing from sets Plant sets outside under cloches when the ground is workable in late spring. Heat-treated sets go in later. Plant them with the tips just showing. Sowing seed Start the seed off indoors in early spring at 10–16°C (50–61°F). Keep them on the cool side when germinated, at 13°C (55°F). Onions grown from seed first send up a crook, a

shoot that forms a loop. Don't try to free it. It is drawing nourishment from the seed in the ground and will straighten itself. When onions reach the crook stage they are ready to be pricked out. Harden off and transplant out when they have two true leaves and the soil is warm enough. For late spring sowings, warm the ground if necessary. Sow seed outside under cloches when the ground is workable. Follow the timings on the packets. Use the thinnings as spring onions. Japanese onions Planting time for Japanese onions is critical. Too early and they may bolt in spring. Too late and they won't survive the winter. Aim for a height of 15–20 cm (6–8 in) by the first frosts. If growing from seed, sow a few outside at two-week intervals through August, earlier in the north and later in the south. Sets are sturdier and can be planted from September to November.

Spacing

15 cm (6 in) apart for average-sized onions, in rows 30 cm (12 in) apart. Adjust spacings for larger or smaller ones.

Cultivation

Aim to grow onions dry and hard. Once established, water only if the plants show signs of wilting.

Harvesting

Lift the bulbs when the foliage dies back. Lay them out in the sun to dry off in a single layer, or bring them under cover. Leave for a week or two until the skins are brown and papery. Don't remove the leaves until they are completely dry or the onions won't store well. They can be hung in nets, made into plaits or laid out on shallow trays in a single layer. You can eat them green.

Problems

Mildews, onion white rot, onion neck rot, onion fly, bolting. Sparrows pull the newly planted onion out of the soil; replant and net if so.

Cooking

There is hardly a savoury dish that isn't enhanced by onions.

Varieties

Globe onions from sets

- 'Centurion' F1 (AGM) – heavy cropper, early maturing, good storer; flattened globe shape; straw-coloured.
- 'Hercules' F1 (AGM), 'Turbo' (AGM) and 'Sturon' (AGM) – resistant to bolting.

Globe onions from seed

- 'Ailsa Craig' – golden oldie.
- 'Red Baron' – red-skinned onion with concentric red-and-white rings inside.
- 'Rijnsburger 5 Balstora' (AGM) – pale yellow globe.

Bulb onions from seed

- 'Buffalo' F1 (AGM), 'Imai Early Yellow' (AGM), 'Senshyi Yellow' – good yields.

Shallots from sets

- 'Golden Gourmet' (AGM), Sante' (AGM) and 'Topper' – good storers.
- 'Hative de Niort' – favourite for exhibition.

Onions, Japanese bunching

Allium fistulosum
ALLIACEAE

The Japanese bunching onion is a development of the Welsh onion, but milder and more refined. Depending on variety, and how long you leave it to grow, it can be used as a spring onion or cooked like a leek. Although perennial, it is usually grown as an annual in the UK. Seed can be sown from spring for cropping six weeks later. Japanese bunching onions can be pulled out, snipped at any time for a bit of flavour or left in the ground where they will continue to grow for months, finally reaching leek proportions. They can go on through mild winters, given cover.

Seed to harvest

Eight weeks for salads.

Varieties

- 'Ishikura' (AGM) – fast grower, with long, white stems.
- 'Kyoto Market' – good for early sowings.

Onions, pickling

Allium cepa
ALLIACEAE

Pickling onions are usually grown from seed outside in spring. Plant them close and don't thin. If you want to keep them white, sow them 5 cm (2 in) deep. They are ready when the leaves die down two months later. Eat fresh or pickle, as they don't store.

Types

Red and white.

Seed to harvest

Eight weeks.

Varieties

- 'Jetset' and 'Shakespeare' – brown skinned.
- 'Paris Silverskin' – pearly white, cocktail onion.
- 'Purplette' – first purple-skinned variety.

Orache / Mountain spinach

Atriplex hortensis
CHENOPODIACEAE

Easy to grow. Ornamental. Grows to 2 m (6 ft) at speed and self-seeds.

Types
Red, gold, green.

Seed to harvest
6–8 weeks.

Min. germination temp.
7°C (45°F)

Situation
Semi-shade in summer.

Soil
Rich, free-draining, sandy soil.

Ideal pH
6.5–7

Sowing and planting
Sow outside in midspring. Make a second sowing a few weeks later. Usually goes to seed by midsummer.

Spacing
25 cm (10 in) apart.

Cultivation
Keep well watered. Remove the flowers unless you want to keep seed.

Harvesting
Pick leaves when young.

Problems
Usually none.

Cooking
Cook as spinach or eat the young leaves raw.

Varieties
- 'Green Spikes' – abundant, pale green leaves.
- 'Opera Red' – deep red variety; retains its colour when cooked.

Onion, Welsh

Allium fistulosum
ALLIACEAE

Welsh onions (from Siberia) are a traditional ingredient in Chinese and Japanese cooking. They resemble coarse chives with hollow stems growing 30–45 cm (12–18 in) tall. They are hardy and need little attention.

Seed to harvest
4–6 weeks.

Sowing and planting
Most die down in winter. The clumps can be dug up, pulled apart, divided and moved around the plot every few years. Sow 23cm (9in) apart, to give them room to clump up. Modern cultivars are self-blanching. Spring-sown seeds should be ready by autumn, and those sown in late summer ready the following spring. Keep weed free. Pick leaves when needed.

Varieties
- 'Welsh Red' – hardy, with strong flavour.

Pak choi

Brassica rapa var. *chinensis*
BRASSICACEAE

Every bit of the plant can be eaten. Pak choi can be harvested at any stage of its development. It grows fast, maturing in about six weeks, making it a good choice for intercropping. Excellent late-season crop if sown in August.

Types
Chinese white (sturdy), Soup spoon (more refined) and Canton types (best flavour). Cultivars bred for European climate. Resistance to bolting and disease.

Seed to harvest
Seedling crop: 2–3 weeks. Maturity: 6–8 weeks.

Min. germination temp.
10°C (50°F).

Situation
Open. Part shade in summer.

Soil
Fertile, moist.

Ideal pH
6.5–7

Sowing and planting
Sow or broadcast seedling crops outside under cover in spring. Grow under netting if flea beetle is a problem. Sow in August for mature plants in autumn. Six weeks before the frosts, sow hardiest types under cover for winter eating. Keep up seedling crops through winter with protection.

Spacing
Thin according to the ultimate size you want and the variety. Medium spacing 20 cm (8 in) apart.

Cultivation
Water.

Harvesting
Harvest at their peak. Eat within two days.

Problems
Flea beetle, club-root, slugs.

Cooking
Salads, stir-fries, greens or garnishes.

Varieties
- 'Autumn Poem' F1 – tender flowering shoots.
- 'Joi Choi' F1 – vigorous; bred for frost and bolt resistance.
- 'Mei Quing Choi' F1 – small heads for close planting after midsummer.
- 'Canton Dwarf' – mini; tolerant of heat.
- 'Pueblo' F1 – bolt resistant.

Parsnip

Pastinaca sativa
APIACEAE

Parsnips are slow to germinate. The tradition is to mark the row with radishes at each end. When the radishes are ready to harvest three weeks later, the parsnip seed should have emerged. Once up, they are hardy and easy to grow.

Types
Bulbous, wedge and bayonet shapes. Canker resistance and faster growth.

Seed to harvest
16 weeks.

Min. germination temp.
7°C (45°F).

Situation
Open, sunny site.

Soil
Manured for previous crop. Stone free and well cultivated for straight roots. If soil less than ideal, make a funnel-shaped hole with a crowbar and fill it with proprietary compost before sowing.

Ideal pH
6.5–7

Sowing and planting
To get round slow and erratic germination, buy fresh seed each year and delay sowing until May. Provide a head start with pregermination, growing in biodegradable modules or by using the fluid sowing technique. If you are sowing directly outside (which parsnips prefer if conditions are right), prepare the ground carefully and warm it for a week or so with polythene. Make drills 2.5 cm (1 in) deep. When the plants are 5 cm (2 in) tall, thin to the strongest.

Spacing
30 cm (12 in) between rows. Sow three seeds at each station, 12.5 cm (5 in) apart for medium-sized parsnips.

Cultivation
Control weeds. Constant moisture.

Harvesting
Harvest when the leaves start to droop in autumn. Parsnips are generally left in the ground, becoming sweeter after the frosts. The leaves die down so mark the spot. Lift crops by the end of February as they will start to grow again. Consider leaving a few for their magnificent, tall flowers the following year to attract beneficial insects.

Problems
Parsnip canker, carrot fly.

Cooking
Traditionally for sweetening cakes, jam and wine. In stews, boiled, mashed or roasted.

Varieties
- 'Cobham Improved Marrow' (AGM), 'Gladiator' Fl (AGM) and Javelin' F1 (AGM) – canker resistant.
- 'Javelin' F1 (AGM) – Wedge-shaped roots. Good yields. Canker resistance.
- 'Lancer' – mini.
- 'Tender and True' (AGM) – old variety. Nearly coreless, sweet-tasting. Canker resistant. Tapering roots for deep soil and exhibition.
- 'White Gem' – broad shoulders, white skin. Resistant to canker. Heavy cropper. Sweet flavour. Not fussy about soil.

Peas

Pisum sativum
PAPILIONACEAE

By choosing different types of peas – garden peas, petits pois, mangetout or sugarsnap – you can have fresh peas from May until autumn followed by peas for drying.

Types

Leafless peas have been developed for mechanical harvesting and need no support. Round-seeded varieties are used for the cooler conditions of spring, autumn and early summer. The sweeter but less hardy wrinkled types are for maincrop sowings.

Seed to harvest

Early: 11–12 weeks. Maincrop: 12–13 weeks.

Min. germination temp.

7°C (45°F).

Situation

A little shade in summer.

Soil

Fertile, light, moisture-retentive soil. Prepare the bed ahead in autumn, adding plenty of well-rotted compost or manure. Peas need a good root run and access to constant moisture.

Ideal pH

6–7.

Sowing and planting

To get good servings of peas you need quite a few plants. It is reckoned that a 5 m (16 ft) row will yield four pickings of 1 kg (2 lb) of peas. In late February or March (for peas in May or June), earlies can be sown 5 cm (2 in) deep in soil under cloches. However, as peas are hardy but the flowers are not, it is safer to germinate early peas on damp kitchen towel and then pot on into modules. Harden off. Transplant into a piece of guttering (this is ideal as you can just slide the plants off undisturbed into a trench) and grow on in a greenhouse or polytunnel until the weather is warmer and the plants can go out. Protect against mice and birds with wire mesh from the moment they are planted out. Carry on sowing every couple of weeks for peas throughout the season. In mid-March to mid-April, change to wrinkled types and round second-earlies. The second earlies usually produce a better crop than the first. For peas in August, move onto maincrop wrinkled types. These are taller, slower but are the best quality if grown well. For autumn peas in mild areas, make a last sowing in July with fast-growing, early, round types, which have mildew resistance. Some new cultivars can be sown at any time.

Spacing

7.5 cm (3 in) apart, to allow for losses. The distance between rows is roughly the same as the ultimate height of the variety of pea.

Cultivation

Mulch to keep in moisture, leaving a little gully between rows to collect rainwater. When the peas have grown to 7.5 cm (3 in) and the first tendrils appear, put a little brushwood around them for the pea tendrils to get a hold and start to climb. Remove the protective wire mesh. Keep plants moist and give them plenty of water, preferably rainwater, when in flower.

Harvesting

Garden peas and petit pois – test a few podded peas to see if they are ready. Pick regularly, supporting the stem as you do so. Mangetout and sugarsnap peas – harvest when the peas are just visible in the pod. If you neglect to catch them at this stage you can use them in the same way as ordinary peas. Peas for drying – leave on the plant to dry out completely before removing the peas from the pods and given a last airing to remove any vestige of moisture.

Problems

Pea weevil, aphids, pea moth, birds, mice, slugs.

Cooking

Classically cooked briefly with mint. Italian risotto primavera. Dried peas for a nourishing winter soup. Mushy peas, pease pudding.

Varieties

Garden peas

- 'Cavalier' (AGM) – late, sweet taste; don't mature all at once; mildew resistant.
- 'Early Onward' (AGM) – popular, early, prolific.
- 'Kelvedon Wonder' (AGM) – old English favourite; good for successive sowing.
- 'Saturn' (AGM) – maincrop; fruitful with a long picking period.
- 'Show Perfection' – high-yielding, maincrop, exhibition pea.

Sugarsnap

- 'Sugar Anne' (AGM) – early, prolific.
- 'Sugar Lord' (AGM) – tall, vigorous, high yields.

Mangetout

- 'Carouby de Maussane' – Ornamental flowers and large, flat pods.
- 'Delikata' (AGM) – Tall, similar to 'Oregan Sugar Pod' but earlier. If not picked regularly, the pods will get strings. Mildew and fusarium resistant.
- 'Oregon Sugar Pod' (AGM) – Extended picking period of medium flat pods which should be picked when young and stringless. Resistant to powdery mildew, common wilt and virus.
- 'Snow Wind' (AGM) – semi-leafless with dark green, sweet-tasting pods; long season.

Mini-sugarsnap

- 'Cascadia' (AGM) – heavy cropper; pods stay tender and sweet for a long time.

- 'Delikett' Dwarf' (AGM) – stringless when young.

Mini-mangetout

- 'Edula' (AGM) – good cropper.

Peas for drying

- 'Carlin' – the traditional, Yorkshire, black, drying pea for mushy peas on Bonfire Night.

Peppers and chillies

Capsicum annuum Grossum Group,
Capsicum annuum Longum Group
SOLANACEAE

Sweet peppers and chilli peppers are more tender than tomatoes but are grown in the same way. If started off with heat at home, or from a small purchased plant, they can be grown on outside in hot summers. The hotter the weather, the more fiery chillis become. You double your chances of success with the new F1 hybrids.

Types

Bell, 'box', 'bonnet' shaped or long and thin. Green turning to yellow, red or purple as they ripen. Chillis red, yellow and white varieties.

Seed to harvest

20–28 weeks.

Min. germination temp.

21°C (70°F).

Situation

Full sun.

Soil

Fertile, free draining.

Ideal pH

6.5

Sowing and planting

Sow seed in propagator in March or April, potting on when there are three true leaves. Keep the plants warm until they can go outside under cloches, when night temperatures are higher than 16°C (61°F). Ideally, this should be when the first flowers are forming. Stake.

Spacing

Sweet peppers 45 cm (18 in). Chillis 30 cm (12 in).

Cultivation

Feed weekly. Keep warm and well watered.

Harvesting

Pick the fruits while shiny and green, to encourage more to develop.

Problems

Whitefly, red spider mite and aphids in the cold frame. Grey mould (Botrytis) in wet weather.

Cooking

Sweet peppers are used in hot and cold Mediterranean stews. Chillis are popular worldwide for spicing and giving heat to dishes – Spanish pimienta, Mexican salsa, Indian vindaloos.

Varieties

Sweet peppers

- 'Ariane' F1 (AGM) and 'Luteus' F1 (AGM) – prolific, yellow fruits.
- 'Canape' F1 (AGM) and 'New Ace' F1 (AGM) – bred for cooler climates.
- 'Gypsy' F1 (AGM) and 'Lipstick' – green, ripening to bright red.
- 'Mavras' F1 (AGM) – handsome, black fruits.

Chillis

- 'Apache' – hot red, round fruits.
- 'Jalapeño' – fiery ingredient in Mexican cooking.
- 'Ring of Fire' – lives up to its name.
- 'Tabasco Habanero' – hotter still; used in West Indian sauces.

Potatoes

Solanum tuberosum
SOLANACEAE

Potatoes are a satisfying and easy crop and the historic allotment staple. With their broad leaves to shade out the competition from weeds and all the digging that goes on, both when planting and harvesting, they are also considered to be a good 'clearing crop' on a weedy site. Buy top-quality seed potatoes from a reputable merchant. They should come with an EU plant passport certified disease-free and carry one of three grades – EEC1, EEC2 or EEC3. Never grow from old potatoes or uncertified ones. Also make sure to dig out the whole crop at the end of the season to avoid self-sown potatoes (known as 'volunteers') or any missed in the previous harvest.

Types

First earlies, second earlies and maincrop. Both types of earlies are eaten fresh as they don't store. As they grow fast, they are less prone to the disease and the slug damage that reaches its peak in late summer and autumn. If you are growing only one type, the earlies are the best choice both for ease of cultivation and flavour. Maincrop potatoes are larger and can be stored over winter.

Seed potato to harvest

First earlies – 100 days, second earlies – 110–120 days, maincrop – 140 days.

Situation

Open, sunny.

Soil

Well manured the previous autumn. Add a good general fertilizer or line the trench with comfrey leaves.

Ideal pH

5–6

Planting

Plant in late March to early May or a month before the last frosts. 'New' potatoes timed for Christmas and winter eating are planted in August in a barrel or bin to keep them out of the cold, wet soil. They need to be kept well watered and covered with straw or fleece when the frosts come. Though not strictly essential, start off seed potatoes is by 'chitting'. Place them in egg boxes or similar with the end bearing the most eyes, or buds, facing upwards. Keep them in a light place out of direct sunlight, at a temperature of 18°C (64°F). Move the seed potatoes to a cooler place when they start to shoot. Around six weeks later, the shoots will be around 2.5 cm (1 in) long and the potatoes will be ready for planting. For fewer but larger potatoes, leave the top shoots and rub off the side ones. Plant in individual holes or in a trench, 10 cm (4 in) deep. Add an extra 2.5 cm (1 in) of soil on top. If they come up too soon, potato plants can be protected with cloches or by earthing up by piling on more soil. You can also grow potatoes in old tyres, stacking them up as the plants grow. To use the no-dig method, place the seed potatoes on top of the soil a little later than normal, at the end of April, when the soil has warmed up. Cover them with straw or organic compost. When the leaves come through, add more straw or organic compost, to keep them covered until the mulch is 15 cm (6 in) thick. A layer of grass clippings will keep the potatoes in the dark and weigh down the straw. You can also grow potatoes through heavy black plastic. This is a good way to combine weed clearance with growing crops. The only downside is that the plastic encourages slugs.

Spacing

First earlies 30 cm (12 in) apart, with 38–50 cm (15–20 in) between rows. Second earlies and maincrop 45 cm (18 in) apart, 65–75 cm (26–30 in) between rows. This is a rough guide only, as potatoes sizes vary.

Cultivation

While excessive water can bring on too much leaf growth at the expense of the tubers, potatoes need to be kept moist. A good dousing every two weeks in dry weather is recommended, as well as extra water when the flowers are forming. As they grow, earth the plants up by drawing soil over them with a hoe, to prevent light getting to the tubers. This will encourage a greater yield from the base. The ideal time to do this is when the haulm (stalks and leaves) are 23 cm (9 in) high. Bury them by about half. Repeat three weeks later, leaving 15cm (6in) of the haulm exposed. Continue to earth up every three weeks until the leaves meet the neighbouring potatoes and shade the tubers. Try to keep the ridge slopes at about 45° and the tops reasonably flat, to help irrigation. Until the ridges are covered, roughen them up with a hoe from time to time to prevent a 'crust' forming.

Harvesting

Earlies – when the flowers open, the earlies are ready and should be eaten soon after harvesting. Check the tubers for size. Dig carefully from the outside inwards, to avoid piercing the tubers. A flat-tined fork is useful for this. Maincrop – lift these potatoes when the haulm has died back and gone brown – usually in September. If potatoes are lifted too early they will taste soapy when cooked. Test by rubbing the tuber. If the skin comes off easily it's not ready. It needs to be dry and more resistant. Choose a dry day and cut the leaves right off before you start. A sickle is the ideal tool for this. If the potatoes come out wet, they need to be laid out in the sun for a couple of hours or brought under cover. Remove any damaged ones for immediate eating. Store the rest in double-thickness potato sacks or the modern equivalent. It is worth befriending the local greengrocer to get a supply of sacks that will cut out the light while letting in air. Store in a cool, frost-free place for up to three months.

Problems

Potato cyst eelworm, potato blight, wireworm, scab, potato blackleg, potato common scab, magnesium and potassium deficiencies, slugs. Companion marigolds will inhibit eelworm.

Cooking

Boiled, mashed, baked, steamed, roasted, sautéed, turned into chips or crisps. Basis of many soups.

Varieties

New cultivars are more expensive, as they carry Plant Breeder's Rights, but choose varieties that have been bred since 1970 if you are looking for disease resistance. For example, new breakthrough potatoes for blight resistance are: the Sárpo range – 'Sárpo Mira', 'Sárpo Axona', 'Sárpo Shona', 'Sárpo Una', purple-skinned 'Blue Danube' and early 'Kifli'. 'Maxine' and 'Picasso' have good eelworm resistance. Some newer varieties are dual purpose. They can be harvested as first earlies and then left to grow on for a second crop later.

First earlies

- 'Amandine' (AGM) – dual-purpose potato; salad potato that can be left to grow on to be a baker.
- 'Red Duke of York' (AGM) – 1942 Dutch variety, with big red tubers; one of the few heritage varieties sold in supermarkets.
- 'Foremost' (AGM) – 1954; gardener's favourite for flavour; waxy; doesn't disintegrate or discolour.
- 'Winston' (AGM) – earliest baker, good for showing.

Second earlies

- 'Kondor' (AGM) – 1984; red-skinned and waxy; good taste, high yields.
- 'Lady Christl' (AGM) – 1996; popular; medium sized, waxy, with creamy flesh; blight and eelworm resistant.
- 'Maxine' (AGM) – 1993; five-star, red waxy potato; excellent for showing; high eelworm resistance.
- 'Nadine' (AGM) – 1987; high eelworm resistance.

Maincrop

- 'Lady Balfour' – 2001; named after the founder of the Soil Association; bred in Scotland with disease resistance in mind.
- 'Desirée' – 1962; universally popular; drought resistant.

- 'King Edward' – 1916; the most famous potato of all for taste.
- 'Picasso' (AGM) – 1992; popular, high yielding; eelworm and scab resistance.
- 'Remarka' – 1992; popular with organic gardeners; all-round disease resistance.

Salad potatoes

- 'Charlotte' (AGM) – 1981; waxy, excellent flavour.
- 'Pink Fir Apple' – late maincrop; Victorian favourite, knobbly, with a pink skin, yellow flesh and outstanding flavour.
- 'Ratte' (AGM) – 1872; French equivalent, better and easier to peel.

Radish

Raphanus sativus
BRASSICACEAE

The summer salad radish grows quickly. It coarsens with equal speed, so sow a few seeds every few weeks. Mouli or daikon radishes have huge, white roots and are usually harvested at the end of summer or in early autumn. The hardy winter radishes can be harvested right through winter. Allow a few plants to flower for next year's seed.

Types

Summer – round or long and tapered. Red, pink, white and bi-coloured. Mouli – long and white. Winter radishes – black, pink or red. Striped. Long or round.

Seed to harvest

Summer – four weeks. Mouli – eight weeks. Winter – 20 or more weeks.

Min. germination temp.

5°C (41°F).

Situation

Open, light shade in summer.

Soil

Fertile, manured for previous crop.

Ideal pH

7

Sowing and planting

Summer – sow summer radishes thinly in situ. Avoid midsummer. Mouli – sow from midsummer onwards. Winter – sow late summer for winter eating and storage. Rotate with the other brassicas.

Spacing

Summer – thin to 7.5 cm (3 in). Mouli – thin to 20 cm (8 in). Winter – 30 cm (12 in), depending on cultivar.

Cultivation

Keep watered, weeded.

Harvesting

Summer – pull up summer ones before they go woody. Mouli – harvest when they are ready and as you need them over two to three weeks. Winter – protect winter radishes from frost. Harvest as you want them or dig up and store in frost-free shed.

Problems

Flea beetle, slugs and snails, cabbage root fly, club-root.

Cooking

Summer – use in salads. Mouli – eat raw or cooked. Winter – can be eaten raw or cooked like parsnips. The tops can be used as greens.

Varieties

Summer

- 'Cherry Belle' (AGM); 'French Breakfast' AGM; 'Rainbow Mix' – red, white and purple.

Mouli

- 'April Cross' F1.

Winter

- 'Black Spanish Round' – old variety.
- 'Green Goddess' – green skinned; mild, good for salads; long lasting.

Rhubarb

Rheum x hybridum (syn. R. cultorum)
POLYGONACEAE

Rhubarb takes up space, but is undemanding. One or two plants will provide for a whole family. It is best grown from sets, or root cuttings. The leaves are poisonous but safe to put on the compost heap.

Types
Cultivars for better forcing, sweeter types.
Set to harvest
Second season for a light harvest.
Min. germination temp.
13°C (55°F).
Situation
Sun or light shade.
Soil
Any, but not soggy. Fertile.
Ideal pH
5–6
Sowing and planting
Purchase sets (certified virus free) or take a division from a plant of three years or more. Plant in late autumn or early spring while still dormant. The buds should be barely covered by soil.

Spacing
Min. 90 cm (3 ft).
Cultivation
Water until established. When four years old, you can force rhubarb to produce succulent stems early. In February, cover the plants with straw to warm them and cover with buckets or bins to block out the light completely. The crop should be ready within six weeks. The plants will need two years to recover before being harvested again.
Harvesting
In the first year, don't harvest. In autumn, cut away the dead leaves and let the frost get to the crown to break dormancy. The following year pull (don't cut) the stems, leaving about half on each occasion. Stop in July, to let the plant regenerate.
Problems
Viruses, slugs, snails, but no problems usually.
Cooking
Crumbles and fools.
Varieties
• 'Early Champagne' – sweet and early.
• 'Timperley Early' – good for forcing.
• 'Victoria' – tried and tested.

Rocket

Eruca vesicaria subsp. *sativa*
BRASSICACEAE

Rocket, the fashionable salad leaf with a peppery kick, is expensive to buy but dead easy to grow.

Types
New, slow-to-bolt varieties.
Seed to harvest
First pickings: three weeks. Maturity: 40 days.

Min. germination temp.
7°C (45°F).
Situation
Light shade during midsummer.
Soil
Moist.
Ideal pH
7
Sowing and planting
Scatter a few seeds every three weeks from late spring to autumn. Continue under crop protection.
Spacing
Broadcast for a seedling crop; 15 cm (6 in) apart, for mature plants.
Cultivation
Keep weeded and watered in dry weather.
Harvesting
Pick individual leaves when young or cut off the tops completely.
Problems
Flea beetle.
Cooking
Salads and garnishes.
Varieties
• 'Apollo' – slow to bolt.
• 'Sky Rocket' – fast grower, tastes like wild rocket.

Runner bean

Phaseolus coccineus
PAPILIONACEAE

Runner beans originated in South America and are frost tender, vigorous climbers, growing to 2.4 m (8 ft) or more.

Types
Dwarf early but less prolific crops under glass. The flowers red, but also white and two-tone. Stringless and less fibrous types.

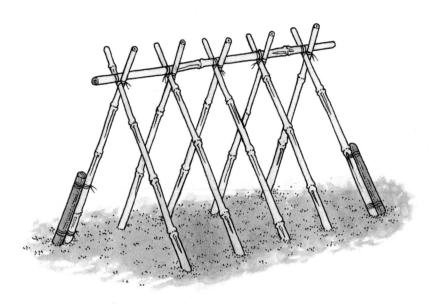

Bean supports

The most practical support is a row of criss-cross poles, tied where they cross and secured further with a horizontal pole across the top. In windy areas, you can reinforce your bean supports by driving a steak alongside one or two corner canes and tying firmly.

Seed to harvest
12–16 weeks.

Min. germination temp.
12°C (54°F).

Situation
Sunny but not baking at midday. Sheltered optimum conditions for bees to pollinate. Good root run. Bean trench prepared autumn before sowing.

Soil
Fertile, moisture-retentive, free-draining topsoil, 38cm (15in) deep.

Ideal pH
6–7

Sowing and planting
Even a whiff of frost will kill runner beans, so wait until May–June before sowing outside. Alternatively, sow indoors in root trainers or biodegradable pots. Set up strong supports before sowing outside. Sow 5 cm (2 in) deep or, to protect plants from cold, 7.5 cm (3 in) deep. Fill the trench to the top once the seeds germinate. Sow a few extras as the germination rate is only 80 per cent.

Spacing
30 cm (12 in) apart in rows. 38 cm (15 in) apart for staggered rows.

Cultivation
Mulch well, keep moist. Tie in the young plants until they are able to self-twine. Pinch out tips when they reach the top of their supports, to prevent them getting top-heavy. As flowers appear, give the plants a thorough soaking. Every day or so, spray the flowers with water when they form to 'set' them and help to produce pods.

Harvesting
Pick the beans as soon as they are ready. Check through the foliage carefully to make sure that there are no old pods lurking as they will stop production. Runner beans usually produce a bumper crop over many weeks.

Problems
Poor setting, birds, slugs, root aphids, halo blight, although usually trouble free.

Cooking
A side vegetable.

Varieties
Trailing varieties

- 'Desirée' and 'Lady Di' (AGM) – almost stringless; prolific croppers.
- 'Enorma' (AGM) – big cropper; good for showing.
- 'Painted Lady' – 1855, the oldest variety of runner bean; scarlet and white flowers.
- 'Scarlet Emperor' – Introduced in 1906, it remains a great favourite. It is said by many to be unbeatable for flavour.
- 'Red Flame' – stringless with red flowers.
- 'Red Rum' (AGM) – early; little foliage, masses of beans; tolerant of halo blight.
- 'White Emergo' (AGM) – Prolific late cropper. Traditional taste and texture. Known for its vigour, which helps it to cope with bad weather.
- 'White Lady' (AGM) – modern, stringless variety; white flowers; prolific.

Bush varieties

- 'Hestia' – miniature and needs no support; disease-resistant; heavy cropper with red and white flowers.
- 'Pickwick' – modern, early dwarf; stringless if picked young.

Salsify

Tragopogon porrifolius
ASTERACEAE

Salsify is an annual meadow plant from the Mediterranean. The white roots grow to 25 cm (9 in) long and taste faintly of oyster, hence the nickname of oyster plant. Not commonly available in the shops, it is easy to grow, though you need quite a few plants to get much to eat. Salsify has pretty, violet flowers that attract useful hoverflies.

Types

Breeding has brought in long-rooted cultivars and increased hardiness.

Seed to harvest

20 weeks.

Min. germination temp.

7°C (45°F).

Situation

Open and sunny.

Soil

Stone free, light, sandy. Manured for the previous crop.

Ideal pH

6–7.5

Sowing and planting

Sow new seed each year in situ in early to midspring. To get straight roots, make funnel-shaped holes, 30 cm (12 in) deep and 23 cm (9 in) apart, with a crow bar or similar tool. Fill with compost or sieved, sandy soil. Sow three seeds per station as germination can be erratic. Thin to one when the plantlets are 5 cm (2 in) high. If this is done carefully, you may be able to transplant them.

Spacing

20–30 cm (8–12 in).

Cultivation

Hand weed to prevent the roots 'bleeding'. Keep consistently watered, to avoid forking.

Harvesting

The roots should be ready by autumn when the leaves die back, though they can be left all winter. Lift with care as they are brittle. Use promptly before they shrivel. For tasty shoots and flower buds ('chards') that can be enjoyed like asparagus in spring, blanch the plant in autumn. Remove any remaining leaves, pile on straw for warmth and put a bucket on top of the plant, to block out light.

Problems

Unlikely.

Cooking

In the Périgord region in France, used in chicken and salsify pie, Tourtière aux salsifis. The cooked roots can be used as a vegetable, for soups and pies, and the leaves added to salads.

Varieties

• 'Giant', 'Mammouth Sandwich Island', 'Mammouth White' and 'White Skinned' – hardy.

Seakale

Crambe maritima
BRASSICACEAE

Traditionally, seakale was gathered from the beaches wild, blanched under a pile of sand and sold in markets. It is easy to grow and will keep cropping well for about six years.

Types

Wild seed. Few cultivars.
Seed or thong to harvest For best crops, two years, then every year.

Min. germination temp.

7°C (45°F).

Situation

Sunny.

Soil

Well drained, light, sandy.

Ideal pH

7

Sowing and planting

Prepare well for the long duration. Add general fertilizer a couple of weeks before sowing or planting. Usually grown from offcuts, or thongs. Rub off all the buds except the strongest. Plant 5 cm (2 in) deep. Or sow seed in spring.

Spacing

45 cm (18 in) apart.

Cultivation

Keep weeded, watered. Feed with liquid seaweed. In autumn, cut away the dying foliage. In February or March, cover the crowns with leaf-mould or sand and cover the whole with a forcing pot, bucket or bin, or a frame covered with black polythene.

Harvesting

The shoots are ready when 20 cm (8 in) long. Cut off with a sharp knife. You should get about three cuts from each plant. After this, remove all the covers and feed well so the plants can build up strength for next year.

Problems

Slugs (but a covering of sand should keep them at bay), club-root, but generally no problems.

Cooking

Shoots like asparagus. The young leaves like greens.

Varieties

• 'Ivory White' – heritage. 'Lily White' – good cropper, fine flavour.

Sorrel

Rumex acetosa
POLYGONACEAE

Easy perennial. May continue through winter with cover. Sow in spring or autumn and renew every four years.

Spinach

Spinacia oleracea
CHENOPODIACEAE

Spinach enjoys cool, damp conditions. It has a tendency to bolt in heat, though modern breeding has curbed this. You need quite a few plants to get a good quantity.

Types
Smooth-seeded, summer varieties are considered superior to the tougher, prickly-seeded, winter ones. New varieties are hardier, more bolt resistant, less bitter. Leaves round, arrow shaped, smooth or crinkly. Red-leaved varieties.

Seed to harvest
5–8 weeks.

Min. germination temp.
7°C (45°F).

Situation
Sunny in spring. Light shade in summer.

Soil
Fertile, moisture retentive.

Ideal pH
7

Sowing and planting
Summer – choose bolt-resistant varieties for first sowing. Early crops can be raised in modules or through plastic on prewarmed soil; otherwise wait until late spring to sow in situ. Soak seed overnight. Sow thinly about 2 cm (¾ in) deep. For a succession, sow every two weeks. Winter – sow in August or September for the following spring. Sow a few batches at two-week intervals as the timing is a guessing game. You want plants to be large enough to survive the winter but not to have bolted before the cold weather. Saladini Sow thinly every couple of weeks from spring to summer.

Spacing
Thin to 15 cm (6 in). Seedling crops: 10 cm (4 in) apart.

Cultivation
Don't let spinach dry out – ever. Give high-nitrogen liquid feed every two weeks. The winter ones will need protection.

Harvesting
Pick outside leaves constantly before they toughen, going from plant to plant. Always leave at least 50 per cent leaves so that the plants can recover.

Problems
Bolting, downy mildew, birds.

Cooking
Wonderfully versatile. Partnered with oil, cheeses, butter, nutmeg. Stuffed pancakes, soufflés and roulades. Soups. Young leaves in salads.

Varieties
- 'Atlanta' (AGM) and 'Sigmaleaf' (AGM) – frost resistant.
- 'Medania' (AGM), Monnopa' (AGM) and 'Palco' (AGM) – vigorous; slow to bolt.

Spinach beet

(Leaf beet, Perpetual spinach)
Beta vulgaris Cicla Group
CHENOPODIACEAE

Spinach beet is more winter hardy than true spinach and easier to grow. It is not grown commercially as it doesn't have a good shelf life. Excellent saladini crops and good winter greens outside under cover.

Types
No cultivars.

Seed to harvest
Ten weeks.

Min. germination temp.
7°C (45°F).

Situation
Can take some shade and wind.

Soil
Manured for the previous crop.

Ideal pH
7

Sowing and planting
The seeds come in clusters. Soak and sow thinly 2.5 cm (1 in) deep. Thin to the strongest. Sow in March or April outside for summer and autumn crops. A second sowing in mid- to late summer will give you fresh leaves through winter. Provide covers for the best crops.

Spacing
20 cm (8 in). Seedling crop: 10 cm (4 in).

Cultivation
Water in summer. Apply high-nitrogen feed if they flag. If leaves coarsen, cut down to the ground for fresh growth.

Harvesting
Pick young leaves from the outside, leaving 50 per cent.

Problems
Beet leaf miner, beet leaf spot.

Cooking
As spinach.

Swede

Brassica napus Napobrassica Group
BRASSICACEAE

Swedes are slow growing but very hardy and can be left in the ground until the new year.

Types

Leaves purple tinged, green- and white-topped. Flesh and skin are yellow. Earlies are for Christmas. Lates for the new year.

Seed to harvest

20–26 weeks.

Min. germination temp.

5°C (41°F).

Situation

Open ground, cool, damp.

Soil

Manured for a previous crop.

Ideal pH

7 or above.

Sowing and planting

Sow earliest crops under glass in root trainers in February. Sow seed outside under fleece in May. Thin when 2.5 cm (1 in) high.

Spacing

23 cm (9 in) apart in rows 38 cm (15 in) apart.

Cultivation

Water consistently through the growing season. Drought makes the roots go woody, while too much water will affect the flavour. If drenched after drying out, the roots may split.

Harvesting

Lift as you want, from autumn until December. Leave a few for winter greens, then clear the whole of the remaining crop. To store, cut the leaves almost to the neck and keep cool and dry. If you want to sweeten the winter greens, blanch by packing in boxes and excluding the light, as for chicory.

Problems

Club-root, downy and powdery mildews, boron deficiency, violet root rot, weevils. Seedlings: cabbage root fly, mealy cabbage aphid.

Cooking

Bashed neeps on Burns' night. Leaves as winter greens.

Varieties

- 'Best of All' – old favourite; hardy and reliable.
- 'Joan' – early sowing. 'Marian' – resistance to club-root and mildew; good flavour.
- 'Ruby' and 'Invitation' – purple varieties known for flavour.

Sweetcorn

Zea mays
POACEAE

Sweetcorn is one crop that is incomparably delicious when home-grown and eaten immediately after picking, before the sugar turns to starch. Given a fair summer and the new, fast-growing cultivars, sweetcorn is no problem to grow.

Types

'Supersweet' and 'Extrasweet'. White, yellow, gold, orange, black, mixed colours and mini-sweetcorn. Early, midseason and late.

Seed to harvest

12 weeks.

Min. germination temp.

16°C (61°F).

Situation

Warm, sheltered.

Soil

Well drained, moisture retentive, fertile.

Ideal pH

5.5–7

Sowing and planting

Sow seed in a propagator in April at 21°C (70°F) in modules or root trainers, as sweetcorn resents disturbance. Plant out in a square block when the seedlings are 7.5 cm (3 in) high. Cover with a frame or plant through polythene, for extra warmth. Alternatively, wait until May or June and sow outside on prewarmed soil that has reached a minimum of 16°C (61°F).

Spacing

35 cm (14 in) apart.

Cultivation

Corn has shallow roots so weed carefully by hand. Keep mulched. For extra root anchorage, earth up as plants grow. A good watering when in flower and when the kernels are swelling will improve the crop. Stake if windy.

Harvesting

When the tassels, or 'silks', turn brown, the corn is ripe. Test further by pushing a fingernail into a kernel. The juice should be milky. Twist off the cobs with one hand while supporting the stem with the other.

Problems

Mice and birds.

Cooking

Best barbecued (with husks on) and eaten very fresh on the cob. American fritters and

chowders. Argentinian humitas –
sweetcorn dip with sweet peppers. Indian
chapatis.

Varieties

- 'Dickson' (AGM) – supersweet; early
  maturing, tall plants.
- 'Dynasty' (AGM) – supersweet;
  midseason variety.
- 'Honey and Cream', 'Peaches and Cream'
  and 'Honey Bantam' – white and yellow
  seeds.
- 'Sundance' F1 (AGM) – early to
  midseason; stocky habit; good vigorous
  variety for the British climate, as is
  'Summer Flavour'.

Mini-sweetcorn

- 'Minisweet' F1 – miniature variety bred
  for sweetness.

Texel greens / Abyssinian cabbage

Brassica carinata
BRASSICACEAE

Texel greens were developed in 1957 from
greens found in Ethiopia. As they grow at
great speed, maturing in six weeks, they
are widely used in agriculture as a catch
crop. If left, they can grow to 1.5 m (5 ft)
and be used to provide game cover in
winter. Very hardy, they do best in the cool
of spring and autumn. If treated as a
seedling crop, they can provide salad
leaves all year round.

Types

No cultivars.

Seed to harvest

Seedling crop: 3–4 weeks or less. Maturity:
Six weeks.

Min. germination temp.

7°C (45°F).

Situation

Open, some shade.

Soil

Firm and fertile, though will grow in poor
soils.

Ideal pH

6.5–7.5

Sowing and planting

Broadcast seed in situ every three weeks
from early spring. Sow in midautumn under
cover, for winter crops.

Spacing

Large plants: thin to 30 cm (12 in) apart.
Small plants: thin to 5 cm (2 in) apart in
rows. For saladini: thin to 2.5 cm (1 in) apart.

Cultivation

Weed and water.

Harvesting

Pick leaves when young, as they coarsen
quickly.

Problems

Club-root, cabbage root fly, mealy cabbage
aphid, flea beetle in hot weather, but
generally healthy.

Cooking

Young leaves can be used for salad
mixtures and stir-fries. The older leaves
can be cooked like spinach.

Tomato

Lycopersicon esculentum
SOLANACEAE

Given the right conditions, tomatoes are
well worth growing as they are markedly
more delicious freshly picked than any
you can buy.

Types

Vine ('indeterminate') tomatoes are tall,
greenhouse types, though some cultivars
for outside. Bush ('determinate') varieties
are more suitable for outdoor cultivation.
These grow faster to catch the best of the

English summer and will fit under cloches
or crop covers. Trailing and dwarf tomatoes
for containers. Beefsteak, plum and cherry.
Green, yellow, purple and striped. Heritage.

Seed to harvest

7–12 weeks.

Min. germination temp.

16°C (61°F).

Situation

Sunny and sheltered.

Soil

Fertile, well drained.

Ideal pH

6–7

Sowing and planting

Raise the seeds in a greenhouse or
propagator, or on a windowsill, in early
April, seven weeks before the last frost.
Sow seed 2 cm (¾ in) deep in seed trays.
Pot on when there are three true leaves.
Harden off about six weeks later, when the
flowers are just forming. Plant out in June,
when warm and sunny.

Spacing

Depends on variety.

Cultivation

Vine types produce a main stem that needs
to be tied onto a sturdy central support to
prevent it from becoming top-heavy. As
they grow, the sideshoots are pinched out.
Towards the end of summer, 'stop' (or nip
out) the leader, to make the plant
concentrate less on growing taller and
more on producing fruits. Bush types don't
need training. Growing in the open air
makes them less prone to disease and
produces tastier crops. Start transplants off
under cloches until well established. Lift off
covers for pollination. All types Feed with
liquid fertilizer on a weekly basis, switching
to a high-potash (tomato) feed when in
flower to help the fruit to form. Keep well
watered throughout. Avoid cold water from
the tap. Mulch to prevent evaporation, and
keep weeded.

Harvesting

Pick as the tomatoes ripen. Gather in the whole outdoor crop before the frosts. Green tomatoes can be ripened by hanging up the trusses in a warm airy spot or by putting them with a ripe banana in a brown paper bag in a drawer. Vine types – ripen by untying them, laying them on a bed of straw on the ground and covering with a cloche.

Problems

Outdoor tomatoes: Blight, eelworm, blossom end rot, mosaic virus.

Cooking

Hugely versatile. Myriad salads and sauces, soups and stews. Green tomato chutney.

Varieties

Vine types for outside

- 'Gardeners Delight' (AGM) – great, old favourite; proper tomato taste.
- 'Gold Nugget' – best grown outdoors; yellow fruits; RHS Collection.
- 'Moneymaker' – all-time favourite.
- 'Shirley' F1 (AGM) – fast; resistance to tobacco mosaic virus, leaf-mould, fusarium.

Bush types

- 'Gartenpearl' – ideal for hanging baskets; easy and prolific.
- 'Legend' – impressive blight tolerance.
- 'Balconi Red' and 'Balconi Yellow' – sweet-tasting cherry tomatoes.
- 'Sub Artic Plenty' – heritage tomato bred for the US Airforce stationed in Greenland in the 1940s; can take cool conditions (not frost) and is a heavy cropper.

Turnip

Brassica rapa Rapifera Group
BRASSICACEAE

Turnips are grown for their fleshy roots, while their leaves can be eaten as mustardy spring greens. The hardier maincrop types will keep going into winter, when fresh produce is scarce.

Types

Flat, cylindrical, round. White, pale yellow, pinkish or black skins.

Seed to harvest

Earlies 5–6 weeks. Maincrop 8–10 weeks.

Min. germination temp.

5°C (41°F).

Situation

Cool, moist. Can tolerate some shade.

Soil

High in organic matter. Prepare the bed in autumn by adding lime if necessary and firming well. Sprinkle on a general fertilizer.

Ideal pH

7 or higher.

Sowing and planting

Sow in situ as turnips don't respond well to transplanting. Earlies – sow in small batches every few weeks in March or April under cloches. Carry on in May in a shady spot. Maincrop – sow in July or August, for eating from October onwards. You can do a further sowing of turnips in autumn, for spring greens in March.

Spacing

Earlies – 2.5 cm (1 in) deep, 10 cm (4 in) apart in rows 23 cm (9 in) apart. Maincrop – 15 cm (6 in) apart, in rows 30 cm (12 in) apart.

Cultivation

Keep weed free, consistently moist. If turnips get too dry, they may bolt or the roots may become woody and unappetizing. If soaked after being dry, the roots may split.

Harvesting

Earlies – these don't store and are best eaten when golf-ball size. Maincrop – catch maincrop turnips at tennis-ball size, before they coarsen. Twist off the leaves before digging they up. Store in a cool shed between layers of sawdust or sand.

Problems

Turnip gall weevil, cabbage root fly, club-root, downy and powdery mildew, violet root rot, boron deficiency.

Cooking

Mashed, roasted, glazed or thinly sliced and stir-fried with greens. Tops as spring greens.

Varieties

Earlies

- 'Ivory' and 'Tokyo Cross' (AGM) – early; fine flavour.

Maincrop

- 'Golden Ball' – fast grower.
- 'Market Express' (AGM) – late, hardy; good flavour when eaten young.
- 'Veitch's Red Globe' – 1882.

fruit directory

soft fruit

Once planted and set up, growing fruit is fairly effortless compared to growing vegetables. It is commonly agreed that the fruit harvest alone will pay the rent for the plot.

Blackberries and hybrids

Rubus fruticosus
ROSACEAE

The blackberry is a wilder character than the raspberry and many crosses between the two have tamed its more uncivilized habits. The resulting hybrids – loganberry, tayberry, boysenberry, tummelberry, veitchberry, youngberry, sunberry, dewberry and Japanese wineberry – are usually earlier, sweeter, less rampant and sharply spined than blackberries. Some are thornless. There is even a thornless blackberry. The stems that grow in the current year will bear fruit in the next. Blackberries and the hybrids can live up to 25 years, so make no rush decisions as to which to grow.

Types
Wide-ranging hybrids with bigger berries, sweeter tasting and less rampant habits. Thornless and disease resistance.

Situation
Blackberries: Sun or partial shade. Hybrids Sun; good air circulation.
Soil
Well-cultivated, fertile, slightly acid soil.
Ideal pH
6.5
Planting
Buy virus-free stock. Erect sturdy post-and-wire supports. The barerooted 'stools' are usually sent off by the nurseries in November and are one year old so should fruit in the first growing season after you receive them. You can also buy them potted up which, though more expensive, gives you leeway on planting times. Cut each stem down to 25 cm (10 in) above ground level, after planting.
Spacing
3 m (10 ft) apart, depending on the variety.
Cultivation
Apply an annual dressing of well-rotted compost. Keep plants mulched and well watered, particularly as the fruits form. Tie in as they grow to stop the stems tangling.

Training blackberries and hybrids

Blackberries and hybrid berries are vigorous and need stout supports – posts and wire, or a good fence about 1.8 m (6 ft) high.

The stool system

After fruiting, cut the plant down to the ground to leave half a dozen healthy new canes. Spread these out into a fan shape to catch the sun and for air circulation and tie them in. Either trim off at the top of the wire or bend them over.

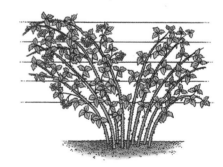

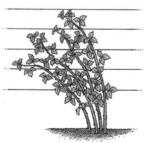

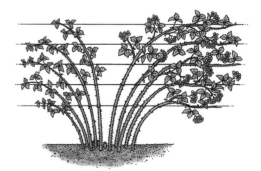

Wire supports

The new canes are tied in along the wires on one side of the support. After fruiting, they are cut right down while the new canes for next year are trained along the other side.

Net plants against birds once the fruits appear. Unless you want to propagate from them, don't let the stems touch the ground as they will root themselves. Pull out suckers as they appear.

Harvesting

Pick fruit with the stalk on, taking care not to handle the fleshy part. Unlike raspberries, the core is part of the fruit when picked. Choose a dry day as fruit deteriorates quickly when wet.

Problems

Raspberry beetle, aphids, grey mould (Botrytis), viruses, rust, purple blotch, birds

Varieties

Blackberries

- 'Fantasia' (AGM) – large, shiny, black berries; full of flavour; vigorous, heavy cropper; sharp spines; midseason to late.
- 'Loch Ness' (AGM) – a thornless variety; long, shiny, black berries; grows short upright canes, making it easy to manage.
- Hybrids are sold under their own name: 'Boysenberry', 'Loganberry', etc.

Blackcurrants

Ribes nigrum
ROSACEAE

Blackcurrants are always grown as large, free-standing bushes 1.5–1.8 m (5–6 ft) tall, though there are compact forms. The current year's shoots will bear the best fruits in the following year. If well cared for, blackcurrants can live for 20 years.

Types

Disease-resistant cultivars. Late flowers. Compact forms. Jostaberry – a vigorous but thornless blackcurrant/gooseberry hybrid producing black fruit the size of gooseberries.

Situation

Open but sheltered position. Sunny is best but can take partial shade. Avoid frost pockets as blackcurrants flower early.

Soil

Deep soil for their roots to spread. Fertile. Slightly acid. Weed well and dig in plenty of well-rotted compost or manure.

Ideal pH

6.5

Planting

Buy a two-year-old, certified virus-free, barerooted 'stool' in autumn. Late varieties are less likely to get caught by the frost. Container-grown plants can be planted at any time, though the best time is between October and March. Plant 5 cm (2 in) deeper than previously, as indicated by the 'nursery' mark on the stem. Cut down to two buds above ground level on each stem. Pile on a mulch of organic matter around the plant, to hold in moisture and keep down weeds.

Spacing

1.5–1.8 m (5–6 ft)

Cultivation

Water well in dry spells. Provide a mulch of compost or manure each spring. Cover with bird netting when in fruit.

Harvesting

Pick whole bunches, or 'strigs', as these keep better than individual berries.

Pruning and training

The best fruits appear on one-year-old wood. The aim when pruning is to maintain as many of the new growths as possible to fruit the following year. In the first year there will be no fruit, so there is no pruning to do. In the second year, start to cut back the old wood. As the bush thickens in subsequent years, in late autumn when the bush is dormant remove up to one-third of the old branches. Cut them right down to ground level. The aim is to be left with for 6–10 healthy stems.

Problems

Blackcurrant gall midge, aphids, capsid bugs, big bud mite, American gooseberry mildew, reversion, leaf spot.

Varieties

- The 'Ben' series have resistance to cold and they flower late, thereby avoiding the frosts.
- 'Ben Connan' (AGM) – compact; exceptionally sweet berries; resistance to leaf midge, mildew and leaf spot.
- 'Ben Lomond' (AGM) – flowers late; has some resistance to frost and mildew; upright habit.
- 'Ben Sarek' (AGM) – a smaller bush than most; big crops of large berries; resistance to gooseberry mildew and leaf midge; tolerant of frost at flowering time; mid- to late season.

Blueberries

Vaccinium corymbosum
ERICACEAE

The 'high bush' blueberry is hardy and ornamental. It has white, bell flowers, blue fruits and dramatic autumn colour. It needs lots of moisture and, above all, extremely acid soil (pH 4–5.5). Unless you have this – which is unlikely – grow it in a container with ericaceous compost and water it only with rainwater.

Types

Modern cultivars have reduced the blueberry from being a huge shrub to a size suitable for container planting.

Situation

Sun preferably or partial shade. Shelter.

Soil

Very acid

Ideal pH

4.5–5.5

Gooseberries

Ribes grossularia
ROSACEAE

Gooseberries are accommodating. They aren't fussy about soil and are not prone to viral diseases. While preferring sun to ripen the berries, they don't mind a little shade – a spot with sun for half the day will suit them fine. They can be grown as bushes, trained as cordons or mop-headed standards, or be grown in a barrel. Gooseberries can also be bought grafted onto other stock, to be grown as standards. They produce fruit from their second year onwards, always providing the first soft fruits of the season. The only disadvantage to this is that they flower so early that frost can destroy the crops. Gooseberries can live for a good 20 years.

Types

Red, green and yellow berries. Jostaberry – vigorous but thornless blackcurrant/ gooseberry hybrid with black fruit the size of a gooseberry.

Situation

Sheltered, well away from frost pockets but with good air circulation.

Soil

Deep so that their roots can spread. Fertile. Free draining. Slightly acid.

Ideal pH

6.5

Planting

Buy a two- or three-year-old, barerooted plant with a clear stem of 10–15 cm (4–6 in). Clear all weeds. Plant it during the dormant season to the same depth at which it was growing in the nursery. Container-grown plants can go in at any time but will need more watering until established. Mulch well.

Planting

Plants are usually sold container grown as two- or three-year-old bushes. Though a single plant will produce fruit, there will be more if it has a companion of a different variety flowering at the same time for cross-pollination. Blueberries take 3–6 years to produce a good quantity of fruit, but after that there is no stopping them.

Spacing

1.5m (5ft) apart.

Cultivation

Water only with rainwater. Mulch with composted bark or pine needles, as these are acidic. Repot into larger containers every two years in autumn.

Harvesting

Harvest the berries over a few weeks when they are ripe and blue. Good for freezing.

Pruning and training

Prune in winter. Cut out about one-third of the old or damaged wood right down to the base. Fruit is grown on two- and three-year-old branches. The aim is to remove any branches more than four years old and keep up the supply of young ones. Trim off the tops in spring, to keep a neat shape.

Problems

Birds, blue mould, but generally healthy.

Varieties

- 'Berkeley' – lush fruits and the bonus of yellow stems in winter; a big spreading plant.
- 'Bluecrop' – the most popular choice, midseason and good flavour; fairly compact.
- 'Herbert' – late variety with extra-large fruits.

Spacing

1.8 m (6 ft) apart.

Cultivation

To keep the fruit away from the ground, where slugs, snails and fungal infections may lurk, sink four canes around the plant at an outward angle and tie string around to lift the branches. Cover with fleece when frost threatens. Net from when the buds form as bullfinches will strip them off at speed.

Harvesting

Wear gloves and long sleeves as gooseberries have sharp thorns. Thin fruits that are close to each other and use for cooking, allowing the remainder to grow into dessert gooseberries. Pick with a short stalk, to avoid tearing the skin.

Pruning and training

On two-year-old bushes, the aim is to achieve a balanced goblet shape with four or five branches that are well spaced to allow for plenty of air circulation. This will be the permanent structure. In the spring after planting, start to prune. Cut out any crossing or rubbing branches and damaged wood, leaving your permanent structure of 4–5 balanced branches. Cut back the new growth on these branches by half.

Problems

Aphids, gooseberry sawfly, American gooseberry mildew, coral spot, grey mould (Botrytis), but generally trouble free.

Varieties

- 'Careless' (AGM) – green, culinary gooseberry; old midseason variety grown outstanding flavour.
- 'Invicta' (AGM) – midseason; green, culinary; thorny, good flavour; mildew resistant.
- 'Leveller' (AGM) – abundant, large, yellow berries with good flavour; not too vigorous; needs good soil and drainage.
- 'Whinham's Industry' (AGM) – a red, dessert gooseberry; prolific, sweet, succulent berries; vigorous; copes with poor soils; prone to mildew.

Japanese wineberry

Rubus phoenicolasius
ROSACEAE

This is usually grown as an ornamental as it produces arching stems, leaves with silver undersides, white flowers and bright red fruit. The fruit is delicious and intensely flavoured, and it ripen conveniently in August in the gap between the summer and autumn raspberries. It rarely falls prey to disease and, because the fruits are protected by bristly calyxes, the birds usually don't bother with them. It is grown in exactly the same way as its near relative, the raspberry.

Raspberries

Rubus idaeus
ROSACEAE

Raspberries are expensive to buy but easy to grow. Autumn raspberries are a doddle, as pruning consists of cutting the whole lot down after fruiting in winter. Another advantage is that they fruit in the first year late in the season, when home-grown raspberries are difficult to come by. Summer raspberries crop in the second year and are a more of a business to prune.

Types

Summer and autumn. Red and gold varieties. Black, purple types are more susceptible to disease but good for jam.

Situation

Airy, with sunshine for at least half the day. As they flower late, frost doesn't usually affect them.

Soil

Fertile, free draining. On the acid side. They don't do well in alkaline soils, or chalk. Soils that are too wet can bring on root rots.

Ideal pH

6.5

Planting

Buy certified virus-free stock. Aphid resistance is also helpful, as aphids carry viruses from plant to plant. Raspberries are usually bought as barerooted plants in the dormant season, or they can be purchased container-grown. The best time to plant is autumn. Put the stakes in before planting. Autumn varieties don't need supports except in windy areas or if you need to conserve space. You can pull them into shape with canes and string, to brace them around the row, or they can be grown on a trellis. If you are growing a row, dig a trench. Clear any weeds thoroughly. Mix in some well-rotted compost or manure. A

Plant supports

Raspberries and other climbing fruits will need support if they are to grow successfully.

The hedgerow system

In the hedgerow system the old canes are cut out after fruiting. The new canes are trained through the double wires and trimmed off in spring at the top of the wire or bent over and tied in.

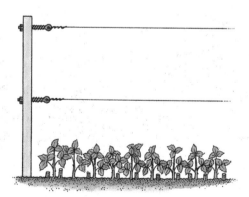

Free standing supports

In allotments there is rarely a fence or wall to train soft fruit and a free standing arrangement with cross posts and double wires makes a satisfactory support for growing the cane fruit.

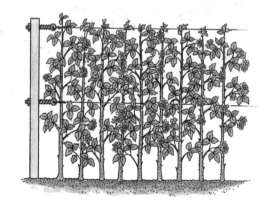

Post and wire supports

Plant young raspberries in the dormant season against a strong post and wire support.

sprinkling of bone-meal or rock phosphate will help rooting. Plant a little below the nursery mark. Once planted, cut the canes back to 15 cm (6 in).

Spacing
40 cm (16 in).

Cultivation
Keep watered and hand weed as the roots are near the surface. A mulch of manure will help to keep the pH low, conserve moisture and keep back weeds. Scatter general-purpose, granular fertilizer over the soil in spring. Raspberries are hungry plants. Net them against birds once the fruits appear.

Harvesting
Pick fruit when still firm, leaving the core and 'plug' on the plant.

Pruning and training
Old wood is brown, and the new season's wood is green and supple. Summer raspberries In autumn, prune the brown canes that bore fruit in summer by cutting them right back to ground level. Tie in about eight of the strongest, new, green canes from each plant to fruit next year. Remove the rest and any suckers that have appeared. If you are dealing with a tangle, it is easier to tackle the pruning from ground level.

In midwinter, cut back lanky topgrowth so canes are 15 cm (6 in) above the top wire. The following summer, when they are growing vigorously, tie the canes to the supports and cut them off when they reach the top. Autumn raspberries Prune in the new year, cutting the old canes back to ground level. Tie in new stems to the supporting wires as they grow over the following months.

Problems
Aphids, grey mould (Botrytis), viruses, raspberry beetle, raspberry cane spot, raspberry spur blight.

Varieties
Summer raspberries
- 'Glen Ample' (AGM) – new variety, getting an accolade; heavy cropper, July onwards; good flavour; spine-free canes; aphid resistant.
- 'Glen Moy' (AGM) – early cropper with berries from late June; spine-free canes; aphid resistant.
- 'Malling Admiral' (AGM), 'Malling Delight' (AGM) and 'Malling Jewel' (AGM) – outstanding flavour.

Autumn raspberries
- 'All Gold' – close relative of 'Autumn Bliss', but sweeter and golden.
- 'Autumn Bliss' (AGM) – crops heavily from August until first frosts; succulent fruits; resistant to root rot and aphids; considered to be the best autumn raspberry.

Purple raspberries
- 'Brandywine' – a hybrid berry between a red and a black raspberry; produces large, luscious fruits in midseason; quite tart but excellent for jam, puddings or pies.

Redcurrants and whitecurrants

Ribes sativum
ROSACEAE

Redcurrants are easy to grow and are fine in semi-shade, while whitecurrants are a nearly colourless variety of the same plant. Though the berries are smaller than blackcurrants, they have novelty value, thinner skins and, some say, a sweeter taste. Red- and whitecurrants fruit in the third year. Unlike blackcurrants, the fruit grows on a permanent framework, increasing in quantity each year. They can be grown as bushes reaching about 1.5 m (5 ft) tall and wide, or can be trained as single or double cordons and fans. Red- and whitecurrant bushes can keep going for up to 30 years.

Types
Late and early varieties. Mildew resistance.

Situation
A sheltered spot to avoid frosts, as they flower early. Can tolerate part shade.

Soil
Deep so that their roots can spread. Fertile. Free draining. Slightly acid.

Ideal pH
6.5

Planting
If you want redcurrants and whitecurrants to grow as bushes, buy two- or three-year-old plants with a single short stem, or 'leg', and well-balanced side branches. If you want to train them as a cordon or espalier, buy a one-year-old plant. There is no virus certificate so rely on a good nursery for best-quality stock. Weed the site well before planting. Don't add manure as it will make plants grow too fast. Plant to the same depth as before.

Spacing
1.2 m (4 ft) apart, depending on variety.

Cultivation
Mulch with straw and water well in dry spells. Give plants a dressing of well-rotted compost every three years. Net against birds when the fruits form.

Harvesting
Harvest by the strig, or bunch. Currants freeze well.

Pruning and training
Bushes Cut the branches back by half to an outward-facing bud and trim off the sideshoots to three buds. You want to have a 15 cm (6 in) leg (or length of clear stem) so the lower branches are kept off the ground. Good fruit suppliers will ensure

this. If there are two stems, cut the weaker out. Once established, cut back the leading shoots by half in early spring, as well as any surplus shoots, so that you have about five branches with plenty of air circulation. You are aiming for a goblet shape.

Problems

Aphids, gooseberry sawfly, American gooseberry mildew, coral spot, grey mould (Botrytis), although generally trouble free.

Varieties

Redcurrant

- 'Jonkheer van Tets' (AGM) – heavy cropper, early fruiter and good flavour.
- 'Red Lake' (AGM) – midseason variety, with plentiful tasty fruits.
- 'Rovada' – very late. 'Stanza' (AGM) – late season (good for chilly places), with lots of tasty fruit.

Whitecurrant

- 'Blanka' – largest berries of whites.
- 'White Grape' (AGM) – midseason variety with plenty of sweet flavour.
- 'White Versailles' – popular; reliable with large, juicy fruits.

Strawberries

Fragaria x ananassa
ROSACEAE

Strawberries are simplicity itself to grow as long as they don't fall prey to soil-borne diseases or viruses. It is vital to start off with certified disease-free plants from a reputable nursery. Strawberries should be moved every three years to fresh ground, and the stock should be replaced completely every nine years.

Types

Summer-fruiting and perpetual. Perpetual strawberries produce small but continuous crops from late summer until the frosts.

The best of these have a wild strawberry taste. The summer (midseason) strawberries crop in the first year.

Situation

Sheltered and sunny. Good air circulation.

Soil

Moisture-retentive, well-drained, humus-rich soil, manured the year before and on the acid side. For luxurious conditions, add well-rotted compost, some leaf-mould and a sprinkling of bone-meal or rock phosphate and a little seaweed meal before planting. If the soil has any tendency at all to waterlogging, raise the bed.

Ideal pH

6.5

Planting

Plant newly bought runners as soon as possible. Strawberries need a period of cold to get going, so autumn is the ideal time to plant. Set the crown – the point where the leaves join the roots – precisely at soil level. If set too low, the plant might rot; if too high, it won't establish well. Strawberries are best grown through a horticultural fabric or protected from slugs by collars.

Spacing

35–45 cm (14–18 in) apart.

Cultivation

Keep moist in dry spells but avoid watering from overhead. Feed well but avoid giving too much nitrogen as this will produce more leaf but less fruit. Net against birds when the fruit forms. Remove runners to conserve the plant's energy until it has stopped fruiting. The early and late varieties should be held back by picking off the flowers in the first year, for a more rewarding crop in the second. As strawberry plants need to be moved every three years, the general practice is to propagate from one-third of the crop every year. Put straw under the plants as the

fruits form, to keep them clean if you haven't grown them through horticultural fabric or collars.

After harvesting

Cut back the plants back to 10 cm (4 in) and remove any scruffy leaves. Clear the straw and burn it. Strawberries should not be grown in the same spot as before, or where raspberries were grown previously, for a minimum of three years. Longer is better.

Problems

Grey mould (Botrytis) – particularly if the plants are overcrowded), powdery mildew in dry weather, aphids, vine weevil, red spider mite, viruses, slugs, snails, birds.

Varieties

Early

- 'Honeoye' (AGM) – firm and glossy with great flavour; fair resistance to grey mould (Botrytis); with cloche protection, fruits from May to early July.

Midseason

- 'Cambridge Favourite' (AGM) – bright red, medium-sized, luscious; copes with a wide range of soils; resistant to powdery mildew, grey mould (Botrytis) and virus.
- 'Hapil' (AGM) – Belgian' high-yielding, vigorous.
- 'Pegasus' (AGM) – vigorous, with big, juicy fruits; resistant to virus, grey mould (Botrytis) and mildew.

Late

- 'Aromel' (AGM) – large fruits; fruits from July to October, even November under cloche protection.
- 'Symphony' – heavy crop of firm berries; vigorous.

Perpetual

- 'Mara des Bois' – wild strawberry flavour.

tree fruits

A recent development in some allotment sites is the advent of the orchard, now allowed by some councils on land where the ground is unsuitable for growing vegetables. Generally though, large trees are banned in allotment plots but small trees trained flat as espaliers, cordons, fans or stepovers are permitted. Apples, pears and plums lend themselves to training in this way. There are also many new cultivars of miniature trees such as nectarines, peaches, figs, oranges and lemons that can be grown in large containers such as half-barrels.

consideration on what to buy

Rootstocks

Generally, cultivated fruit trees are not grown from seed as the results are unreliable. Instead they are budded and grafted onto rootstocks, usually from a different variety or a close relative of the same type of fruit tree. This is done by joining a shoot from one tree onto the root system of another. It is the root, rather than the shoot, that determines the eventual size of the tree, so be sure to choose a plant with the right rootstock for you. Each type of fruit has an individual set of rootstocks numbers. When planting, take care to plant to the same depth as in the nursery. If you plant near or above the graft, the shoot on top of the graft may put out its own roots and make the tree too vigorous. It is a complicated subject and worth getting advice from a specialist nursery.

Pollination

Some tree varieties, such as the 'Victoria' plum, are self-pollinators, so you will get some fruit with a single tree. However, you will get more fruit if they can cross-pollinate. Most fruit trees, however, need to be fertilized by the pollen of a different variety of tree of the same type. If you are buying several fruit trees that need cross-pollination, look for different varieties of the same fruit tree (such as apples), making sure that they flower at the same time. Take advice from the nursery, as some trees are ineffectual pollinators. Most fruit trees are pollinated by insects, particularly bees, so avoid windy areas where they will be blown off-course. If your trees flower early before the bees are about, you can hand pollinate them with a soft paintbrush, moving from flower to flower.

Tips when buying fruit trees

• Always buy certified stock where possible. Certificates are not available for all fruit trees but cover commonly grown apples, pears and plums. These will have been grown in accordance to the Department for Environment, Food and Rural Affairs (Defra) Certification Scheme and will be guaranteed to be substantially free of pests and disease as well as being true to name;

• Award of Garden Merit (AGM) is particularly worth looking for as trees will last for decades. The AGM is awarded by the Royal Horticultural Society following extensive and rigorous trials;

• Always go to a reputable nursery. Fruit trees are generally lifted for sale in November. They usually come as one-year-old 'maidens' or 'whips'. 'Feathered maidens' will have formative branches or sideshoots. You can also buy a two- or three-year-old, partially trained and shaped by the nursery. Though more expensive, these will give you a head start, possibly worth it if you only want one or two;

• The cheapest option is to buy fruit trees barerooted. If you buy them pot grown, make sure they are not pot bound, with roots so congested that they can't spread out comfortably in the soil. A good nursery won't mind if you check the bottom of the pot. If a tangled mass of roots is poking out, you can be sure that it is pot bound and is likely to be dehydrated; look for late-flowering types in cold parts of the country, as frost will ruin your chances of a fruit crop if it gets to the flowers. Plant your trees in a sheltered spot and be ready to cover them with fleece when frost threatens.

cultivation

Fruit trees are a long-term investment so it is worth getting the conditions as perfect as possible. Don't plant where there were fruit trees before as they can get replant disease. They need sun for the fruit to ripen. The topsoil should be 60 cm (24 in) deep, well drained and slightly acid (pH 6.5). Trees develop big roots, so dig a generous planting hole, mix in plenty of well-rotted compost or manure and sprinkle on bone-meal for good rooting.

Put a stake in first and plant to the same depth as the tree was growing at the nursery. Firm the soil by stamping around the tree. Give it a tug to see if there is any movement, and stamp some more if not yet firm enough. Water well to get rid of any air pockets.

An organic mulch around the tree to cover the root run will keep in moisture and keep back weeds. Don't let it touch the trunk of the tree, however, as it could set off rot. Keep well watered in the first summer until the roots get a good hold.

If you are buying barerooted trees, don't let the roots dry out any further. Plant as soon as possible. If the ground is frozen or waterlogged when they arrive, cover

them with wet sacking or heel them in. To do this, in a spare piece of soil dig a trench deep enough to cover the roots and lay the young trees at an angle of 45 degrees. Cover loosely with damp soil until you can plant the trees properly.

Protection against animals
Rabbits can cause great damage by nibbling the bark off young trees. If they chew the bark off all the way round the tree, it will die. If you have rabbits around, encircle the trunk with rabbit netting buried 30 cm (12 in) deep. Birds will be after your fruit. Bullfinches don't even wait for them to form. They will strip apples, pears and plums of the fruit buds. With dwarf stock, however, it is easy to net them before the fruits form.

training fruit trees

Where there is no room for a fruit tree, or the rules don't allow them on your allotment, you can often get away with training them flat, into a espalier, cordon, fan or stepover. The form you choose depends on the amount of space, the type of fruit and how much time you are willing to spend. Make sure you have the appropriate rootstock. You can buy fruit trees partly trained by the nursery.

Espalier is an elegant form suitable for apples and pears. It take up quite a lot of space;

Cordon is also useful for apples and pears and takes up less space;

fan is suitable for the stone fruits particularly plums;

Stepover is a low, single cordon, usually grown in a series like a hoop edging. Start with a one-year-old whip as it will be the most flexible.

To train one yourself, it is best to start with a one-year-old whip, as it will be highly flexible, or with a two- or three-year-old feathered maiden. Choose specimens with strong, straight stems and plenty of sideshoots. It will take you a couple of years to make a good framework. Winter pruning encourages fast growth, while summer pruning slows it down. Shortening the secondary growth throughout summer lets in light and air to the flowers and fruits and keeps the shape of the tree. Keep your secateurs to hand and trim off unwanted growth regularly. If you are training apples and pears, you need to buy the common spur-bearing types, which have short shoots that bear flowers and fruits right along the branches rather than in clusters at the tips, like the tip-bearing types. Training the branches down towards the horizontal encourages more fruit, while

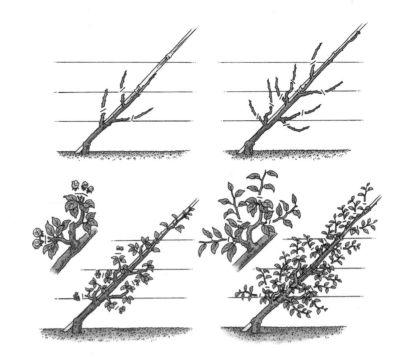

Tree shapes
The cordon

The cordon doesn't take up much space and is particularly suited to apples and pears. Secure a cane against a wire support at a 45° angle, plant and tie in the young tree to it. Cut back the leader by the third and trim the side shoots to some 7 cm (3 in). Though the summer keep trimming the side shoots. Carry on over the years until the tree reaches the top of the supports.

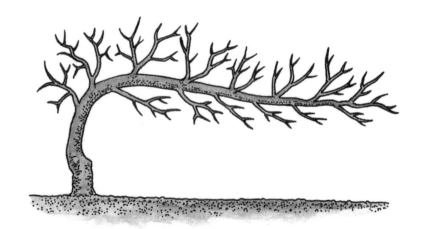

The stepover

The stepover is a low, single cordon, usually grown in a series like a hoop edging. Space 60 cm (24 in) posts about 1.5 m (5 ft) apart and stretch a wire between them. Start with a one-year-old whip as it will be flexible. Plant at an angle of 45° and attach the tip to a peg and twine which you will gradually tighten through the summer until the young tree is at an angle of 90°. Shorten the laterals (side branches) to three buds and snip off the leader to a bud when it has grown to the right length.

Training

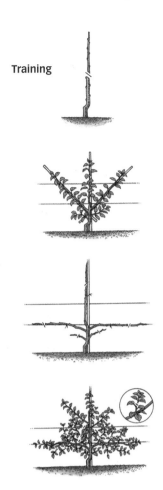

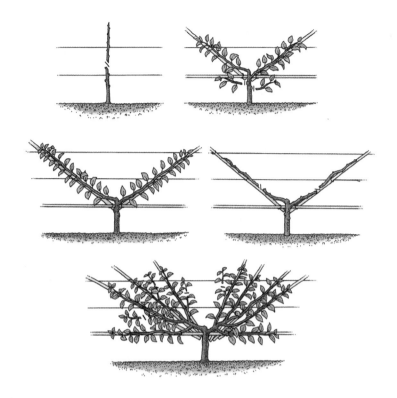

The fan

The fan suits stone fruits, such as plums and greengages, particularly well. Choose a feathered maiden with two strong side shoots about 25 cm (10 in) from the ground. Tie onto canes strapped onto the framework at 45°. Cut the leader off slightly higher than the side shoots. Encourage well-placed side growth while trimming back extra shoots to two buds.

The espalier

The espalier is particularly suited to apples and pears. It is grown tier by tier and requires a strong support. Choose a feathered maiden with near perfectly spaced side branches or a one-year-old whip. Encourage the upper most buds to shoot sideways by cutting back the leader above a pair of buds each winter, ensuring there are two buds in the right place to make lateral branches. Tie in a strong upper shoot to make the new leader. When the new shoots appear tie them to a cane at about 45°. At the end of the growing season, lower them to the horizontal and tie them in. Continue until you achieve the desired height and trim off the leader in summer to slow growth down.

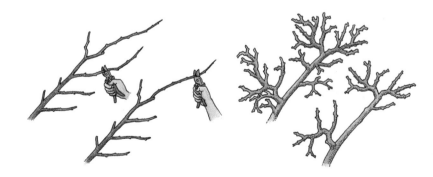

Pruning fruit trees

Shorten the secondary growth of fruit trees to three buds through summer to build up a network of short fruit-bearing spurs.

slowing down growth. Therefore, if you find that one sideshoot is more vigorous than its partner, lower it to dampen its ardour. Tie the weaker one at a more upward angle until it has caught up.

Golden rules when training fruit trees
• Use tools that are sharp, clean and well within their capacity to do the job;
• Always cut just above a joint or bud to prevent dieback;
• If taking out a whole branch, cut back to the main stem;
• Remember that new growth will shoot in the direction that the bud is facing;
• Always cut to an outward-facing bud so that the new growth grows outwards and not back towards the centre of the tree.

Apples
Malus domestica
ROSACEAE

Apples are hardy and late flowering by fruit-tree standards. They flower in mid- to late spring, so are a good choice for colder areas. The vast majority need to be cross-pollinated

Types
Dessert, cooking and cider. There are so many varieties that it is generally recommended that you choose by tasting lots of different ones. Bear in mind any local varieties. If you are going to train the apple trees as a fruit fence, remember to get a 'spur bearer'. It will produce fruit along the length of the branches and not just the tips (as does a 'tip bearer'). Look also for resistance to frost and disease, and for late flowering. Take advice from the nursery on which varieties will cross-pollinate successfully and also grow well in

your area. Some of the most outstanding apple varieties can be quite difficult to grow. The favourite-of-all-time, 'Cox's Orange Pippin', for example, is prone to disease and doesn't do well in the cold. Rootstocks M27 – 1.2–1.8 m (4–6 ft); is a very weak tree that will need support throughout its life; suitable for horizontal cordons and stopovers. M9 – 1.8–3 m (6–10 ft); is good for spindle bushes, cordons and pyramids; will also need support. M26 – 2.4–3.6 m (8–12 ft), if left to grow to its full height; is more robust than M27 and M9 and is the most widely used rootstock for trained fruit trees.

Situation
Sunny and sheltered.

Soil
Well drained and slightly acidic.

Ideal pH
6.5

Planting
It is best to plant during the dormant season. Water well beforehand. Dig a hole large enough for the tree to spread its roots. Add some well-rotted compost and a sprinkling of bone-meal or rock phosphate, for good rooting. Stake if necessary before planting and firming in well. Plant to the same depth as before, making sure that the union or grafting mark is kept clear of the soil. Water well and mulch.

Spacing
Calculate the distance according to the ultimate spread of the tree, plus extra space for access.

Cultivation
Keep up watering in dry spells in the first year. For good-quality fruit rather than quantities of it, it may be necessary to thin the fruit. To get less but larger and more luscious fruits, pick a few off as they form to get even spacing of 10 cm (4 in) between each fruit.

Harvesting
Apples are ready when they come off into a cupped hand with a small twist of the wrist. Store them wrapped in brown paper in boxes in a cool, airy shed.
Problems: canker, codling moth, apple sawfly, aphids, capsid bug, caterpillars, mildews, brown rot, blossom wilt, winter moth, birds.

Varieties
• 'Falstaff' (AGM) – late crisp sweet fruits; reliable with some frost resistance.
• 'James Grieve' (AGM) – juicy, green apple on the sharp side; quite early flowering.
• 'Laxton's Epicure' (or 'Epicure') (AGM) – crops late summer; interesting aromatic taste.
• 'Sunset' (AGM) – delicious, like a 'Cox's Orange Pippin'; small tree, very reliable; fruits in early autumn.
• There are very many other varieties. Go to an apple tasting at a fruit farm for ideas.

Cherries
Prunus avium, Prunus cerasus
ROSACEAE

Sweet, eating cherries flower early and need the heat of a really warm wall and a winter screen to protect them against frosts. They can be grown as multi-stemmed trees, or bushes, and they respond well to training as a pyramid or fan.

Types
Growing large, sweet cherries (*Prunus avium*) presents a problem as they are the favourite fare of birds and need to be netted. The acid culinary cherry (*Prunus cerasus*) is a more practical choice for the allotment. It needs a little less heat and flowers later in mid- to late spring. It is

more compact than a sweet cherry and so a 'Colt' rootstock works out well. Acid cherries are self-fertile and a single tree will provide plenty of fruit.

Rootstocks

There has been no proven dwarfing stock. The smallest is 'Colt', which is suitable for a fan of around 5 m (16 ft) across and 2.4 m (8 ft) high. However, a new introduction is semi-dwarfing 'Gisela 5' – 2.4–3 m (8–10 ft). Ask the specialist nurseries for further information.

Situation

Can be grown on a north- or east-facing wall or fence.

Soil

At least 45 cm (18 in) deep. Moisture retentive.

Ideal pH

6.5

Planting

Prepare the ground well and incorporate plenty of organic matter. Put up stakes and wires prior to planting. Water plants well beforehand. Dig a hole large enough for the roots to spread out comfortably. Add some well-rotted compost and a sprinkling of bone-meal or rock phosphate, for good rooting. Take care to plant to the same depth as in the nursery. Mulch well. Don't attempt to prune until budburst, to avoid any danger of silver leaf disease.

Spacing

Bushes and fans: 3.5–5 m (11 x 16 ft).
Pyramids: 3 x 3.5 m (10 x 11 ft).

Cultivation

Protect plants in early spring against frosts. Give them rain cover as for peaches in winter. Keep well watered. Dryness followed by wet can split the fruit. Feed with phosphate annually. Protect against birds.

Harvesting

Pick by the sprig when the fruit is ripe.

Pruning

Delay pruning until spring or summer as cherries are susceptible to silver leaf disease. Acid cherries fruit on wood from the previous season, so the aim is to take out some old wood and to encourage new growth while keeping a balanced shape.

Problems

Birds, silver leaf disease, aphids, fruit fly, bacterial canker, blossom wilt, brown rot, scorch, magnesium deficiency.

Varieties

Acid

- 'Morello' (AGM) – most famous cooking cherry.
- 'Nabella' – new variety from Germany.

Sweet

- 'Stella' – a highly popular dessert cherry self-fertile and prolific.
- 'Sunburst' – Late season Canadian cherry with large, sweet fruits; self-fertile.

Peaches and nectarines

Prunus persica
ROSACEAE

Peaches and nectarines are most successfully grown in warm areas with the protection of a south-facing wall or a fence or in a lean-to arrangement. The flowers, which are not hardy, come early, and the fruits need masses of sunshine to ripen. Most are self-pollinating. They respond well to fan training.

Types

Peaches – pink, yellow or white flesh. 'Cling' peaches cling onto the stone. Nectarines are really just peaches with smooth skin. They are less hardy and produce less fruit than peaches.

Rootstocks

Until recently only 'St Julien A', 3–4 m (10–13 ft), was used for peaches and nectarines.

Situation

Extremely warm and sheltered.

Soil

Deep, well-drained but moisture-retentive soil on the acid side. Prepare the ground by adding generous quantities of organic matter.

Ideal pH

6.5

Planting

Plant in autumn, as peach and nectarine trees start growth early. Water plants well before planting. Dig a hole large enough for the tree to spread its roots. Add some well-rotted compost and a sprinkling of bone-meal or rock phosphate, for good rooting. Plant to the same depth as at the nursery, making sure that the union or grafting mark is kept well clear of the soil. Mulch well.

Spacing

Calculate the distance according to the ultimate spread of the tree, plus extra space for access.

Cultivation

Peach and nectarine trees are mostly self-pollinating but, as they blossom before there are many insects about, it is a good idea to hand pollinate as extra insurance.

Keep them well watered and feed regularly with seaweed. Make a temporary shelter over them in late winter to keep the rain off as it will spread peach leaf curl on the new leaves as they open. Thin the developing fruits for a good crop.

Harvesting

Pick carefully when ripe, taking care not to bruise the fruit.

Problems

Peach leaf curl, scale, red spider mite, aphids.

Varieties

Peach

- 'Avalon Pride' – medium vigour; breakthrough resistance to peach curl.
- 'Duke of York' – self-fertile; delicious, heavy crops; does well on a south-facing wall.
- 'Peregrine' – reckoned to be best for growing against a wall.

Nectarine

- 'Fantasia' – semi-dwarf, up to 2.4 m (8 ft); reckoned to be the best outdoor variety.
- 'Lord Napier' – heritage (1860); popular; bears big fruits.
- 'Necterella' – dwarf; full-sized fruits despite its diminutive size; needs to be moved under cover in winter.

Pears

Pyrus communis
ROSACEAE

Pears need more sun than apples, and they flower several weeks earlier than them. In gardens they are happiest planted against a warm wall. They respond well to hard pruning and can be trained flat in any form, even grown in a tub. Pears fruit well for up to 40 years. All pears have to be cross-pollinated, so you will need two trees unless there is one on a neighbouring plot.

Types

Take advice on which varieties are compatible. Look for late flowerers if you are in a frosty area and be prepared to give them protection.

Rootstocks

'Quince C' – the smallest, at 2.4–3 m (8–10 ft); is generally recommended for cordons and espaliers for pears. 'Quince A' – 'semi dwarfing', at 3.6–5 m (12–16 ft).

Situation

Warm and protected from frost.

Soil

At least 45 cm (18 in) depth of well-drained but moisture-retentive soil on the acid side. Pears don't do well on chalk.

Ideal pH

6.5

Planting

If growing as a fan or a cordon, set up the posts and wire frame first. Pears work particularly well when trained as fans, because they like to put out a strong leader. Water each tree well before planting. Dig a hole large enough the tree to spread its roots. Add some good compost and a sprinkling of bone-meal or rock phosphate, for good rooting into the hole. Stake if necessary before planting and firming in well. Plant to the same depth as before, making sure that the union or grafting mark is kept well clear of the soil. Mulch.

Spacing

Calculate the distance according to the ultimate spread of the tree, plus extra space for access.

Cultivation

Keep watered in dry spells in the first year. For larger and more luscious fruits, thin the forming fruits to get even spacing of 10cm (4in) between each one. Net against birds when the fruits form.

Harvesting

Early pears that ripen in midsummer can be eaten off the tree. The later ones are picked when the fruits are hard and ripened indoors.

Problems

Pears are less prone to pests and diseases than apples. Pear leaf blister, pear midge, aphids, codling moth, canker, pear scab, brown rot, blossom wilt, replant disease, winter moth, birds.

Varieties

• 'Beth' (AGM) – midseason, reliable cropper with small but tasty fruits.

• 'Concorde' (AGM) – midseason; compact form, juicy fruits.

• 'Conference' (AGM) – early, very reliable and scab resistant.

• 'Doyenne de Comice' (AGM) – late, heavy pear; absolutely delicious.

Plums, greengages and damsons

Prunus domestica
ROSACEAE

Plums are grown in much the same way as pears. They need warmth and shelter but flower even earlier, so they are not recommended for places with late spring frosts. Plums are ready for harvesting in August onwards, and they taste sweeter if left on the tree until fully ripe. Greengages make smaller trees than plums and are more sensitive to frost. Otherwise they are grown in the same way. Damsons, which are hardier than true plums and fruit later, are not usually trained but are left to grow into full-sized trees. This rather rules them out on an allotment.

Types

Dessert and cooking. For fans and cordons, look for the more compact types. There are many self-fertile cultivars. If you are growing a few cross-pollinators, get guidance from the tree nursery on flowering times and compatibility.

Rootstock

'Pixie' – 1.8–2.4 m (6–8 ft) usual for training. 'St Julien A' – 3–4 m (10–13 ft); is semi dwarfing.

Situation

Sunny and sheltered. Grown against a warmth of a wall is ideal.

Soil

Any reasonable soil. Good drainage is important.

Ideal pH

6.5

Planting

If growing as a fan or a cordon, set up the posts and wire frame first. Water plants well before planting. Dig each hole large enough for the tree to spread its roots. Add some well-rotted compost and a sprinkling of bone-meal or rock phosphate, for good rooting. Plant to the same depth as previously growing in the nursery, making sure that the union or grafting mark is kept well clear of the soil. Mulch.

Spacing

Calculate the distance according to the ultimate spread of the tree, plus extra space for access.

Cultivation

Keep watered in dry spells in the first year. To get large fruits, thin the forming fruits to get even spacing of 10 cm (4 in) between each fruit. Net against birds when the fruits form. Never prune plums during the dormant season as it can expose them to silver leaf disease and canker.

Harvesting

Harvest when the fruit is ripe.

Problems

Silver leaf, plum leaf curling aphid, brown rot, plum moth, winter moth and blossom wilt.

Varieties

Plums

• 'Blue Tit' (AGM) – compact, midseason cultivar; juicy, blue fruits reliable.

• 'Czar' (AGM) – late-cropping, compact, very reliable, blue cooking plum; frost resistant and self-pollinating.

• 'Early Laxton' (AGM) – sweet-tasting, yellow fruits with red tints; compact cultivar.

• 'Opal' (AGM) – late-fruiting, compact cultivar; reliable with sweet-tasting, orange fruits.

• 'Victoria' (AGM) – famous and classic golden plum; fully self-fertile and reliable.

Greengages

• 'Cambridge Gage' (AGM) – reliable with sweet, green fruits.

herb and flower directory

growing herbs and flowers

Herbs are classified as plants that are useful to mankind whereas garden flowers are often dismissed as being merely decorative. Both can be useful in practical ways for the vegetable grower.

For the gardener cook, of course, herbs are essential ingredients and go hand-in-hand with vegetable growing. But there are many garden flowers that are edible too, and they add creative and unusual touch to the cook's repertoire. You cannot buy petals in supermarkets as they wither within the hour and have no shelf life. Flowers of all sorts draw in pollinators with their tempting nectar as well as the friendly predators that keep down pests. They help to camouflage your crops from pests that go by sight or smell. Last but not least, flowers give enormous pleasure.

Most culinary herbs are ancient plants, little changed from their wild forebears. It is generally best for growers to buy the ordinary ones (look for 'officinalis' after their name) as these generally have the most potency and flavour. Of course you may want special flavours such as mint plants that taste of chocolate (surprisingly like an after-dinner mint) or basil that tastes of cinnamon or has frilly leaves. As herbs have provided the only medicine

over thousands of years, they come with much folklore attached and the weight of practical experience and common knowledge.

Lavender, rosemary, mint and thyme put off pests with their pungent volatile oils, as do onions and garlic. Tansy is an old strewing herb, powerful and not recommended for eating. However it protects its neighbours from damage by cutworms, ants, flies, mosquitoes and the fruit moth. The wormwoods have toxic roots so it is not advisable to plant them near your crops. *Artemisia vulgaris* was called the 'midge plant' by the Anglo-Saxons, for its deterrent properties. It is useful to have growing near fruit trees as it will stave off fleas, mosquitoes, cabbage butterfly, slugs and mice. Southernwood (*Artemisia arbrotanum*) was traditionally tied up in sachets to repel moths and fleas. Dried herbs mixed with seed when sowing are said to keep off mice, birds and slugs. Marigolds are considered to be the gardener's best friend. *Tagetes minuta*,

relative of the French marigold (otherwise known as 'Stinking Roger') releases sulphur compounds known as thiophenes from its roots and these inhibit the growth of nematodes or eelworms. Tansy is said to concentrate potassium in the soil. Camomile is known as the plant's physician for improving the health of its neighbours when they are a little below par.

Many pests go by sight or smell, so if you plant a lot of one type of vegetable in one spot you will be turning it into a sitting target. Best practice for the organic gardener is to have a rich array of different types of plants, including plenty of flowering ones. There is no need to be too fussy about which flowers you grow. Nearly all are good for wildlife in one way or another. The only ones to avoid are cultivars that have been so overbred as to be sterile or so distorted that insects can't physically reach the nectar. Single-flowering types rather than cultivated doubles are the best bet.

culinary herbs

Culinary herbs are generally easy to propagate, either from seed or cuttings, depending on type. To a certain extent, you can't grow too many as they make useful gifts or can be sold at the farmers' market. The flowers of all the culinary herbs are edible and can be sprinkled around as unusual garnishes or frozen in ice cubes, to decorative effect.

Basil

Ocimum basilicum
LAMIACEAE

Tender perennial, grown as an annual in the UK. Sow seed in spring at minimum of 13°C (55°F) or directly outside after the frosts in a sheltered, warm spot. Pinch out the growing tips through summer, to stop the plant getting straggly, and take off any flowers. Harvest completely before the frosts. Basil is a classic accompaniment to tomatoes.

Bay

Laurus nobilis
LAURACEAE

Evergreen shrub that can grow to tree size (6 m/20 ft) but can be kept in check with clipping and also grown in a large tub. It needs a sheltered, sunny position as it is quite tender, particularly when young. Ingredient of bouquet garni. Believed to deter weevils when packed between dried fruit or pulses.

Bee balm / Bergamot

Monarda didyma
LAMIACEAE

Easy-to-grow, tall perennial. The leaves are used for tea with an Earl Grey taste and lemon bergamot (*M. citriodora*) for lemon tea. The petals can be used in salads and fruit salad as well as punch or other cold drinks. The red varieties M. 'Cambridge Scarlet' and M. 'Adam' are said to have the best flavour being spicy, strong and minty. Bee balm is hugely popular with bees.

Borage

Borago officinalis
BORAGINACEAE

Borage tastes strongly of cucumber and is best known for flavouring Pimms. The star-shaped, periwinkle-blue flowers look fabulous in salads. You can also freeze them in ice cubes or add them to iced tea. You can eat the leaves as well. Prepare the flowers by removing the hairy sepals. Do this by pinching the middle of the flower and pulling the petals off the corolla. Borage is easy to grow from seed sown in spring in situ, as it does not move well. Is very attractive to bees and is reputed to be a good companion to strawberries.

Camomile

Chamaemelum nobile
ASTERACEAE

Sow from seed in full sun. Use the flowerheads, fresh or dry, or combine them with the leaves of other herbs, such as lemon verbena or mint, for tea and tisanes. If there is any left over, a spray of camomile tea is said to prevent damping off in seedlings.

Chervil

Anthriscus cerefolium
APIACEAE

Biennial treated as an annual in the UK. Chervil tastes mildly of aniseed and parsley, is hardy and useful in winter. The seed doesn't last longer than a year, so make sure you have a fresh supply. For summer use, sow in late spring in light, moist soil in dappled shade. Chervil grows happily slotted between tall, leafy vegetables. It should be ready to pick in about seven weeks. As long as it is not allowed to flower, it will carry on through summer. For winter use under cloches, make a second sowing in midsummer. Chervil is said to repel slugs, ants and aphids if planted near lettuce.

Chive

Allium schoenoprasum
ALLIACEAE

Perennial that makes an attractive, onion-tasting garnish and the mauve, drumhead flowers are decorative in salads. You can pull the flowers apart and use them in the same way as the leaves when chopped, or you can use the flowers whole as a decoration or garnish. They look wonderful in herbal vinegars. Chives spring readily from seed when the soil temperature is 19°C (65°F) in late spring. However, if you can get hold of an existing clump, it is even easier to dig it up, pull the mass of little bulbs apart and replant them. They need to be divided every three years anyway. Chives like moist, rich soil and five hours of sunshine in summer. If they look tired, cut back to 2.5 cm (1 in) to encourage fresh new growth.

Coriander

Coriandrum sativum
APIACEAE

The leaves and seeds of this annual are a key flavour in oriental cooking. You need to grow a quite a lot to get a reasonable quantity. Coriander likes sunshine and to be kept quite dry. As it is likely to bolt if it is transplanted, sow seed straight out after all danger of frost. Cover thinly with fine soil. For a continuous supply, sow every three weeks through summer. It will self-seed and also cross-pollinate with fennel and dill. To prevent this, pull up the plants when the seeds are almost ripe.

Dill

Anethum graveolens
APIACEAE

The dill leaf is the classic partner for fish and spinach. The seeds, which have a stronger taste, are used in cooking. Sow in midspring outside in sun in well-drained soil. Dill can grow to up to 1.5 m (5 ft), so it may need staking. Water in hot weather to prevent bolting. Cut back regularly to encourage the production of fresh leaves. Don't let dill seed itself or cross-pollinate with coriander and fennel. The flowers are very attractive to beneficial insects.

Fennel

Lovage

Levisticum officinale
APIACEAE

Perennial growing to 2 m (6 ft). Lovage tastes like celery. Both leaves and seeds can be used for flavouring soups and stews, and the leaves can be cooked like spinach. Lovage needs a period of cold so sow outside in autumn in sun or partial shade. Prepare the ground well, incorporating plenty of well-rotted manure or compost. Keep clipping the plants in summer to encourage fresh, young leaves. Once it has established after a year or two you can divide it in spring or autumn. Cut off the flowering stems when the seeds are nearly ripe.

Marjoram / Sweet marjoram

Origanum majorana
LAMIACEAE

Half hardy and treated as an annual. There are many members of the oregano family but the undoubted culinary star is sweet

Fennel

Foeniculum vulgare
APIACEAE

Like dill, fennel, with its aniseed taste, is traditional in fish dishes. It needs space as it can grow to 2 m (6 ft). Sow seed in a sunny spot in well-drained loam after the frosts, or in spring under cover in biodegradable modules. Water in dry spells. Fennel will die back in winter. Tidy it up at the end of the season and replace every three years. The leaves can be frozen in ice cubes and the seed saved for cooking. The flowers are attractive to beneficial insects. *Foeniculum vulgare* var. *dulce* is the much smaller vegetable type of fennel, with the swollen stem that can be eaten in salads or braised.

Lavender

Lavandula officinalis
LAMIACEAE

This highly scented, evergreen shrub propagates easily from cuttings. It needs full sun and to be kept on the dry side and protected with mulches in winter when young. Trim immediately after flowering. Try to keep the bush neat and avoid cutting into old wood as it doesn't put out new growth easily. The flowers can be crystallized and used to flavour sweets. The oil is widely used in perfumery. Lavender has always been associated with washing and has antiseptic properties. It is known to deter moths and other flying insects.

Lavender

Marjoram

Mint

marjoram. A popular ingredient in Italian and Greek cooking, it is sprinkled on tomatoes and other salads or added at the last minute to soups and sauces. Either buy plants or sow seed outside after the danger of frost has passed. Alternatively, sow indoors at 16°C (61°F). Choose a sunny, well-drained site. Marjoram grows to 60 cm (24 in) and is well suited to container growing. Trim after flowering in summer.

Mint

Mentha x piperita
LAMIACEAE

The common perennial garden mint needs no introduction. However, there are dozens of types including ginger and chocolate, so finding a pure seed strain is difficult. The best policy is to buy a plant or to get a root cutting from a neighbour. Any time during the growing season you can dig up an established plant and pull the roots apart, making sure that each division has some roots and shoots. Replant in sun or shade.

Rosemary

Mint is a great colonizer, so sink a container into the ground and plant in that or grow it in a pot. Trim the plants back in summer for fresh growth. In autumn dig some up and plant in pots to go inside.

Parsley

Petroselinum crispum
APIACEAE

Perennial, treated as an annual. Curly-leaved parsley is used mostly as a garnish and the flat-leaved variety has a stronger flavour for cooking. As parsley has a hungry taproot, sow it in situ in deep soil from spring to summer with a further sowing in early autumn. Keep well watered. Be patient as parsley can take up to six weeks to germinate. For summer picking, sow in partial shade, and for winter sow (under cloches) in a sunny, sheltered spot. Cut off flowers as they appear. It is best to start afresh each year as parsley runs to seed quickly in its second season. Take precautions against slugs.

Rosemary

Rosmarinus officinalis
LAMIACEAE

Perennial, quite tricky to grow from seed. It is easier to buy a small plant in spring or grow it from cuttings. Find a sheltered, sunny spot in soil with good drainage. Mulch young plants in autumn to protect them against cold. Trim immediately after flowering. Try to keep the bush neat and avoid cutting into old wood as it doesn't put out new growth easily. With its delicious (to us) volatile oils used for flavouring stews, rosemary is also said to repel mosquitoes.

Parsley

Sage

Purple sage

Sage

Salvia officinalis
LAMIACEAE

A short-lived perennial. You can grow sage from seed outside or from cuttings in late spring to early summer, or you can buy a small plant. Site it in a warm spot with free-draining, neutral to alkaline soil. Trim back after flowering in summer, to keep the shape. Prune again in spring, to encourage young shoots. Protect young plants in winter in their first year with mulch.

Savory

Satureja hortensis, Satureja montana
LAMIACEAE

The savouries are pungent and peppery. They are used sprinkled on salads and in rich stews and for flavouring vinegars and oils. Summer savory (*S. hortensis*) is an ingredient of Herbes de Provence along with rosemary, thyme and marjoram. It is an annual with fine seed and is easiest to sow indoors in spring. Don't cover the seed as it needs light to germinate. Transplant into well-drained soil on the alkaline side after all danger of frost has passed in a sunny place. Keep picking the leaves to stop it going straggly and don't let it flower or it will go over. Dig it up at the end of the season. Winter savory (*S. montana*) is a coarser plant but useful for fresh leaves in winter. It is a perennial and can be propagated from softwood cuttings taken in spring. Protect it against the frosts and harvest the leaves as you want them.

Winter Savory

Tarragon

Tarragon

Artemisia dracunculus
ASTERACEAE

There are two types of tarragon – Russian and French. The French type is by far the best. As it can be propagated only by dividing underground runners, if you don't know someone who can give you one, buy a small plant. The roots spread profligately, so it needs to be planted in a bottomless bucket to prevent the plant from getting out of hand. When you want more plants pull the roots apart in spring. Plant tarragon in full sun. When it dies back in winter, give it a mulch of leaves or straw. In cold areas, take root divisions in autumn.

Thyme

Thymus vulgaris
LAMIACEAE

Thyme is a classic ingredient in French cookery, used in soups, casseroles and stews, as the flavours blend deliciously in slow cooking. It can be grown from seed in late spring, but it is much easier to propagate from cuttings in spring or summer or to start with a new plant. To develop the strongest and best flavour, thyme needs sun and to be kept fairly short of water. Trim plants after flowering to promote new growth and to stop the plant becoming woody. Thyme needs to be protected from harsh winds and winter damp. There are many different cultivars including lemon thyme (*T. citriodurus*) and caraway thyme (*T. herba-barona*). The tiny flowers can be used as garnishes, separated and sprinkled onto dishes or incorporated into cheeses and flavoured butters.

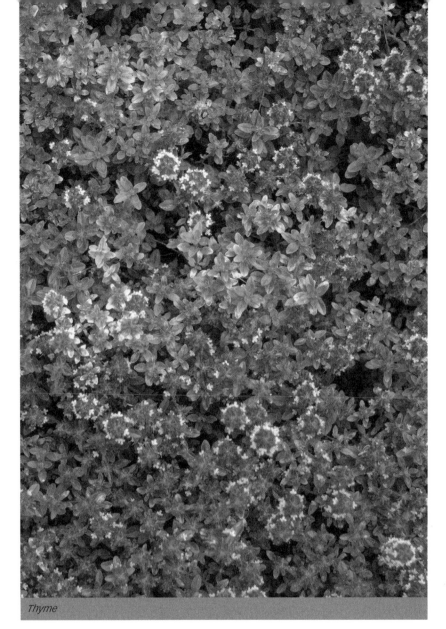
Thyme

edible flowers

Part of the fun of growing your own is to have produce that you can't buy in the shops. Shops don't stock flower petals as they have a non-existent shelf life. Yet they always look wonderful as decorations on food and some are very tasty. They are a great addition to the gardener-cook's repertoire and a satisfying bit of one-upmanship for the home grower.

warning about edible flowers

Don't eat any flower unless you are sure you know what it is and that it is safe to eat. For example, don't confuse garden peas with sweet peas! Don't confuse geranium (*Pelargonium*) with cranesbill (*Geranium*); avoid any flowers that come from florists, nurseries or roadsides, as they may have been treated with pesticides or be polluted; as a general rule, only eat the petals unless specified otherwise. Always taste them first before going ahead as some can be bitter, depending on variety.

Begonia

Begonia x tuberhybrida
BEGONIACEAE
This has a light, lemony taste and a crisp texture. It makes for a showpiece garnish whole or the petals can be used in salads and sandwiches. Begonia needs good rich soil, plenty of water, filtered sun and to be dug up like dahlias and kept frost free through winter.

Chrysanthemum

Chrysanthemum spp.
ASTERACEAE

Perennial. The petals have a strong, rather bitter taste. The easiest types to prepare in the kitchen are the open-petalled varieties. They can be sprinkled on salads, used in stir-fries or to garnish soups. Chop suey greens or 'Chrysanthemum greens' (*C. coronarium*, syn. *Xanthophthalmum coronarium*) is the only type grown for its leaves.

Day lily

Hemerocalis spp.
HEMEROCALLIDACEAE

Day lily is commonly used in Japanese tempura and the buds are used for soups. They can also be sautéed or baked in the same way as courgette flowers or used as an elegant garnish.

Geranium

Pelargonium spp.
GERANIACEAE

This has different flavours depending on variety: *P. tomentosum* tastes of peppermint; *P. citronellum* and *P. crispum* have a distinct lemon flavour. They can be used as a garnish or to flavour sweets, jellies and tarts. They candy well.

Marigold

Tagetes spp.
ASTERACEAE

Another easy-to-grow annual that flowers continually for months. T. 'Lemon Gem' and T. 'Tangerine Gem' are considered to be the best for eating, as they have a citrus flavour. The petals can be sprinkled on salads.

Tropaeleum

Marigold

Nasturtium
Tropaeolum majus
TROPAEOLACEAE

This has a good mustard kick. It was widely eaten during the war and is making a comeback. You can eat both leaves and flowers. The tiny seedheads can be used like capers. Nasturtium types are trailing, climbing, small and large. Some of the climbers can reach 3m (10ft). Nasturtium grows easily from seed. It likes full sun and needs little attention. When it goes over, pull it out and shake it, to reseed for next year. If you get too many, nasturtiums are easy to pull out.

Pink
Dianthus spp.
CARYOPHYLLACEAE

The old cottage pinks are spicy and taste of cloves. The blossoms can be made into syrups and sorbets, used to garnish cakes and sweets. Sometimes the white base of the petals is bitter, so taste a petal and remove the base if so.

Viola

Pot marigold
Calendula officinalis
ASTERACEAE

Known as 'the poor man's saffron'. The petals can be used to colour rice or junkets or be chopped up to colour butters and cheese. The petals can be dried and stored through winter. Pot marigold is easy to grow from seed. It flowers continually all summer and can tolerate light frost.

Rose
Rosa spp.
ROSACEAE

Rosebuds are lovely for candying as decoration. The petals can be used for jellies, rose waters or fruit syrups. Remove the bitter, white section at the base of each petal.

Strawberry
Fragaria spp.
ROSACEAE

Flowers can be sprinkled on salads or candied as decorations.

Tulip
Tulipa spp.
LILIACEAE

Petals are crisp and taste surprisingly like peas. If you remove the pollen and stigma, the whole flower can be eaten stuffed, or the petals can be used as decoration. Some people are allergic to tulips, so be cautious.

Viola and pansy
Viola spp.
VIOLACEAE

These taste rather like lettuce. They make pretty garnishes, fresh or candied.

culinary vegetable flowers

If you leave the odd vegetable to flower (sometimes you have to wait until the following season for the biennials, such as parsnip and carrot) you can produce many delicious flowers. They have the added advantage of drawing in bees like a magnet.

Broccoli

Brassica oleracea Italica Group
BRASSICACEAE

Sown in spring for summer eating or in summer for winter eating. If you don't harvest it you will soon get the flowers which can be used whole as decoration. They taste mildly of broccoli.

Courgette

Cucurbita pepo
CUCURBITACEAE

Hugely prolific in both flower and fruit. Courgette flowers can be stuffed with cheese, breadcrumbs or meat mixtures and either baked or deep fried. Keep the stems on. They look tickly but are smooth out when cooked.

Garlic

Allium sativium
ALLIACEAE

Flowers can be added to any dish that you are flavouring with garlic for an extra kick.

Pea

Pisum sativum
PAPILIONACEAE

It is really worth leaving a few to flower as the flowers taste like the freshest pea. Absolutely delicious on salads. They can also be candied.

Radish

Raphanus sativus
BRASSICACEAE

Dainty flowers in different colours are produced if you leave radishes (or when they bolt). They are quite tasty and provide colour to dishes.

Rocket

Eruca vesicaria subsp. sativa
BRASSICACEAE

Rocket flowers are hot and punchy and a good addition to salads.

Runner bean

Phaseolus coccineus
PAPILIONACEAE

The pretty flowers taste pleasantly of peas and beans. They look great as decoration on bean soups or sprinkled on salads.

flowers for predators

Flowers are useful for bringing in helpful predators that will demolish the pest population. Best known amongst these are ladybirds, lacewings and parasitic wasps.

Parasitic wasps are tiny and completely harmless to humans. They lay their eggs on the aphid or cutworm larvae, for their young to devour when they hatch out. These tiny insects like small flowers that are in proportion to themselves. Top favourite nectar plants are the umbelliferae family – carrot, coriander, fennel, dill, parsnip and parsley. Apart from coriander, these are biennial so you need to leave a few to flower in the second year. Parsnips produce very dramatic umbels on a 1.5 m (5 ft) stem, a highly visible magnet for predators, particularly good hoverflies as they need an open flower to get at the pollen with their short feeding tubes.

Bees love the daisy family, Asteraceae. Its flowers may appear to be large but in fact they are composed of many small florets. Simple, daisy-type flowers in yellow or orange are particularly popular. These include yarrow, sunflowers and dahlias. Bees also relish flowers of asparagus, all the brassicas, broad beans and runner beans. Honey bees love herbs including borage, sage, lavender, rosemary, marjoram, all the mints and thymes as well as bee balm.

To extend the season, and provide nectar in winter, plant a few wallflowers for spring and Michaelmas daisies for autumn. If you grow buckwheat, clover or lupins as green manures, let a few flower for the beneficial insects. The green manure *Phacelia tanecetifolia*, otherwise known as the scorpion weed, has beautiful, blue flowers and is so effective in bringing in hoverflies that some farmers sow it in the field margins to protect their crops.

Alyssum

Lobularia maritima
BRASSICACEAE

Ground-hugging annual. If sown from March to May, alyssum will produce highly scented, white flowers from June to September. Sunshine and good drainage.

California poppy

Eschscholzia californica
PAPAVERACEAE

Fast-growing annual and great self-seeder. Sow in situ in spring in sunshine. The delicate, papery flowers come in all shades of yellow to orange and white. Plant in poor ground in sun.

Cosmos

Cosmos spp.
ASTERACEAE

Half hardy so usually treated as an annual. Germinates readily from seed in spring. Tall with feathery foliage and elegant saucer-shaped flowers in pink, white or red, from June right through to October if it is deadheaded. Popular with nectar feeding insects including bees. Attracts the hummingbird hawk-moth. Well-drained soil in sun.

Evening primrose

Evening primrose

Oenothera biennis
ONAGRACEAE

A tall plant up to 1.2 m (4 ft) with highly
fragrant yellow flowers that open at
night is especially attractive to night-
flying insects. It is a biennial so seed
sown one year will flower in the second.
It self-seeds prolifically however. Full
sun, good drainage.

French marigold

Tagetes patula
ASTERACEAE

Half-hardy annual that germinates within
a week of sowing and is an ideal
companion plant. The pungent smell is
known to repel most pests, including
aphids and ants, yet is attractive to
hoverflies. The seed is popular with
goldfinches. T. 'Golden Gem' is reckoned
to be one the best types for predators.
Plant in moist, well-drained soil in sun.

Marigold

Marigold

Calendula officinalis
ASTERACEAE

Flowers non-stop right into autumn and
will self-seed merrily year-in-year-out.
Excellent companions for vegetables that
suffer from aphid damage (broad beans or
fruit trees). Wide variety in sunset shades.
Tolerates light shade but best in sun and
well-drained soil.

Morning glory (dwarf)

Convolvulus tricolor
CONVOLVULACEAE

Bushy, compact plant with bright blue,
trumpet flowers with yellow throats.
Morning glory is hugely attractive to bees,
hoverflies and moths including the hawk
moth. Sow in autumn or spring. Prefers
light, well-drained soil in sun.

Morning glory

Linum rubrum

Poached egg plant

Nasturtium

Tropaeolum spp.
TROPAEOLACEAE

All species of nasturtium are invaluable but possibly the best is T. majus – an annual that grows at extreme speed up to 3 m (10 ft) and comes in glorious fiery colours. T. 'Alaska Mixed' with its marbled leaves is recommended as it doesn't run. Nasturtiums will grow almost anywhere from June until the first frosts.

Poached egg plant

Limnanthes douglasii (AGM)
LIMNANTHACEAE
Low-growing ground cover with jolly, saucer-shaped flowers with yellow centres in a white surround, which gives it its common name. Poached egg plant is an excellent companion for vegetables, being highly attractive for bees and hoverflies. In time it will naturalize and flower at different times – as early as April and as late as July.

Red campion

Red campion

Silene dioica
CARYOPHYLLACEAE

Perennial wild flower of the woodland edge. The pink flowers appear on tall stems over a mat of oval, hairy leaves. Red campion is a care-free plant with a long flowering season right up until autumn. It attracts aphids and also ladybirds. Plant in well-drained fertile soil in light shade.

Scarlet flax

Linum grandiflorum 'Rubrum'
LINACEAE

A hardy annual that flowers non-stop through summer until autumn. Scarlet flax needs little attention and provides nectar and pollen to bees, wasps and other pollinators and predators. Sow in late spring. Prefers well-drained soil in sunshine.

Achillea

Echium

Viper's bugloss

Echium vulgare
BORAGINACEAE

Biennial wild flower of the chalk downs, viper's bugloss is regarded as the topmost bee plant. it is easily grown from seed in late summer. From then on, it will self-seed. Prefers well-drained, light, chalky soil in sun.

Yarrow

Achillea filipendulina 'Gold Plate' (AGM)
ASTERACEAE

Tall perennial up to 1.2 m (4 ft) with flat, plate-like, yellow flowers enjoyed by nectar-feeding insects, including bees and butterflies. It flowers from early summer to autumn and needs little attention, being drought and heat tolerant. Plant in full sun and well-drained, preferably chalky soil.

Tansy, Batchelor's buttons

Tanacetum vulgare
ASTERACEAE

Native plant found on waste ground. This strong-smelling 'strewing herb', with its fern-like leaves and saffron-coloured, button flowers, is attractive to a wide range of insects, including hoverflies and bees. It can be invasive so don't allow it to self-seed. Sow in well-drained, light soil in sun.

Verbena

Verbena bonariensis (AGM)
VERBENACEAE

Short-lived perennial, borderline hardy but a wonderful self-seeder. This verbena is tall and airy with flat-topped, purple flowerheads. Reputed to beat even buddleja as an attraction for butterflies. Sow in spring to flower from August onwards. Mulch in winter to protect it in cold areas. Plant in well-drained, light soil in sun.

meadow on a roof

Roof greening is catching on. It is fun to see what comes up, how the flora changes in the seasons. A green roof makes a desirable, undisturbed habitat for wildlife. It is not difficult to do on a small garden shed as long as it is good and sturdy and can take the weight. If you have any worries about its strength, check with an architect or structural engineer. You will probably be able to reinforce it with a few simple girders. The roof must be either flat or have a pitch of less than 30 degrees. It must also be waterproof.

The thinnest, lightest green roofs, and possibly the most practical but also the least inspiring, are the traditional sedum roofs. These contain little stonecrops that grow wild in rock crevices and need minimal water, practically no soil and almost zero attention. They are also fairly evergreen. They can be bought ready planted in a growing medium and rolled out like a carpet or turf onto the prepared roof. More interesting for the nature lover is to make a little roof meadow. It will need a slightly greater depth of growing medium – usually a lightweight mix of aggregates and soil – of around 7.5 cm (3 in).

Green roofs are made up of several layers. For the simplest shed roof, you can probably get away with butyl lining (pond lining material) as waterproofing. Above this, use a layer of geotextile to protect the waterproofing from weed roots. The growing medium, or 'substrate', is the next layer. The last layer is the plants themselves. On a flat roof, you would need a drainage gully and a down pipe. You might decide to put a wooden frame on the roof to contain the substrate, particularly if the roof is on a slant.

You can buy wildflower turf ready to roll out, or you can use your own mix and insert little plants. Some manufacturers specialize in native wild flowers growing in biodegradable felt. If you want to go one step further with native wild flowers particular to your area, log onto the Postcode Plants database at the Natural History Museum (www.nhm.ac.uk/nature-online/life/plants-fungi/postcode-plants) and enter your post code. Don't include grasses in your seed mix as they are likely to dominate and overwhelm the wild flowers.

the problem pages

pests, diseases and other annoyances

Knowledge is power when it comes to dealing with pests and disease. Study the pests, their lifestyles and breeding habits so that you can outwit them. Be observant so that you can deal with problems before they develop. Grow plants in top health so that they will shrug off disease. Aim for a fair balance, not perfection.

Most allotment holders would agree that the whole point of growing your own food is to feed the family on the very best – the tastiest, healthiest and least contaminated crops. They should be so fresh that there can be no comparison with shop-bought produce. Given this scenario, allotment growing has got to be organic. Getting out of trouble with a squirt of chemicals is an entirely outmoded concept, causing collateral damage both to wildlife and the soil. This doesn't mean that the organic gardener has less than a full arsenal of weapons at his or her disposal. The aim is not to eliminate each and every pest but to create a good ecology and a healthy balance so that it will need the least possible amount of intervention from you for plants to stay healthy. Aerial attacks can be snookered effortlessly with netting and attacks from below ground with collars.

netting (or fleece)

Very many pests fly in to lay their eggs near a host plant for their larvae to eat when they hatch out. Nets will defeat them completely. You can avoid the numerous pests that plague brassicas (such as cabbage moths, cabbage whitefly, cabbage white butterfly and cabbage root fly) by the simple contingency of growing them under nets from start to finish. Bear in mind that nets need to go up before the pests arrive and the gauge of mesh needs to be in proportion to the pest. They may need to be lifted when in flower for those vegetables that require pollination.

collars

Placing these around young plants will prevent soil-borne grubs from creeping up the stems. Brassica collars doubled up (so there are no gaps) will keep out soil-borne creatures effectively. If you haven't put on nets they will also prevent flying pests laying their eggs right next to the host plants for the larvae to feed on when they hatch out.

good husbandry

Raising plants to be in top health, so that they will shrug off pests and disease, comes down to good husbandry – knowing the precise needs of your plants. Provide them with their individual needs of soil, pH, temperature, sun or shade and timing. Go with the grain and raise them quickly (before pests and disease can take hold) by growing them in the optimum season for them. Supply them with sufficient water and nutrients, but don't overdo it as this will make them soft, sappy and attractive to pests. After a few years, the annual addition of well-rotted, bulky organic matter will have made the soil so fertile that plants will rarely need extra fertilizer. Don't overcrowd plants by sowing or planting them too close together, and don't let them get choked by weeds. Nurse them when they are young and vulnerable. Avoid stressing them.

disease-resistance

Disease-resistant cultivars are a godsend. Thanks to scientific breeding, many of the worst pests and diseases are more avoidable than ever before. For soft fruit, tree fruit, potatoes and other plants prone to viruses, always use certified virus-free stock where it exists.

Knowing the enemy

Some pests are large enough to be seen and identified, many are not or appear only at night. Detection skills come in here, either by night vigils with a torch and magnifying glass, or by finding clues from the type of damage.

If there are holes in the leaves of a plant, the chances are that they are being eaten by slugs, snails or caterpillars. V-shaped holes in peas and beans signify weevils. A meandering pattern of damage inside a leaf will be leaf miners. Leaves curling over could well harbour a colony of aphids eating the sap on the reverse side. If it's the roots that are damaged, this has probably been done by underground larvae. Decapitated vegetables are usually the work of cutworms. Mice are the likely culprits when newly planted seedlings disappear without trace. If your young onions sets are unearthed, blame the birds.

Distortions, mottling or mosaic patterns and unnatural colouring are the signs of virus. Moulds signify fungus diseases. Diseased material should not go on your compost heap but can be sent to the council's recycling scheme. Their heaps reach such high temperatures that all disease is destroyed.

Generally creatures that move fast are chasing prey and the slow ones are after your vegetables. But not always – a ladybird larva, for example, could easily be mistaken for an enemy. On close inspection, you will see the tell-tale spots. Some creatures can be both friend and foe. Birds and wasps are invaluable in keeping down pests but will have an eagle eye on your fruit. There has to be some give and take.

Catch problems early and dispatch them

Many problems can be dealt with if you catch them quickly. Cut away diseased material before it has a chance to spread. Take care not to shake the spores around. Pick off pests by hand before they multiply. If you are quick enough, a good sharp shower of water can be all that it takes to deal with a problem.

Encourage predators

Pests have natural predators. Entice them in to help you. Ladybirds, hoverflies and lacewings demolish aphids, mites, scale insects, mealy bugs and small caterpillars at an astonishing rate. A single ladybird eats an average of 400 aphids every week. Ground beetles eat slugs, underground larvae and root aphids. Parasitic wasps will eat caterpillars. Other wasps eat grubs, scale insects, maggots and flies. The braconid wasp injects her eggs into aphids and the larvae of other insects. Centipedes eat slugs and snails. Earwigs eat caterpillars, aphids and the eggs of codling moths. Frogs, toads, hedgehogs, newts, shrews and slowworms demolish slugs and many other pests. Birds and bats eat a wide range of pests. Robins relish caterpillars, cutworms and other soil-borne grubs. Starlings will go for wireworms, while thrushes are skilled at dealing with snails.

Crop rotation

This is vital to help prevent a build-up of pests in the soil, especially on those allotments where the same land has been used for the same crops over many years.

Camouflage

Don't let your plants become a sitting target – they can't run away. Disguise them by mixing in flowers, alternating with rows of green manure or edging your beds with pungent herbs or marigolds (the ultimate companion plant). Many pest insects fly in a random and inaccurate way looking for specific crops. They need a big landing area. If you have small beds with different crops in them they may well miss the target altogether.

Hygiene

Be wary of cross-infection. Dip your tools into disinfectant or alcohol between plants when pruning fruit as they are prone to viruses. Viruses usually start on a single plant and are spread by aphids or anything that moves from plant to plant – and that includes you. Keep pots and containers well scrubbed. Mind where you tread if you have visited another plot where there may be diseases in the soil. Be wary of accepting gifts of plants. On an allotment it is truly unwise to exchange potatoes, brassicas or onions. They may carry any of the worst of the soil-borne diseases – eelworm, potato blight, club-root or onion white rot.

Traps

Car grease spread on a board will trap flea beetles when the plant is shaken. Commercially bought sticky grease bands are effective against the wingless winter moths that crawl up the trunks of apples, pears and plums to lay their eggs. Jars of beer sunk into the ground will send slugs off into drunken oblivion. Pheromone traps lure codling moths looking for a mate. They indicate their presence so you can take further action in the early stages.

Timing

Early potatoes are less prone to disease because they grow fast and are out of the ground before blight has got going. Overwintered broad beans are too tough for the black bean aphid to enjoy much. Early carrots are usually out before the breeding season of the carrot fly. Texel greens and other oriental vegetables grow so fast that they can even beat club-root – with luck.

biological pest control

The use of nematodes and parasites to target specific pests is temporary but effective. The nematodes and parasites are usually obtained by post and are watered on at certain specified times and when the temperature is right for the particular target.

An effective caterpillar treatment is *Steinernema caposcapsae*, which can be sprayed onto brassicas in three bursts over three weeks to catch all the hatchings. Others include microscopic nematodes that will effectively deal with slugs underground, where you can't get at them, and are particularly useful for potatoes. This is best applied a couple of weeks before planting out.

pesticides

Most (even organic) pesticides have been outlawed over the last few years with good reason.

● Soft soap is effective while insecticidal soap, which is a mixture of potassium salt soaps, packs a bigger punch destroying aphids, red spider mite and sawfly amongst others on contact while being harmless to people and pets. Insects breath through the skin so they drown as the soap breaks the surface tension of the water. Washing up liquid and detergents should not be used.

● Soot or sulphur was traditionally used as a fungicide. Now that people don't burn coal, however, they are not so easy to come by. However, sulphur for garden use can be bought as a spray or dust and is effective against powdery mildew, rusts, leaf blights and fruit rots. Fungus is spread by rain. Applications of sulphur are most effective if applied early in the growing season and within four hours of a rain shower or a wet period.

● Pyrethrum (a natural plant product from the chrysanthemum family) deals with small caterpillars and aphids, flea beetles and red spider mite. The new slug pellets based on ferric phosphate are harmless to wildlife – killing only slugs and snails. They last for several weeks before breaking down to iron and phosphate nutrients as part of garden soil.

The latest organic pesticides are mostly based on plant and fish oils or biological enzymes. Check the catalogues as new organic products are being trialled all the time. To be marketed as organic, they must meet the standards of the Soil Association and the UK Register of Organic Food Standards (UKRAFS).

Golden rules for effective pest control

- identify the problem accurately;
- target precisely;
- follow the manufacturer's instructions to the letter;
- store chemicals away from children in the original labelled container;
- use sound equipment and wash thoroughly afterwards, having disposed of any leftover;
- spray only on windless evenings when the good insects have turned in for the night;
- wear a mask, to avoid breathing in the sprays;
- don't spray open flowers for fear of harming bees.

Marigolds attract beneficial insects and camouflage your crops.

common pests and diseases

Whereas pests are fairly easy to identify by the type of damage, the trail, the timing or the presence of eggs or larvae, diseases may need a more scientific analysis to pin point the problem. As a general rule, common sense and a guide is all you need to work things out. However, if you are seriously concerned, you can get a professional analysis done by The Royal Horticultural Society and other organizations that advertise in gardening magazines.

American gooseberry mildew

This fungal disease is usually caused by high humidity or too much nitrogen feed. The first symptoms are a white, powdery fungal growth on the stems and leaves. Young leaves may drop off and the fruit may become discoloured. Cut off affected parts as soon as you see the first signs. Prune to allow plenty of air circulation. Look for disease resistance in future plantings.

Anthracnose

Fungus badly affecting dwarf and runner beans. First symptoms are sunken, brown spots on the stems. The leaf veins may go red and the leaves drop off. The pods may get infected. Remove all sick plants and start again using resistant cultivars.

Aphids

There are many aphid types such as green fly and black fly, mealy cabbage aphid, black bean aphid – to name but a few. They breed rapidly, suck the sap, weakening the plants, and they spread viruses as they move from plant to plant. They secrete honeydew, which attracts creates sooty moulds. This is a harmless fungus, but it blocks out the light and can cause the leaves to drop off. As aphids travel from plant to plant they can spread viruses. The picture is compounded by sugar-eating ants, which herd and move aphids around physically to protect their food source. Pick off affected leaves, wash off aphids with a jet of water or squash them by folding the leaves over and rubbing them out. Catch them early in the season as a single aphid will have a hundred offspring. Beat the black bean aphid season by planting early under cover. If you get caught, cut off the tops of the plants where they congregate. Encourage their numerous predators – hoverflies, lacewings, parasitic wasps, spiders, earwigs, birds and ladybirds. Grow plants under horticultural fleece, though not when they need to be pollinated. Last resort: spray with soft or insecticidal soap. Root aphids work unseen to weaken plants. Different types live among the roots of lettuce, runner and French beans and Jerusalem artichokes. They are tiny, yellowish and secrete a fluffy wax. To avoid them: rotate crops; buy aphid-resistant cultivars; be vigilant and pick and shower off; and spray with soft or insecticidal soap. Last resort: Pyrethrum.

Apple and pear scab

This fungus shows as black or brown scabs on fruits and leaves. These can spread until the fruits are blackened, distorted and cracked, eventually falling off the tree. Practise good hygiene and remove all affected fruit. Prune back branches, to allow good air circulation. Last resort: spray with sulphur.

Apple sawfly

This spends the winter in the soil and lays its eggs in spring on immature fruits. The resulting maggots, which are white with brown heads, burrow into the fruit, leaving a trail of excrement. By the time they have reached the core, the fruit will fall off the tree. Sometimes the maggots die in the fruit – the apple will grow on to maturity but it will be distorted. Pick up any fallen fruits before the maggots get out and back into the soil. Rake back mulches and cultivate around apple trees, to expose the maggots to the birds.

Asparagus beetle

The chequered, black-and-yellow adults stay hidden around the plants through winter and emerge in spring to lay their eggs. Both adults and the grey larvae defoliate asparagus and skin the stems. Watch out for them in late spring and remove them. Burn the foliage at the end of the season when you cut it down. Clear away hiding places where they may hibernate.

Bacterial canker

See *Cankers*, page 350.

Bean chocolate spot

This is a fungus that shows as brown spots on leaves, stems, pods and flowers. Destroy the crop. In future, avoid damp conditions and grow on well-drained soil. Plant further apart, for good air circulation.

Bean mosaic virus

See *Virus*, page 360.

Bean seed fly

The adults emerge in spring and lay their eggs near seedlings. The resulting maggots eat pea and bean seeds while they are just germinating, completely destroying the crop. To avoid the problem, sow under cover and plant out transplants.

Bean weevil

Pea and bean weevil beetles make U-shaped holes in the edges of leaves of peas and beans. The larvae of tiny grey beetles live in the soil and feed on the nitrogen fixing nodules of the roots and the adults emerge in June or July. Generally, they don't do too much harm except to young and vulnerable plants. Move to new ground and keep the adults off with cloches or nets when you sow.

Beet leaf miner

The larvae of the leaf mining fly, small white maggots, burrow inside the leaves of beetroot and spinach eating the internal tissue. This causes the leaves to develop big brown patches. Spot the problem quickly and remove the affected leaves.

Beet leaf spot

A mild fungal disease affecting the beet family. First signs are small, rounded spots, each with a purplish edge and pale centre. The overwintering fungus is spread by rain, tools or hand, and it flourishes in hot and humid weather. Clean up the plants, removing affected leaves. Use fresh seed next time.

Big bud

Caused by blackcurrant gall mites. Tiny, white grubs feed and breed inside the flower buds through winter, causing them to swell. They will affect the health of the bush and can spread viruses. Remove and dispose of all affected buds. If very bad, cut the bush to ground level, to start afresh the following year.

Birds

When soft fruit is ripening, birds can strip it with the speed of light. Pigeons are partial to young brassicas and can devastate a crop. Netting is the most effective deterrent, but take care that the pigeons can't get trapped inside. Bird scarers – anything that flaps in the wind – will help. Old CDs tied along lines are effective as they flash as the light catches them. Humming lines will also put birds off. Bits of snake-like hose might hoodwink them briefly. In practice, birds usually see through our silly attempts to hoodwink them, so change the types of bird scarers regularly.

Black bean aphid

Black aphids (see *Aphid*, opposite) that arrive in number to the undersides of the leaves notably of broad beans but also globe artichokes and many flowers, including nasturtiums. Generally they don't cause too much damage though they can weaken the plant if not caught in time. They

leave a sticky mould (honeydew) which attracts ants. Watch out for them and remove affected leaves. Pick off the tender top leaves of broad beans when they reach the desired height before the aphids arrive. Encourage predators.

Blackcurrant gall midge

Minute, white maggots feed on the tips of young leaves, causing dryness and making them drop off. Choose resistant varieties. Spray the maggots with insecticidal soap.

Blackcurrant reversion

This is spread by the big bud mite. Symptoms are small, yellowing leaves, reduced flowers and cropping. There may also be symptoms of mite infestation and, typically, swollen buds. Remove plants and start with fresh certified stock.

Blossom end rot

Shows as a tough, leathery patch at the 'blossom end', or base, of tomatoes and occasionally peppers. It may not affect all the fruits. It is caused by dryness at the roots, which can result in calcium deficiency as plants need water to take up calcium, or by soil that is too acid. Pick off the affected fruits and water the plants well and regularly.

Blossom wilt

An air-borne fungus carried by wind or insects. Blossom wilt affects apples, pears and all the stone fruits. The spores rest in cankers over the winter, and the fungus

Collars around brassicas.

spreads onto the blossom, killing it and moving onto the leaves. Small, beige pustules appear on the affected areas. It may be quite localized at first. Prune out infected areas before it spreads, removing cankers.

Bolting

When a plant feels under pressure, it is inclined to panic and flower early, rendering it useless as produce. Try to meet the plants individual needs, to avoid stress.

Boron deficiency

Usually caused by excessive lime. Root vegetables are most susceptible. Boron deficiency shows as cankers on the roots and rotting. Increase acidity with manure and compost.

Botrytis

See *Grey mould (Botrytis)*, page 353.

Brown rot

Caused by various air-borne fungi that penetrate tree fruits (particularly apples) through broken skin. They trigger the formation of rot and whitish pustules. The fruit will either fall off or wither away. Birds often cause the injury by pecking at the fruits, and they can carry it from tree to tree. Rain will spread brown rot also. Remove affected fruits and destroy them. Prune back any diseased spurs. Net against birds.

Cabbage aphids

See *Aphids*, page 344.

Cabbage moth

The green or light brown caterpillars of cabbage moths eat holes in the leaves of brassicas and burrow into the hearts of cabbages. They also go for onion leaves. Pick them off before they burrow, or grow the brassicas under fine netting.

Cabbage root fly

A bad pest particularly for brassicas, though it can destroy root crops as well, making them inedible. The adults look like small horseflies but it is the small white maggots that do the damage. The eggs are laid near or on the plants and the pupae overwinter in the soil. Symptoms are wilting and poor growth. The worst damage is likely in late spring, but second and third generations can make this a summer-long problem. A covering of net or fleece covers should thwart the cabbage root flies completely if put in place immediately after planting. If the pupae have already burrowed, brassica collars – doubled up so there are no gaps – are highly effective. A trick for confusing the fly is to blur the outline of the crop by interplanting it with rows of green manure.

Cabbage white butterfly

The caterpillars of the cabbage white are large and yellow with black markings. They feed on the outer leaves of brassicas, leaving holes, and they can strip a plant with speed. You will find the eggs on the undersides of leaves. The larvae of the small white cabbage butterfly are velvety and camouflaged green. They eat the hearts. There are two to three generations a year in spring and early autumn. Watch out for them and try to catch them before they burrow in. Inspect and pick off the affected leaves from July onwards. Prevent completely by growing under fine mesh.

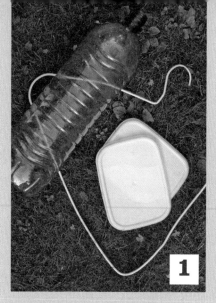

1 You will need a water bottle, wire clothes' hanger, drill, a thin plastic lid and a craft knife.

2 Carefully drill a hole in the bottom of the bottle.

Making a bird scarer

3 Drill a hole in the top.

4 Straighten out the coat hanger and thread it through the bottle...

5 ...and out at the top.

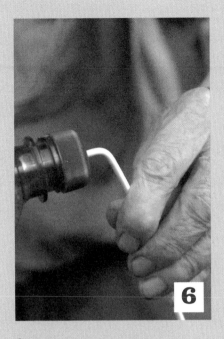

6 Bend the end of the coat hanger at the top end so that it will stay put.

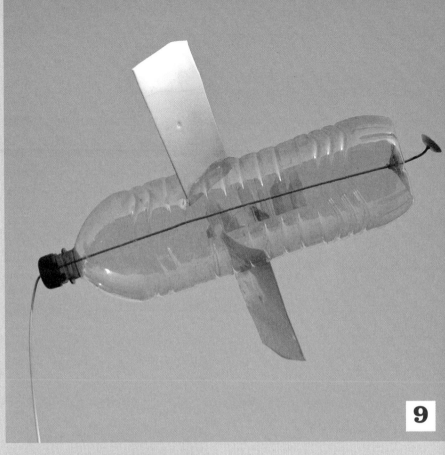

9

9 Attach the long end of the coat hanger to a stake and watch the bottle spin.

7 Carefully make a slit each side of the bottle.

8 Cut the plastic lid to make 'wings' and stick the lid into the slots.

Cabbage whitefly

Sap-feeding pest for brassicas. The tiny, white-winged adults fly up when disturbed while their scaly, brown young stay still on the undersides of leaves. A slight infestation causes little harm but don't let it get out of hand. Symptoms will be leaves that are sticky with honeydew and sooty moulds. The insects are around throughout summer and start laying eggs from mid-May onwards. Clear away all brassicas debris at the end of the season. Douse infected plants with a good jet of water. Last resort: spray weekly with insecticidal soap.

Calcium deficiency

See *Blossom end rot*, page 347.

Cankers

These are caused by a group of fungi and bacteria and can be devastating to fruit trees. They are most likely to occur in wet weather in spring or autumn. Cankers enter the fruits from the smallest wound. The first signs are an area of bark sinking inwards, and resin may ooze from cracks and fissures. The entire tree may then start to die. Remove diseased parts, cutting back to healthy tissue. Improve growing conditions. Last resort: sulphur.

Capsid bug

Small, shield-shaped, flying insects suck sap from the tips of the shoots, particularly of currants, apples and potatoes. The common green capsid will feed on the leaves, buds and flowers of all tree and bush fruits, leaving a trail of irregular holes and distorted fruits. They eat at night and travel at speed. Usually the damage is not life threatening unless they are carrying a virus. Attract birds and remove any fallen leaves where the bugs may lurk.

Carrot fly

The females lay their eggs around root crops and the resultant larvae tunnel unseen into carrots, celeriac, parsnips, parsley and celery, destroying the crop. There are usually two generations, one in late spring and another in midsummer. To defeat them entirely, either grow the whole crop under fleece or erect vertical barriers of fleece, finest mesh, heavy cardboard or sacking at least 60cm (24in) high. This will thwart carrot flies as they fly close to the ground and in straight lines. Earthing them up so that the shoulders of the carrots are concealed from view is also effective. Other methods are to sow in late spring, to avoid the first wave and make the second less serious as the population won't have built up. There are disease-resistant cultivars (e.g. 'Resistafly'), which are unappetizing to the flies. Crop rotation is important. Companion planting with onions can confuse both the onion fly and the carrot fly as they track by scent.

Celery fly

See *Leaf miners*, page 353.

Celery leaf spot

A disease caused by a fungus, usually in the seed. Celery leaf spot generally appears first as tiny, brown spots on the leaves and can spread over the plant rapidly in damp conditions. Cut away any infected parts of the plant. Use fresh, disease-resistant seed next time.

Chocolate spot

See *Bean chocolate spot*, page 345.

Club-root

An incurable, widespread fungal disease affecting brassicas and sometimes turnips and swedes. The roots become distorted, forming an elbow-like 'club' or a series of tuberous swellings, known as 'fingers' or 'toes'. If your brassicas are wilting, although they have enough moisture, dig one up and check the roots. If affected, dispose of the whole crop without delay before the disease spreads. Avoid using the same soil for brassicas for as many years as possible, bearing in mind that club-root can live in the soil for 20 years.

Take every precaution to avoid club-root. Keep the soil on the alkaline side, by adding lime to bring it up to pH 7 or more. As some common weeds, such as shepherd's purse, are in the brassica family and can harbour club-root, be conscientious about weeding.

Be very strict about cleaning tools, and remember that you can spread it on your boots. Buy transplants from a reliable source if you haven't grown them yourself. Choose disease-resistant varieties and grow them fast. Start plants in sterile compost, or if sowing outside make a bigger hole than usual and fill it with new proprietary compost.

Codling moth

This moth lays its eggs on the fruit and leaves of apple trees and less so of pears. The resulting pink, black-headed caterpillars tunnel into the fruit, often without trace as they tend go in near the stalk. After about four weeks when the fruit is spoilt, they head off to pupate. Pheromone traps, put up from May to July, will catch some or at least warn you of the presence of codling moth.

A sticky fly trap.

Coral spot

A fungus gets into a wound or a dead branch and causes dieback. Currants are particularly vulnerable. Prune out all affected stems down to healthy wood.

Crown rot

An individual or joint attack by fungi and bacteria in the soil. The effect is a rotting off of the crown, the point at which the leaves join the root. Sometimes you can save the plant by cutting off the infected areas back to healthy tissue. Improve growing conditions.

Cucumber mosaic virus

See *Virus*, page 360.

Cutworm

Big caterpillars may sever the stem entirely of a wide range of young vegetables and strawberries. They are the larvae of a group of nocturnal moths that lay thousands of eggs around the stems of plants in summer. The soil-borne caterpillars, which are in shades of brown, yellow and green, and curl into a C-shape, will work their way through a row of vegetables by night. The first signs are plants that have been severed just below the soil level. You will find the caterpillars under the surface. Clear weeds, which the moths like for egg laying, and put a collar of carpet underlay around the stems to protect them when transplanting. Turn over the soil for the birds to find the cutworms in winter or let chickens peck around the area at the end of the season.

Damping off

Caused by fungal infection common in seedlings. First symptoms are wilting. As the plants die back, patches of fluffy, white fungus appear. To avoid it, use strict hygiene – scrubbed tools, pots and trays, sterilized compost and only tap water. Don't leave seeds in the heat longer than necessary for germination and sow thinly in modules, to avoid crowding.

Downy mildew

A disease caused by various fungi that penetrate into plant tissue. They live in the soil and in plant debris for up to five years. Discoloured areas appear on the leaf surfaces with correspondingm white or pale grey fungal growth on the undersides. If unchecked, the leaves will die and drop off. Downy mildew thrives in damp, warm conditions and is common on a wide range of crops, particularly when young. Remove infected leaves and destroy them. Improve air circulation and clear weeds. Water at the base of plants, to avoid spreading this disease.

Eelworm

See *Potato cyst eelworm*, page 355.

Flea beetle

Small and shiny, this jumping beetle emerges in spring and can fly long distances to find food. First signs are little holes in leaves and stems. Its larvae feed on the roots. A bad attack will check older plants and can kill seedlings. Protect crops by growing under cloches or fleece. Grow plants fast in the right season and conditions to get them through the vulnerable period. Flea beetles don't get going until the midday temperature is 20°C (68°F). If you get an infestation, put up sticky, yellow traps. Alternatively, use boards smeared with car grease or slow-drying glue. Place these under the plants. Give the plants a shake and the beetles will leap into the trap. Clear debris round plants where flea beetles hibernate.

Gooseberry sawfly

This is a green caterpillar with black spots about 2.5cm (1in) long. It can completely defoliate gooseberry bushes if not checked. Look out for gooseberry sawflies from spring to autumn. Pick them off from the undersides of leaves before they cause too much damage. In autumn, rake away any mulches and turn over the soil lightly, to invite birds to find them. The biological caterpillar treatment Steinernema carpocapsae is effective or, when plants are small, spray with pyrethrum.

Grey mould (Botrytis)

This is a common problem in damp summers, causing leaves, flowers and buds to rot. It's a fluffy mould that releases clouds of spores, infecting everything around it when disturbed. Avoid overcrowding, and clear any rotting vegetation around plants as it will harbour grey mould. Provide good air flow. Remove all diseased plants.

Halo blight

Bacterial disease particularly affecting dwarf French and runner beans. The first symptoms are dark spots in the centre of a pale 'halo' on the leaves. This is followed by yellowing between the veins. The disease comes in the seed and rain spreads it. If you catch halo blight in time, you might save the crop by picking off the leaves. However, next year start with new seed from a fresh source.

Leaf miners

A generic term for many different insects that have larvae that burrow around inside the leaves of plants. Eggs are laid under the leaves in spring. You can detect the larvae by the meandering pattern of damage, which eventually makes the leaves go dry and brown. If you hold the leaf up to the light you may spot the culprit. They leave brown patches on the leaves of beetroot and spinach beet. Generally they are not too harmful. Pick off and destroy the affected leaves. The caterpillars of leek moths bore into the stems of leeks and onion bulbs. There are two generations – late spring and late summer. They pupate in cocoons on the leaves. Pick off the cocoons when you see them. If you cut the leeks down to the base, they will quickly reshoot afresh. If the damage is too great, start again.

Leaf spot

A general term for both fungal and bacterial diseases that cause spotting on a wide range of plants, including peas and broad beans. The spots are dead areas and. as they spread, leaves drop off. Leaf spot is generally not very damaging. Remove affected leaves and burn. Make sure the plants have plenty of air circulation and don't water from overhead, as this can spread leaf spot.

Leek moth

See *Leaf miners*, above.

Leek rust

A fungus that affects the onion family at large. The leaves get covered with vivid orange pustules filled with spores. Remove affected leaves. Generally no other damage will have occurred. Remove all debris around the plants. To avoid leek rust in future, use new ground, space widely for air circulation and don't overfeed with nitrogen as this will produce vulnerable soft growth.

Lettuce root aphid

See *Aphids*, page 344.

Magnesium deficiency

Caused by acid soil and the overuse of high-potash fertilizers. Magnesium is easily washed out by heavy rain. The symptoms are yellowing along the edges and in the areas between the veins of the older leaves. As the leaves deteriorate, they may go red, purple, yellow or brown. Foliar feed with Epsom salts. Lime the soil to reduce acidity. Avoid potash fertilizer.

Mealy cabbage aphid

See *Aphids*, page 344.

Mice and voles

Mice steal seeds and seedlings, particularly peas and beans, and will raid your shed. Grow plants under cover and transplant when less vulnerable. Voles like beetroot, carrots and potatoes. Use cloches to protect plants and if necessary put down traps.

Mildews

See *Downy mildew*, page 353, and *Powdery mildew*, page 355.

Mosaic virus

See *Virus*, page 360.

Onion fly

Having spent the winter below ground, the onion fly emerges as an adult in May. It lays its eggs on and around the host plants – onions in particular, but also leeks, shallots and garlic. The resulting small, white maggots cause havoc with the crops. They bore holes into them, eat the roots and cause the plants to rot. Remove any affected plants and destroy. Plant sets rather than grow from seed or cover plants with fine net or fleece before the flies arrive. Practise crop rotation. Dig the land over and let the birds find these pests.

Onion neck rot

This fungal disease is exacerbated by wet weather. The signs of damage don't usually appear until the onions have been in store for a couple of months, when they become soft and discoloured. A grey, fluffy, fungal growth develops, particularly around the neck of the bulb. The fungus lurks in onion debris and on the soil. Grow your onions by the book – use top-quality sets and allow for plenty of air circulation while they are growing and during storage. Don't store any onions that are damaged. Practise crop rotation.

Onion white rot

A fatal disease caused by soil fungus. The entire onion family is susceptible. A fluffy, white fungus dotted with little, black specks spreads over the base of the bulbs and the roots, and the leaves turn yellow and wilt. The black specks are 'sklerotia', or 'fruiting bodies' that will lurk in the soil for up to seven years, waiting for the next host. Dispose of the crop and avoid using the same land for the onion family for eight years if possible.

Parsnip canker

Rough, brown, red or black patches appear usually on the shoulder of the roots. Parsnip canker is a fungal infection that enters through a wound. It could be through a tiny hole left by a carrot fly. There isn't a cure. Buy disease-resistant seed next time.

Pea and bean weevil

U-shaped holes appear in the edges of leaves of peas and beans. The larvae of tiny, grey beetles live in the soil and feed on the nitrogen-fixing nodules of the roots, and the adults emerge in June or July. Generally, they don't do too much harm except to young and vulnerable plants. Move to new ground and keep the adults off, with cloches or nets, when you sow.

Pea moth

This moth lays its eggs on pea flowers to hatch out inside the pea pod. Plant early or late in the season to avoid the breeding time. As peas do not need to be pollinated, cover them with fine mesh when in flower. Turn over the soil for the birds to get at this pest in winter.

Peach leaf curl

A fungus that attacks the unfurling leaves of peaches and nectarines. It causes the leaves to twist and curl, change colour, develop red blisters and drop off. Peach leaf curl is spread by rain and is prevented by covering the plants from late winter to spring. This is done by constructing a wooden frame and hanging clear-plastic curtains, with a roof piece, over the entire plant and tucking the ends into the soil. Open up on dry, early spring days for pollination. Pick off any affected leaves and burn.

Pear leaf blister

Pear leaf blister is more unsightly than harmful. Microscopic gall mites burrow into the leaves, resulting in yellow or pink blotching and blistering. There is no real cure apart from removing affected leaves promptly.

Pear midge

Tiny larvae of a fly or gall midge which burrow into young pear fruits slowly turning them black and causing them to fall off. The maggots go back into the soil to pupate for the following year. Pick fruits at the first signs and destroy. Disturb the soil for the birds. There is no cure for a bad infestation.

Pear rust

See *Rust*, page 356.

Pear scab

See *Apple and pear scab*, page 345.

Plum leaf curling aphid

Green, winged aphids feed on the leaf sap of plums and greengages. The symptoms are curled and crinkled leaves in spring, with the aphids nesting inside. They fly off after a few weeks and the trees will put out new leaves. They return at the end of summer to lay their eggs ready for the next season. Encourage predators, squash them or hose them off. Remove affected leaves. Last resort: insecticidal soap.

Plum moth

The plum moth produces little, pink and brown caterpillars that feed inside plums and leave their excrement in it. They burrow out to overwinter in fissures in the bark. A pheromone trap in late spring will warn you of their presence and disrupt mating. Pick up any fallen fruit and dispose of it. There is no cure for an infestation.

Potato and tomato blight

This serious fungal disease caused the Irish potato famine of the mid-19th century. First signs are brown marks on leaves and stems with a downy, white mass of fungal spores on the undersides. The spores wash down into the soil, and the tomato fruits and potato tubers develop sunken areas. Tomatoes can also get leathery patches. Other fungi and bacteria join in to induce a fast-spreading, highly infectious soft rot. Blight is most likely in hot, damp weather. The Potato Council will send you free blight warnings if you sign up www.potato.org.uk/blight.

Destroy the tomatoes. If you catch the blight early enough, you may be able to save the potato crop by removing the leaves and digging up the potatoes quickly. In future, buy resistant strains (e.g. the Sarpo series such as 'Sarpo Mira, 'Sarpo Shona'). Space plants widely for air circulation, and water at ground level. Earth up and mulch potatoes with straw, to prevent the spores reaching the tubers. Dig up all potatoes at the end of the season. Any left will infect the next crop. Use crop rotation.

Potato blackleg

This is caused by soil-borne bacteria. First signs are stunted leaves and blackened rot at the base of the stem. The potato will also be rotting as the bacteria will have entered the potato through a break in the skin and may be isolated to a single potato plant in a crop. Potato blackleg is more likely in wet conditions. Avoid damaging potatoes, particularly when lifting them. Only store tubers with unbroken skin. Buy certified seed potatoes.

Potato common scab

A bacterial disease usually occurring in dry weather and on sandy soils, particularly if newly cultivated. Circular, scabby patches appear on the tubers, which can usually be peeled off. Increase the acidity of the soil and its water-holding capacity (by digging in well-rotted organic matter). Keep the crop well watered. Buy resistant cultivars.

Potato cyst eelworm

Potato cyst eelworm is to be avoided at all costs as there is no cure. Each microscopic nematode female can lay 500 eggs, which stay in the ground for ten years or longer, waiting for a host plant to arrive before they hatch. On an allotment where much potato growing has taken place over years, eelworm eggs are likely to be lurking in the soil. The larvae feed on the roots. The first symptoms are drying, dying leaves starting from the bottom, followed by poor crops. If allowed to build up there will be crop failure. Look for varieties with resistance where possible. Avoid bringing the eelworm in on your boots or tools from other parts of the allotment site that may be infected. Keep up the crop rotation with as big a gap as possible before returning to the original potato patch. Put on lots of well-rotted compost and manure, to bring in nematode predators. When the ground is fallow, plant mustard green manure (Sinapsis alba) as it inhibits eelworms. It is said that they don't care for marigolds either.

Potato powdery scab

A fungal disease mostly found on heavy soils where potato crops have been grown over the years. The potatoes form scabby patches that burst to release thousands of spores into the soil. Destroy the crop and abandon the site for potato growing for a minimum of three or four years. Improve the drainage for future crops.

Powdery mildew

First signs are a whitish, powdery growth – typically on the upper sides of the leaves but can be almost anywhere – on a wide variety of plants. Powdery mildew is caused by a group of fungi. If left to develop it can cause yellowing, distortion, dead spots on leaves and leaf drop. In severe cases it can kill. Powdery mildew thrives particularly on young plants in dry soil in humid conditions. Catch it early and remove affected leaves. Keep the plants watered at the base, to avoid spreading the fungi. Don't overfeed plants with high-nitrogen fertilizers as they will produce soft, lush growth. Look for cultivars with disease resistance.

Raspberry beetle

This beetle feeds on raspberry flowers and lay its eggs on raspberries, blackberries and the hybrids. The yellow larvae burrow into the fruits, making them dry up and shrivel. Expose the ground around the canes for the birds to find the overwintering pupae. If there is a bad infestation, cut all the canes right back to ground level. You will miss next year's fruit but this should do the trick.

Raspberry cane spot

A fungus that shows as purplish spots with a white centre on the young stems of raspberries, blackberries and the hybrids. In extreme cases it can split the canes and cause leaf drop. Prune out affected canes as soon as you see it before it spreads.

Raspberry spur blight

A fungus that first appears on the buds of new raspberry and loganberry canes, leaving deep purple splotches. If left unchecked, it will spread to the canes, turning grey with tiny, black spots of 'fruiting bodies' in winter. The result is a poor crop. The fungus spreads rapidly in wet or overcrowded conditions or where too much nitrogen has caused soft, sappy growth. Prune out diseased canes before

the fungus spreads and thin for the following season.

Red spider mite

Microscopic, brown mites flaring to brilliant orange-red may appear in winter. They attack outdoor strawberries and other soft fruit. The effect is a silvering of the leaves, followed by a mottled yellowing. Red spider mites are a new and increasing problem outdoors in hot summers. They like dry conditions best, so a squirt of water or misting on a regular basis will help to keep them at bay, with or without the addition of insecticidal soap. Clear all debris. The fruit tree red spider mite on apples, plums, damsons and pears is difficult to control once it has taken hold.

Replant disease

This disease is generally associated with roses, though it occurs with fruit trees as well. It happens when you replace a fruit tree with another of the same species in the same spot. If you cannot find a fresh site for new plantings, the only way to prevent replant disease is to dig out the topsoil to a minimum depth of 45cm (18in) and put in fresh soil from another part of the plot.

Rust

Various fungi cause discoloration, withering and die off on foliage and stems. First signs are bright orange or dark brown pustules. Rust is most common in tree fruit in damp situations. Remove infected leaves. Improve conditions. Last resort: spray with sulphur.

Scale insect

Mostly found in greenhouses, but also outside. Scale insects are sap feeders that attack the leaf veins or stems of plants,

weakening them. They develop a waxy shell or scale. Scale insects look like tiny, brown specks. Control them by catching them early on the undersides of leaves and destroying them.

Scorch

Burnt, bleached or brown patches on leaves or petals caused by the sun, particularly where droplets of water magnify the rays.

Shot hole

A general term for bacterial and fungal infections that cause holes edged with a brown ring to appear in the leaves. Remove affected leaves and destroy. Keep up air circulation and remove weeds.

Silver leaf

A fungus that enters through wounds, affecting only individual branches at first and causing a slight silvering. Plum trees and cherry trees are particularly vulnerable. Leaves drop off and branches will die in time. Eventually the whole tree will perish. Prune only in summer, as wounds heal more quickly when the tree is growing vigorously. Cut back to healthy wood and bin any infected prunings. Clear away dead timber where the spores lurk.

Slugs

There are four common species of slug. Some live underground and attack roots and burrow into potato tubers unseen. Slugs like warm, moist weather and come out to feed at night. They shelter and breed under stones, in amongst piles of leaves, under garden debris, in the soil, and under mulches. They have many predators – frogs, toads, birds, hedgehogs, shrews, slow worms and beetles. Hens are remarkably efficient in clearing them out.

Mulch around your plants with inhospitable mulches to help protect from slugs.

Cover small plants with cloches. Surround plants with inhospitable sharp or dry mulches – bran, gravel, egg shells, wood chips, soot, ash, or lime. Do torchlight vigils and catch and destroy slugs by dropping them into a salt solution. Using tongs or rubber gloves makes this slightly less repellent. Trap and drown them by sinking plastic pots of beer or milk into the ground, changing the bait from time to time and stopping if you catch beetles. Slugs will gorge until they die on bran. Scooped-out melon and grapefruit skins make hiding places for them to congregate, as do old planks or wet newspaper – they can then be collected and destroyed. Lay out alternative food sources. Slugs will choose rotting vegetation over fresh, so old lettuce leaves kept moist under the cover of a tile will draw them away to where they can be collected. Nematodes will kill the slugs above and below ground and provide you with at least six weeks of peace – time for plants to get growing. Use the new organic slug pellets that are harmless to all other wildlife.

A slug barrier offers excellent protection.

Snails

The same treatments are effective as for slugs, though frogs won't eat snails nor will parasitic nematodes be able to get at them effectively.

Soft rot

A bacterial and fungal disease that results in decay of plant tissues. Soft rot affects swedes and turnips, showing as a greyish, mushy rot on heavy, wet ground. Start again, trying raised beds for better drainage.

Sooty mould

Results from the honeydew excreted by aphids, whitefly and mealy bugs. Though unsightly as leaves get covered with grey to black mould, sooty mould is not in itself harmful except that it reduces light and air getting to the leaves. The only way to deal with it is to destroy the aphids.

Tip burn

Affects lettuce and chicory, turning the leaf edges brown. Tip burn is usually caused by calcium deficiency due to dry roots or the soil being too acid. Water well and, if your soil is acid, lime it before planting lettuce next time.

Tomato blight

See *Potato and tomato blight*, page 355.

Turnip gall weevil

At first glance, turnip gall weevil can be confused with club-root. The adult beetles lay their eggs on the roots of turnips, swede, cabbage, cauliflower, brussels sprouts or broccoli. The ensuing grubs make the plants produce swellings to encase them. The weevils may not affect the green leaves of the cabbage family, but the turnips and swedes should be discarded. Use new ground next time. Cover with net or fleece immediately after sowing, to prevent the eggs being laid.

Vine weevil

The tell-tale signs are irregular holes around the edges of leaves caused by the adult beetles. The larvae, which hatch out in spring, do the most damage, having fed on the plant roots all winter. Little, black beetles emerge in May or June, and each one lays hundreds of eggs around the roots of host plants. Plants in containers and those in the greenhouse are particularly at

risk. The larvae, which are white with a brown head, C-shaped and 10 mm (⅜ in) long, can be controlled with biological control Steinerema kraussei.

Violet root rot

Filaments of violet fungal threads cover the roots, crown and stems of plants. Violet root rot affects asparagus, beetroot, carrots, celery, parsnips, potatoes, strawberries, swedes and turnips. The first signs are yellowing and stunting. It is most commonly found in wet, acid soils. Remove and destroy the crop before it disintegrates and sheds its spores. Change the soil conditions before trying again.

Virus

This comes in many forms, all incurable. The first signs are loss of vigour, stunting and distortion, followed by strange colour changes and patterns on leaves including mosaic patterns, flecking and mottling. Viruses can be caused by soil-borne nematodes and fungi. More commonly they will be passed from plant to plant by aphids or even gardeners as they move around handling different plants. Try to prevent the spread by strict hygiene and keeping the aphid population at bay. Buy certified virus-free stock where possible. Remove infected plants as soon as a virus is detected.

Whitefly

Sap-feeding insects that can be spotted on the underside of leaves. Whitefly excretes honeydew, which leaves sooty mould on the leaves – not harmful in itself but it prevents light and air getting to them. If you shake the plants the whiteflies will fly up and you can suck them up with portable vacuum cleaner or shower them off with a jet of water.

Winter moth

In October, the wingless females of the winter moth emerge from the soil and climb apples, pears and plums to mate. The resulting looper caterpillars emerge at budburst in spring and can cause considerable damage to emerging fruits, flowers and leaves. Protect trees by applying grease bands in October and keeping tree stems well greased until April.

Wireworm

The larvae of the click beetle. The beetles lay their eggs in summer and the larvae live underground for up to five years and bore holes into carrots, brassicas, strawberries, lettuce, onions, tomatoes and potatoes. They feed on turf, so as your plot becomes more cultivated with less grass, they will diminish in number. You can trap wireworm by burying carrots, cabbage or a potato on a stick to draw them away from your crops. Keep the ground free of weeds and dig it over in winter for the birds to find these pests.

bigger pests

There is little that you can really do that will to discourage big wildlife from demolishing your crops and causing havoc other than building fortifications against them and putting your crops safely under siege.

Badgers

These are becoming an increasing problem in allotments. Like foxes, they are a protected species. They live mainly on earthworms but also eat beetles, voles, mice, frogs, snails and wasp grubs, acorns, beech nuts, fruits, roots and bulbs. Badgers have a particular love of sweetcorn and will knock down quite hefty barricades to get at it. As they are big clumsy animals, the main damage comes from them digging big holes and knocking things down. They can heave themselves over wire fences and walls so barriers have to be extremely strong and difficult to climb to keep them out.

Foxes

Although a common feature of allotments, foxes are protected by law from inhumane and poisonous control methods. Despite popular belief, they are not dangerous, except to chickens and rabbits. These must be secured safely in their hutches, houses and runs, particularly in late spring when foxes are rearing their cubs. It is rare for a fox to attack a cat and they do not fight dogs either, unless cornered. However,

foxes do disrupt crops when digging for worms, leave highly pungent excretions usually on exposed spots, and their mating calls – eerie screaming sounds – can keep you up at night should you live near enough to the allotment site during their courtship months – December to February.

Like dogs, foxes can scent food from a great distance, so don't leave temptation in their way. Deterrents on the market include liquids that mimic scent-marking odours of foxes, to give the impression that another fox has marked the territory. There are citronella products that can be used to protect specific areas of the plot, and sprays that can be introduced after clearing up excrement that removes the associated territory scent. The best protection is to cage your crops off with thick wire mesh – or to decide to live and let live. Foxes may deal with the rabbit population.

Rabbits

Wild rabbits are a real pest for the vegetable grower as they will gnaw their way through your crops and chew off the bark of young trees. The only really effective prevention is to put up barriers.

These need to be only 90cm (3ft) high but should be buried 30cm (1ft) down and bent outwards in an L-shape at the bottom, to prevent rabbits burrowing through. Trees can be protected with tree guards to the same height. If the rabbits are already in your part of the allotment, you could try the humane catch and release traps. Any caught rabbits need to be taken a good distance away or they will find their way back. Rabbits generally have a large home range (6 hectares/15 acres), which they like to stick to throughout their lives. There are also products on the market that are said to trigger fear of death in a rabbit. The home version is dried blood meal. You can buy it in garden centres and scatter it around the allotment beds.

CANES

	EACH
3 FT	12p
4 FT	~~14p~~ 16p
5 FT	24p
6 FT	26p
7 FT	28p
8 FT	~~30p~~ 32p

off the plot

reuse and renew

It has always been a matter of pride amongst allotment people to make do and mend. They set a great example when it comes to recycling. Below are a few ideas.

here and there...

- hefty cardboard, the sort that washing machines are packaged in, makes a good, light-excluding mulch, as do silage bags, though these are not biodegradable;
- old drawers can be turned into cold frames with a piece of glass or plastic on top;
- old bits of timber and floorboards can be used for raised bed edging;
- fish or scaffold netting makes a framework for peas to climb;
- plastic water bottles make cloches for individual plants with the bottoms sawn off and the lids removed;
- the inner cardboard tubes of toilet rolls and kitchen towel can be used root trainers for seeds. If you make three cuts around the bottom you can tuck them into each other to make a base for each container;
- cardboard egg boxes make starter containers for seeds of small plants;
- old tin cans, ice cream tubs and yogurt pots will serve as containers as long they are well scrubbed and have drainage holes in the bottom;
- polystyrene cups make cosy containers for winter seedlings;
- polystyrene boxes from the fishmonger are useful for warmth under seedlings in winter;
- bubble wrap is often thrown out by big shops and is free to anyone not too proud to pick it up; it makes good insulation in the greenhouse or for a cold frame;
- old CDs or silver foil dishes can be strung up as bird scarers;
- pallets have multiple uses and, nailed together, make excellent compost bins or storage boxes for people without a shed;
- potato sacks come free from vegetable stalls if you ask stallholders nicely;
- if you are short of compost, go to a vegetable market at the end of the day before the road sweepers get there, to gather up the waste vegetation;
- an old sandpit can be made into a pond or a child's flowerbed.

from the council...

Compost
Depending on the area, allotment sites may be able to get compost made from recycled garden and kitchen waste delivered in loose, 5 tonne loads from the recycling departments of the local waste authority. This is usually free to allotment sites, providing access is good, and it can be tipped easily. Council compost is tested for contaminants to the industry standard (PAS100) and will have reached sufficient heat for all the pathogens to have been destroyed. It won't have been sieved, but should be good for soil improvement.

Leaves
Councils will generally supply leaves in autumn, to rot down for leaf-mould. Specify that you want leaves from parks not from the roads as they might be contaminated.

Wood shavings

Worth asking the council. Wood shavings make luxuriant carpeting on paths.

Manure from stables and city farms

When buying or collecting manure from stables, check the source if you have any fears of contamination. In recent years there has been a serious problem with the weedkiller aminopyralid in products such as Forefront, Pharoah and Banish, which have been sprayed on arable land as a herbicide for docks, nettles and thistles. The chemical in the resulting hay appears to be harmless to animals that eat it, but is so persistent that, even after it has gone through the digestive system, it remains active in the manure. The effect is stunted growth and distortion in broad-leaved plants including peas, beans, carrots, parsnips, potatoes and tomatoes. Contaminated vegetables will be inedible but will not affect health according to the Pesticide Safety Directorate.

If you have any worries, do a test. Fill three flowerpots with ordinary compost, and three mixed with manure. Mark the pots. Sow a broad bean in each and note the result. If you already have a heap that is contaminated, return it to source by adding it to the council waste scheme, or leave it to rot down for two years before testing again. The Health and Safety Executive reports that, if weedkiller is already incorporated it into the soil, it should be inactive after six months and the soil should be safe to use again for growing vegetables. For updates, advice and the helpline, go to:
http://www.dowagro.com/uk/grass_bites/faq/allotment.htm

The trading hut. If there isn't a on your site, encourage the management to start one. They can buy in bulk, making great savings for all the plotholders.

good old tools

The basics, that you will use almost every day, are a good spade, fork, hoe, rake, trowel and secateurs. Buying new, cheap tools is a false economy. They break easily.

Shafts snap and blades bend. The alternative to buying top-priced quality tools is to search out the great, old classics. You can find them in country markets or in auctions of goods and chattels. Sometimes there are stalls for old tools at flower shows, and you can buy them on the internet.

Throughout the 19th century, the British garden tool industry earned itself a worldwide reputation. The great, old tool names to look out for include Elwell, Skelton, Brades and Parkes & Nash. They are all lost to us in the manufacturing melt down but, in garden sheds throughout the world, their tools survive.

what to look for

Blades and heads
Spade blades are made of carbon steel – iron and carbon forged at high temperatures and tempered by reheating at lower ones. This makes them extremely strong, inflexible and able to take a razor-sharp edge. Rakes and other tools with tines are made to be a little less rigid, with the addition of manganese – depending on the function.

Tool handles
The best handles are made of selected hard woods. The favourite is straight-grained ash as it is strong but not brittle. The best handles are the D- and Y-shaped ones. To make the Y-shape, the ash handle is split, steam bent and a wooden crosspiece is attached with a steel cap. The simple T handle suits gardeners who wear thick gloves. It is a question of preference. Try different handles and weights to see what feels comfortable and that the tool is the right height for you. Standard lengths are rather like adult trouser sizes, from 70 cm (28 in) to 80 cm (32 in). The tool should be a comfortable weight. Give it a swing to test it before buying.

Spades
A spade, sharp enough to split open a compost bag, is a precision instrument. At the same time it needs to be strong enough to take your weight when digging. With it you can cut straight edges, make trenches and take off spits of turf cleanly. The back is used for breaking down clods of earth or banging in stakes. The ones with metal treads of top of the blade are more comfortable on the soles of your feet, especially if you garden in gumboots.

Forks
A garden fork's sharp individual tines can penetrate hard ground. Forks are used for sifting stones, breaking up clay soils and for harvesting potatoes and root crops. For heavy work, the English garden fork with its chiselled tines is hard to beat. The small border fork, which is a third of the size, is a niftier tool for lighter work.

Hoes
Throughout the growing season the hoe will be used almost daily to whip out weeds before they get much root. Weight in the handle helps. There are numerous types:
● draw hoes are generally recommended for cutting off the tops of light weeds. You

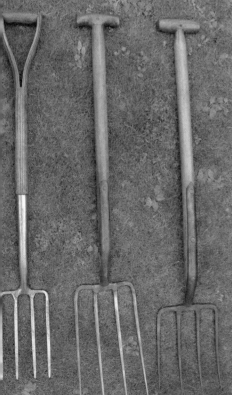

have more control over them than with a push hoe;

- push, or Dutch, hoes come in many forms, including diamond-shaped and moon-shaped ones. They should have a sharp edge so they can be angled into nooks and crannies. If you choose a swan-necked Dutch hoe type, the soil won't build up behind it;
- warren hoes, with their narrow triangular or heart-shaped blade, are designed to make sowing drills and are good for hooking out weeds;
- wheel hoes (invented by Jethro Tull) make weeding and cultivating down straight lines between rows on light soil as effortless as pushing a pram.

Trowels

These are indispensable for planting and transplanting, for making small planting holes and digging out weed roots. The tip of the trowel is useful for scooping spoonfuls of fertilizer or for breaking up the soil surface. Deeper-bowled trowels can carry more compost while the narrow ones are better for precision work.

Rakes

With a good flathead rake and a little practice you can transform a rough patch of ground into that most desirable of garden ideals – a fine tilth. Drag stones and debris out on the pull and level on the push. Turn the rake over and you can make a flat track. The bowhead rake is very handy for making straight, wide rows, following a line marked out with pegs and string, and for dragging out stones as it does so. In autumn, you may need a springbok rake, the most efficient tool for gathering up leaves.

watch out for

A bit of rust doesn't matter – you can rub that off with emery paper – but make sure the steel isn't bent or cracked. All the rivets should be sound and the woodwork should be free of splits. Look for shafts and handles that have a close, straight grain on the front and back, where the main leverage is going to be. The wider, weaker grain and any knots in the wood should be at the sides.

where not to economize

Secateurs

These are invaluable. You should never be without them. If possible, buy a pair of new, professional-quality ones. They will last you a lifetime. They should feel comfortable in the hand, the spring should work smoothly, and the safety catch and the blades should slide together like a well-oiled machine. A holster will guarantee that they are always to hand. Always use tools that are more than capable of the job in hand. When you have heavy pruning to do, you will need to upgrade from secateurs to loppers or a pruning saw.

Stakes

Encourage the trading hut to get hold of hazel peasticks and stakes. The only reason that you don't see them in the garden centres is because they don't stack neatly and take up too much space. Using hazel will be helping to support Britain's coppiced woodlands. Apart from providing you with lovely rustic stakes and peasticks, a hazel is a superb tree for wildlife.

Seeds

If your allotment is a member of NSALG, the management will be able to get seeds at around half price from Kings Seeds (www.kingsseeds.com). However, most seed companies will do a bulk deal. Many allotment people grow from dried pulses – certainly worth a try. Do a germination test before sowing them. Best of all, though, is to use your own seed (see page 148–152). In the end, you may develop strains that particularly suit your conditions. There is nothing like seeing your own seed come up for a rush of pure satisfaction.

other places for horticultural bargains

Trading hut

If there isn't a trading hut on your site, encourage the management to start one. They can buy in bulk, making great savings for all the plotholders.

Boot fairs

Though you rarely find good old tools in boot fairs, you can often find other bargains. Gardening gloves, watering cans, fertilizers, working boots and old deckchairs, also plug plants in trays are often sold very cheaply.

Commercial forestry suppliers

For woodland tree (e.g hazel for coppicing) at a fraction of the price.

The internet

If you are looking for machinery in particular, browse the internet for fierce competition on price.

the law and allotments

Many aspects of allotment gardening, from who should provide plots to how you can be evicted, are governed by "allotments acts" of ancient vintage and mind-numbing complexity, wrapped in enduring myths and qualified by subsequent and seemingly unrelated laws.

acquiring a plot

Nowadays most allotments are provided by local authorities: the lowest tier of local government in a particular area is also the "allotment authority", which has a duty to provide a sufficient number of allotments where it considers a demand to exist (Small Holdings and Allotments Act 1908 s23). Myth has it that if you ask for an allotment the council has to give you one. What's the reality?

First, the allotment authority has to judge whether there is demand for allotments. Where there is some provision already it can look to current usage levels and waiting lists as a guide, and if you are on a waiting list, you can remind your local councillor of that fact. Where there is no provision, you can force the issue by asking five other council taxpayers to join you in requesting allotments: the allotment authority is then legally obliged to take this into account (Small Holdings and Allotments Act 1908 s23), and you can request evidence that it has done so. The National Society of Allotment and Leisure Gardeners (NSALG, www.nsalg.org.uk) should be informed if your council refuses to assess its allotments provision, and may be willing to support you in legal action. The local planning authority (which may be a higher level of government) is also required by planning guidance (Planning Policy Guidance Note 17) to undertake a robust audit of its open space provision, including allotments.

Once it agrees that there is a demand, the allotment authority must consider whether it has provided a sufficient number of allotments. Contrary to myth, there is no enforceable national standard as to what a sufficient number might mean: the same planning guidance advises that standards of provision should be set locally. Where it has plots already it may find that the demand can be accommodated by tightening up on cultivation standards,

or splitting plots in half. If you are on a waiting list you are likely to take offence at the sight of a poorly maintained plot, but there may be a good reason behind non-cultivation, such as illness or a new tenant only just starting. Good practice guidance in managing cultivation standards has been issued by the Local Government Association (LGA, A Place to Grow), and you can challenge your council on whether it is in compliance, although the guidance is not legally binding. Plot splitting is unpopular with growers who aim for self-sufficiency, but it is permitted by the failure of the allotment acts to spell out a minimum size for an allotment (although there is a maximum), and smaller plots can suit people with busy lives.

Where these measures are insufficient, then the allotment authority is obliged to secure more allotments to meet demand, and can do so if needs be by compulsory lease or purchase of land (Small Holdings and Allotments Act 1908 s25 and s39). Crucially, however, the law sets no deadline on this action. Furthermore, in Inner London (where waiting lists are longest) local authorities have been long since been released from the duty to provide allotments, although they can choose to do so (London Government Act 1963 s55), and in Northern Ireland (which, along with Scotland, has separate allotments legislation), provision has always been at the local authority's discretion (Allotments Act (Northern Ireland) 1932 s1). Local government everywhere has many competing claims on its resources, and allotments can seem very expensive when the number of beneficiaries is taken into account, so reluctance to act quickly is not surprising. A Place to Grow includes guidance on how to drum up support for new allotments from beyond the immediate circle of keen gardeners, by achieving wider community and environmental benefits, and also advises allotment authorities to have a strategy in place to meet demand. Why not ask your council what its strategy is?

You may think it important that the local authority provide other facilities along with your new plot, such as secure fencing, parking, a water supply and a shed. Most do provide extras, but they are under no legal obligation to do so, and where allotment rents do not even cover recurrent costs (as is usually the case), additional facilities mean additional contributions from general taxation. Higher rents could make a contribution, but concessionary rents (which are allowed by the Allotments Act 1950 s10) may be required to ensure that people on low incomes are not excluded. Case law (Howard v Reigate and Banstead BC 13 November 1981) indicates that allotment rents should be set in a way that is comparable with charges for other municipal leisure facilities, although there are many possibilities for establishing such comparability, not all of which would support low rents. The alternative way forward (for both new and well-established sites) is to set up an association and seek a devolved management agreement with the local authority, which will improve access to grants and other forms of support. Such agreements are allowed in law (Local Government Act 1972 s123 and s127). Further information on the practicalities are provided in another LGA good practice guide, Growing in the Community (2nd Edition), through the network of experienced Allotment Regeneration Initiative (ARI) Voluntary Mentors (www.farmgarden.org.uk/ari), who can provide free hands-on support, and through the NSALG.

what can I do with my plot?

An allotment garden (a plot to the rest of us) is defined in law as a parcel of land "which is wholly or mainly cultivated by the occupier for the production of vegetable or fruit crops for consumption by himself or his family" (Allotments Act 1922 s22). This definition clearly precludes commercial enterprise, although the disposal of unplanned surpluses to others is not illegal. The cultivation of a plot by a group requires special tenancy measures to remain lawful – for example, by securing individual tenancies for defined segments of the plot, or obtaining temporary release of the land for another use (Small Holdings and Allotments Act 1908 s27), although the latter is difficult to justify when there are waiting lists.

A variety of restrictions within and beyond the allotment acts constrain the way in which the plot can be used. Chickens (but not cockerels) can be kept (Allotments Act 1950 s12), for example, but the way these are kept must comply with public health and animal welfare laws and guidelines, which can be impossible on some sites. There is nothing in the allotment acts to restrict bonfires, but good relations with neighbours and the need to avoid creating a statutory nuisance often give rise to local regulations. These restrictions find practical expression in the terms of the allotment tenancy that you will be required to sign, and any rules or regulations to which the tenancy makes reference. The details of such documents vary widely, though good practice models can be obtained from the NSALG and ARI. It is essential that you retain these documents and comply with them as far as you are able, and seek advice from whoever is running the site when ambiguities arise. For example, you may wish to bring carpet, timber and other material on site to support raised bed cultivation between permanent beds, but you should check that these are not deemed to be waste deposited on the plot in contradiction of the rules. Problems also arise in respect of "no dig" methods when the allotment tenancy requires "cultivation", and in whether children are permitted to roam unsupervised (as they are prone to do) beyond the confines of the plot. In simple terms, however, you are unlikely to fall foul of the rules if you keep in mind the need to be a good neighbour, and to keep the plot in a well-cultivated condition. And if a rule seems unfair or unreasonable, find out who is responsible for it (it may be the local authority, or it may be something agreed by the sites' own association), and be prepared to query it.

One thing you cannot automatically do with your plot is pass it on, in whole or in part, to someone else. If you give up the plot for any reason, it will normally go to the next person on the waiting list. You should inquire as to local arrangements for passing on a plot to a partner in you are obliged to relinquish the tenancy: it may be possible to establish a joint tenancy, or your partner may be allowed to join the waiting list and sit at the top of the list until the plot becomes vacant.

losing the plot

Provided that you keep to the tenancy agreement, your tenancy may continue indefinitely, although legally you can be required to relinquish your plot within a year without due cause (Allotments Act 1922 s1), provided that notice is served in accordance with detailed provisions of the allotment acts, and you can also lose your plot if you move a mile or more outside the local authority's boundary (Small Holdings and Allotments Act 1908 s30), although this provision is rarely enforced. In practice, tenancies are usually lost because of non-compliance, or because the site itself is lost to another use. What protection does the law provide in either circumstance?

Provided that the tenancy agreement itself does not contradict the law – which is unlikely, given the durability of standard model agreements – your main protection is to honour its terms. Sometimes this is straightforward. The agreement should specify, for example, how much rent should be paid to whom, and when. Failure to pay within a specified period is likely to lead to an irrevocable notice to quit (Small Holdings and Allotments Act 1908 s30). But other infringements are subjective. One of the side effects of long waiting lists, for example, has been to throw a particular spotlight on non-cultivation, which can mean very different things to different people. The LGA guidance A Place to Grow suggests fair and appropriate procedures for dealing with this issue, and in the event of dispute you may wish to challenge your local authority – or the allotment association if management is devolved – on whether it complies with this guidance. If your association is not in compliance, you might wish to check if this constitutes a breach of the devolved management agreement with the local authority. You should also check that there is an appeals procedure in place, and take advantage of it if you believe you have a good case.

When the site itself is under threat, a key issue is whether it was originally acquired for the purpose of providing allotments (such sites are known as "statutory allotments"), or for some other purpose. The latter, which are also known as "temporary allotments", have no more protection in law than plots provided privately. Local authorities cannot dispose of statutory allotments, however, without going through a defined legal procedure (Allotments Act 1925 s8), in which they must demonstrate to central government that there is insufficient demand for the plots despite evidence of active promotion, and that existing plotholders will be relocated elsewhere if at all possible. The NSALG must also be consulted. Disposal is not allowed simply because the local authority has a different use in mind for the land, and if disposal is approved, the proceeds should be directed in the first instance to making alternative provision for displaced plotholders and upgrading the allotments estate (Small Holdings and Allotments Act 1908 s32).

If the worst happens, and you are forced to surrender your plot through no fault of your own, you will be entitled to compensation for the value of any crops lost and the residual value of any manure applied to the land (Allotments Act 1922 s2). Many authorities ban the cultivation of fruit trees and perennial crops, in part to restrict their liability for compensation. If you have a shed or greenhouse, you may be obliged to remove it.

If you are surrendering a plot voluntarily because your personal circumstances have changed, and the tenancy will consequently pass to someone else, the local authority has no obligation to compensate you, nor to obtain any remuneration for you should you choose to leave a shed or other structures behind. And in the worst case, the authority has the right to seek compensation from you if it has to restore your plot to cultivable status (Allotments Act 1950 s4). If you are in difficulty but do not wish to abandon allotment gardening altogether, check if your landlord would be willing to reduce the size of the plot, to accommodate a newcomer, or perhaps allow you a privileged position on the waiting list as a reward for surrendering the plot while it is still in good condition. Once again, A Place to Grow defines good practice in such matters.

further help

You can look up all the allotment acts for yourself on the Office of Public Sector Information website (www.opsi.gov.uk/legislation/about_legislation), a source which helpfully indicates which provisions are still valid. For a discussion of allotment law in depth, the authoritative source is Paul Clayden's The Law of Allotments (5th Edition, 2008 London, Shaw and Sons). Useful free resources that include coverage of legal issues include Allotments: A Plotholder's Guide (www.farmgarden.org.uk/ari/documents/plotholdersguide.pdf) and A Place to Grow (www.lga.gov.uk/lga/aio/9027597). Growing in the Community, which can be downloaded for a fee (www.lga.gov.uk/lga/publications/publication-display.do?id=5403533), contains a good summary of relevant legislation, and captures many of the environmental and community benefit arguments for creating new allotments and retaining existing ones. If you are campaigning for a new site, the web-based resources Allotmoreallotments (www.allotmoreallotments.org.uk)is invaluable. Additional support for associations is available free from the Allotments Regeneration Initiative, and for heavyweight legal advice and support, consult the NSALG.

Dr Richard Wiltshire
School of Social Science and Public Policy
King's College London

index

Page numbers in *italic* refer to illustrations

useful addresses

organizations

National Society of Allotment and Leisure Gardeners
www.nsalg.org.uk
Represents allotments nationwide with membership to allotment societies and gardeners.

National Allotment Gardens Trust (NAGT)
www.nagtrust.org
Promotes the environmental benefits of allotment gardening.

The Federation of City Farms & Community Gardens (FCFCG)
www.farmgarden.org.uk
Supports, represents and promotes UK community-managed farms and gardens.

Allotments Regeneration Initiative
www.farmgarden.org.uk
Launched by the FCFCG to help regenerate old allotments and create new ones.

Soil Association
www.soilassociation.org
Membership charity campaigning for planet-friendly organic food and farming.

Garden Organic
www.gardenorganic.org.uk
The national charity for organic growing. The Heritage Seed Library preserves old varieties that are not registered.

Landshare
www.landshare.org
Puts gardeners and gardens together.

The Women's Environmental Network (WEN)
www.wen.org.uk/your-wen/local-food
Offers training and support to groups of women growing food in urban areas.

Brogdale
www.brogdale.org
Home of the National Fruit Collection.

Thrive
www.thrive.org.uk
Small but impressive national charity that aims to change the lives of disabled people through gardening.

Gardening for the Disabled
www.gardeningfordisabledtrust.org.uk
Voluntary organization providing grants to help disabled people get back into gardening.

Bees British Beekeepers Association
www.britishbee.org.uk
Information and training for beekeepers.

Waste & Resource Action Programme (WRAP)
www.wrap.org.uk
WRAP's mission is to help develop markets for material resources that would otherwise have become waste.

suppliers

Unwins
www.unwins.co.uk/seeds-for-kids-cid5.html
Seeds for children.

Thompson & Morgan
www.thompson-morgan.com
Seeds, bulbs, plants and gardening equipment.

Suttons
www.suttons.co.uk
Seeds, bulbs, plants and gardening equipment.

Growing Success
www.monrobrands.com
Garden-safe chemicals.

Just Green
www.just-green.com
Environmentally friendly products and tools for the home and garden.

Lindum Turf
www.turf.co.uk
Suppliers of wildflower green roofs.

Tamar Organics
www.tamarorganics.co.uk
Seeds, biological controls and sundries.

Chase Organics
www.chaseorganics.co.uk
Organic extracts. Specialists in seaweed extracts.

Organic Gardening Catalogue
www.organiccatalog.com/catalog
Wide range of gardening supplies.

Suffolk Herbs
www.suffolkherbs.com
Heritage and unusual vegetables, wildflowers and herbs.

acknowledgements

Greatest thanks for their hospitality and valuable time to Ken Blakeley from the Isle of Dogs Allotment Society; to Jamie Blood, Grove Lodge Meadow Allotments; to Ahmet Caglar, Culpeper Community Garden; to Pru Coleman, Compton Road Allotments; to Paul and Louis Goddard, Redland Green Allotments; to Anne Gray, East Hale Allotment Society & Living Under One Sun Community Growing Project; to Timothy Hague; to Madeleine Groves, the Vacant Lot Gardens, Shoreditch; to Allan and Alma Kimber, Boundary Way Allotment; to Gareth Morgan of Forest Farm Peace Garden; to Imogen Radford, Hoxton Manor Allotments; to Oliver Thake, Haymead Lane Allotments; to Geoff Sinclair, Allotment Forestry and to Mike Woodhouse at Fishponds. My very sincere thanks also to Janet Reilly, Derek Bolton, Andy Strachan and Charlotte Corner at Garden Organic for their generous and inspiring contribution.

My heartfelt thanks for a delightful collaboration to Rosemary Wilkinson and Emma Pattison from New Holland Publishers. Special thanks also to Dr. Richard Wiltshire for agreeing to write the legal chapter for this book and for his ever wise and knowledgeable council. Last but by no means least, thanks to my daughter, Francesca, for taking the photos and being an entertaining driving companion up and down the country on the trail of allotments.